Accepting Authoritarianism

Accepting Authoritarianism

STATE-SOCIETY RELATIONS IN CHINA'S REFORM ERA

Teresa Wright

Stanford University Press

Stanford, California

Stanford University Press
Stanford, California

© 2010 by the Board of Trustees of the Leland Stanford Junior University.
All rights reserved.

Printed in the United States of America on acid-free, archival-quality paper

Library of Congress Cataloging-in-Publication Data

Wright, Teresa.
    Accepting authoritarianism : state-society relations in China's reform era / Teresa Wright.
        p.   cm.
    Includes bibliographical references and index.
    ISBN 978-0-8047-6903-7 (cloth : alk. paper) — ISBN 978-0-8047-6904-4 (pbk. : alk. paper)
    1. China—Politics and government—1976–2002.   2. China—Politics and government—2002–   3. Authoritarianism—China.   4. China—Economic conditions—1976–2000.   5. China—Economic conditions—2000–   I. Title.
    JQ1510.W69   2010
    331.10951—dc22
                                                                        2009045980

Typeset by Westchester Book Group in 10/14 Minion

To Matt, Nicholas, and Anna

CONTENTS

ACKNOWLEDGMENTS

OVER THE MANY YEARS that this book has been percolating in my mind, I have benefited from the feedback and support of a multitude of people. From start to finish, my colleagues in the Political Science Department at California State University–Long Beach have given me indispensible advice and encouragement. I am grateful to all who have read and commented on my work at the department's research colloquia, and I give particular thanks to Chuck Noble, Rich Haesly, Cora Goldstein, and Geoff Gershenson for their extensive verbal and written comments. It has been an honor and a privilege to have such intelligent, supportive, and good-natured colleagues and friends. Also deserving special mention and thanks is Dorothy Solinger, who has been an inspiration and mentor to me for more than a decade. I am immensely grateful to her for taking the time to read virtually every word of the manuscript—often in multiple drafts—and for asking the tough questions. One would be hard-pressed to find a scholar with a keener intellect or wider knowledge of China. Also deserving of great thanks is Chris McNally; I had the good fortune of working in an office next to his during my stays at the East-West Center in Honolulu. Happy to read multiple versions of every chapter, Chris was indispensable as an incredibly sharp and knowledgeable scholar with whom to puzzle through various aspects of the argument and as a friend and colleague with whom to commiserate and laugh. In addition, my sincere gratitude goes out to Kevin O'Brien, Merle Goldman, Bjorn Alpermann, Elizabeth Perry, Rudra Sil, Marcus Kurtz, and Ben Kerkvliet for their thoughtful feedback on various chapter drafts.

In terms of institutional support, three summer stipends and a year-long academic leave granted by Cal State–Long Beach were crucial—as was the generous and cheerful help of the Political Science Department's administrative staff, Nancy St. Martin and Amelia Marquez. Of equal importance, the research and writing of this book would not have been possible without a Visiting Fellowship from the East-West Center in the summer of 2006 and a Visiting Fellowship and Visiting Scholar position at the Center during the 2007–2008 academic year. To the Center's friendly, helpful, and highly competent staff (especially Lillian Shimoda), I express my warmest mahalo.

Finally, I am deeply grateful to the friends and family members with whom I have spent so many good times; your smiles and our many adventures have enabled me both to think freely and to buckle down in the office when need be. To my old friends on the mainland and my relatively new Oahu ohana, you have added immensely to my life. To my extended family, you have been a bedrock of support, as well as a source of great fun. And to my "little family"—my husband, Matt, and my children, Nicholas and Anna—I can hardly express how grateful I am to have you in my life. Thanks for putting up with my trips away from home and my long hours in front of the computer—and for making me keep things in perspective. Your love and laughter have brought me profound contentment and tremendous joy.

1 INTRODUCTION

ASK MOST AMERICANS whether it is possible to have economic freedom without political freedom, and the answer will be an unequivocal "no"—yet this seemingly contradictory and unstable situation has characterized China for more than thirty years. Despite the country's dramatic economic growth and liberalization, political freedoms have been severely constrained, and the Chinese Communist Party (CCP) has allowed no challenge to its rule. With the exception of village elections, there have been few signs of increased political liberalization, and in fact there is some evidence of political constriction.

What accounts for this counterintuitive reality, and what might lead toward liberal democratic change? Unlike other countries, where authoritarian political leaders have faced international constraints that have pressed them to undertake democratization, today's China is almost entirely invulnerable to foreign threats and entreaties. The world's other major powers tend to tiptoe around the Chinese leadership, out of fear that angering China will inhibit profitable economic relations with its market. Thus, to a large extent, China's political future will be determined by relations between the ruling party-state and the Chinese people. Without public pressure for systemic political reform, the current ruling elite is unlikely to initiate it.

Given this political environment, it is crucial that we understand the concrete ways in which China's dramatic economic reforms have changed state-society relations, both in terms of politics and economics. Indeed, because relations between the ruling CCP and society have *not* become increasingly strained, China has flouted the expectations of Western policy makers and academics, especially since the early 1990s. Despite a marked upsurge in popular unrest in China since that time, public pressures for systemic political change have been virtually absent, and public support for CCP rule has remained high. Although this does not preclude the development of societal pressure for democratization in the future, the present political proclivities of the citizenry cry out for an explanation.

This book argues that the political attitudes and behavior of the Chinese public derive from the interaction of three key factors: (1) state-led economic development policies; (2) market forces related to late industrialization; and (3) socialist legacies. Throughout China's reform era, these factors have shaped popular political attitudes and behavior by influencing public perceptions of socioeconomic mobility, material dependence on the party-state, socioeconomic status relative to other groups, and political options. In the post-Mao period, and especially since the early 1990s, these variables have given most major socioeconomic sectors—including those that in other countries have pressed for democratic change—reasons to tolerate or even support continued CCP rule and to lack enthusiasm for systemic political transformation.

First, this confluence of state-led economic development policies, market forces, and socialist legacies has led to upward socioeconomic mobility for large segments of the population, including private entrepreneurs, profession-als, rank-and-file private sector workers, and farmers. This is not to argue that economic improvement alone has caused political satisfaction. The crucial factor is that in China, most citizens appear to believe that the authoritarian national government has facilitated the country's—and, therefore, individual citizens'—economic rise.

Second, key sectors—particularly private enterprise owners and state-owned enterprise workers—have had privileged relationships with the CCP. In China, the state has retained control of key economic resources; consequently, groups enjoying a special connection to the state have been rewarded with economic prosperity and security. In turn, this has given those groups a mate-rial interest in perpetuating the political status quo, along with a reason to fear liberal democratic reform that might threaten their political advantage.

Among rank-and-file state sector workers, further considerations have been in play. China's late opening to global markets has engendered intense competition for desirable jobs. When coupled with lingering socialist poli-cies that have provided special benefits to state sector workers, these individu-als have had a material interest in protecting their privileged status. In addi-tion, because members of this group have espoused socialist values such as support for state-mandated social welfare guarantees, the continued socialist rhetoric and policies of the central regime have given these individuals an ideal interest in supporting the political status quo.

Farmers and private sector workers have been far less materially reliant on the party-state in the reform era. The relative economic independence of these groups has diminished their incentives to support the existing political system, making them more open to political change. Yet, inasmuch as socialist policies have continued to guarantee land rights to these individuals, their basic livelihood has been protected by a state-provided safety net. Further, as with state sector workers, to the degree that farmers and private sector workers believe that such protections *should* be provided by the government, these groups' potential ideal interest in systemic political transformation has been undercut.

Third, state-led development policies and market forces associated with China's late opening to the global capitalist system have engendered a polarized socioeconomic structure with an economically well-off minority and a poor majority. Within this highly skewed socioeconomic hierarchy, private enterprise owners and professionals have been at or near the top. From the perspective of most members of this wealthy minority, liberal democratic rule has not been appealing. The wide gulf between the rich and poor has bred divergent lifestyles and interests that have limited any potential feeling of common cause or trust between the upper and lower "classes."[1] Without such feelings, wealthy individuals have had little motivation to press for mass political empowerment or to desire majority rule. For private enterprise owners who have profited by paying low wages and by working their employees relentlessly, the political enfranchisement of the lower "class" has been particularly undesirable—especially because relatively poor individuals have displayed clear socialist economic expectations and values.

Farmers and rank-and-file workers in both the state and private sectors have constituted the vast lower tier of China's polarized economic hierarchy. Although these groups would seem to benefit from majority rule, they have had countervailing reasons to accept the political status quo. As noted earlier, state sector workers have continued to receive benefits from the party-state that have been unavailable to other poor individuals. Meanwhile, farmers and private sector workers, who have generally been rising in socioeconomic status, have tended to feel that the central party-state has facilitated rather than thwarted their economic advancement. In addition, their basic sustenance has been protected by the government's guarantee of land rights to those with rural residence registration.[2] The socialist values of individuals in China's lower socioeconomic tier also have worked against their potential interest in systemic political change.

At the same time, socialist legacies have privileged urban residents over those with rural residence registration, engendering clear divisions within China's lower "class." Rather than feeling a sense of common cause and interests, unskilled laborers with urban and rural residential registrations have tended to view each other as competitors and with mutual disdain. As a result, they have had little inclination to press for their common political enfranchisement.

Fourth, the reform era has witnessed a perceived widening of political options within the existing system and a diminution of appealing political alternatives. Since 1987, rural residents—including both disgruntled farmers and prosperous private entrepreneurs—increasingly have been able to elect local leaders. In addition, the general citizenry has had a growing ability to voice its grievances through petitions and legal adjudication. Although in some authoritarian countries such a partial political opening has led to greater public pressures for democratization, in China this widening of possibilities for political participation has been perceived as an attempt by central authorities to rein in corrupt and ill-intentioned local elites. As a result, potential political dissatisfaction with the overall political system has been undermined.

CHANGES IN STATE-SOCIETY RELATIONS IN THE ERA OF REFORM

The variables just outlined have aligned in somewhat distinct ways in the first and second phases of China's post-Mao era.

The Early Reform Era (Late 1970s to the Early 1990s)

In the first phase of China's reform era, which encompassed the late 1970s through the early 1990s, China's form of state-led development featured relatively gradual and circumscribed economic reforms that allowed individuals to engage in commerce in limited markets and to form small-scale private enterprises. Meanwhile, socialist economic policies generally persisted in the state sector, such that most urban workers (especially those in central state-owned enterprises) continued to receive welfare benefits provided by the party-state. Externally, as China slowly opened its economy to the international capitalist system, it faced an increasingly competitive and integrated global market wherein a surplus of unskilled workers was readily available to mobile capital owners.

Economic Inequality During this era, economic inequality rose in comparison to the Maoist period (1949–76), leading to a substantial rise in socioeconomic polarization. When China embarked on economic reform in the late 1970s, its Gini coefficient—a statistical measure of wealth distribution—was among the lowest in the world, standing at 0.15 (with 0 reflecting perfect economic equality, and 1 indicating perfect inequality). Indeed, the degree of economic polarization in China was low even in comparison with other socialist states. China's level of material inequality more than doubled over the course of the 1980s, reaching a Gini coefficient of 0.386 in 1988. Viewed against the backdrop of China's recent egalitarian past, this economic imbalance generated substantial public discontent among those at the lower end of the socioeconomic spectrum—especially given the widespread belief that those at the top garnered their riches through unjust or corrupt practices. At the same time, during this period the vast majority of China's rural residents experienced substantial improvement in their financial circumstances, and most urban dwellers also enjoyed rising or stable economic conditions.

Economic Dependence and Political Options In addition, this era witnessed a gradual but general decline in levels of economic dependence on the party-state. Farmers were allowed much more independence in growing and selling crops; increasing numbers of urban college graduates were not assigned jobs by the state; and skilled and savvy state-owned enterprise workers began to enter the private sector. In terms of political options, many citizens harbored bitter memories of the tumult and hardship of the Mao era, yet their dissatisfaction with the political system was undercut by their relief at the rise of party leaders with a more pragmatic orientation toward economic and political development.

Political Unrest The confluence of these factors from the late 1970s through the 1980s paved the way for some political unrest in China, which materialized in such cases as the Democracy Wall movement of 1978–80, the student protests of 1986–87, and the massive student-led demonstrations of spring 1989. Yet even before the brutal crackdown of June 4, 1989, the vast majority of citizens showed little interest in pursuing systemic political change. Although some of the protests of this period—especially those in spring 1989—involved large numbers of citizens, participants generally were urban students and intellectuals, with some state-owned enterprise workers as well. Few private entrepreneurs were involved, and virtually none of China's rural residents— who at the time constituted roughly three-fourths of the population—took part. Further, even when protestors of this period called for "democracy," many exhibited an explicit commitment to socialist economic values.[3]

The Late Reform Era (Early 1990s Through the Present)

The second phase of China's reform era began in the early 1990s and continues today. This era has featured a dramatic acceleration and expansion of state-led economic privatization and marketization. In addition, the CCP leadership has moved from tolerating the private sector to embracing it—and has even invited private businesspeople to join the Communist Party. In the process, many of China's private entrepreneurs have become extremely wealthy. At the same time, the restructuring of large state-owned enterprises has resulted in the unemployment of tens of millions of state sector workers, as well as a substantial diminution of the social welfare benefits formerly provided to them by the party-state. Further, increasing numbers of rural migrants have moved to the cities, improving their economic fortune (as well as that of their families back in the countryside) by working in China's burgeoning private enterprises. Meanwhile, since 1992, China has much more fully opened its economy to the international capitalist system, leaving its unskilled laborers more vulnerable to the vicissitudes of the global market.[4] These factors have influenced popular perceptions of socioeconomic mobility, dependence on the state, relative socioeconomic status, and political options. The result has been greater public tolerance of, and even support for, the existing CCP-led political system.

Socioeconomic Inequality: The Numbers Perhaps the most important overall feature of the late reform period has been the development of an even more highly polarized socioeconomic structure. By 1995, economic inequality had grown to such an extent that China's Gini coefficient stood at 0.462. As of 2007, estimates ranged from 0.496 to 0.561.[5] By way of comparison, in 2004 the Gini index of the United States was around 0.45, and in 2005, Brazil stood at roughly 0.56.[6] Thus, within three decades, China moved from a position among the most economically equal countries in the world to the ranks of the most unequal. Reflecting this imbalance, as of 2006 the wealthiest 20 percent of Chinese citizens earned more than 58 percent of China's income, while the poorest 20 percent took in only 3 percent, making for a top-to-bottom ratio of more than 18 to 1. In contrast, the top 20 percent of the United States' population earned just over 50 percent of the national income, and the bottom 20 percent earned slightly more than 3 percent, with a top-to-bottom ratio of roughly 15 to 1.[7] Further, in China, this inequality has emerged suddenly, under the same political system that until recently castigated the evils of economic polarization.

The overall result is a socioeconomic structure that resembles an "onion dome," with roughly 15 percent of the population occupying the narrow upper level and the remaining 85 percent forming the wide base. Using the income categories of China's National Bureau of Statistics, in 2007 those in the top level earned 60,000 yuan or more per year. In official statistics, this included both the "upper stratum" and the "middle stratum." With earnings between 60,000 and 500,000 yuan/year, the "middle stratum" represented approximately 12 percent of the population. Those in the "upper stratum" (with more than 500,000 yuan/year in income) included no more than 3 percent of the citizenry.[8] The remaining 85 percent earned less than 60,000 yuan/year. In reality, most in this group lived on far less, as China's national per capita income in 2006 was only about 16,000 yuan.[9]

Socioeconomic Inequality: Public Perceptions   In a 2006 survey, 2.3 percent of China's citizenry described themselves as "wealthy" (*furen*), while 75.1 percent described themselves as "poor" (*qiongren*).[10] A separate 2006 study presented a less stark picture: .5 percent self-identified as "upper class," 5.4 percent as "upper middle class," 39.6 percent as "middle class," 29.1 percent as "lower middle class," and 24.5 percent as "lower class." Still, even in the more moderate findings of the second study, more than half of the respondents considered themselves to be of "lower" economic status. Further, this latter study finds that, between 2002 and 2006, the percentage of the population who perceived themselves to be "middle class" shrank, while the percentage of those who viewed themselves as "lower class" rose.[11]

The Onion Dome, Sector by Sector   In the second phase of China's reform period, the onion dome's narrow "middle" and "upper" strata have included owners of medium and large private enterprises (defined by the party-state as having eight or more employees) and professionals (such as lawyers, medical doctors, accountants, and engineers). As noted earlier, many members of this group have had strong incentives to perpetuate the political status quo. Given the polarized economic structure, as well as the socialist economic preferences of those at the lower end of China's socioeconomic spectrum, liberal democratic (or majority) rule likely would result in policies (such as higher taxes to support income redistribution) that would threaten the prosperity of well-off individuals. For private entrepreneurs who have garnered their wealth through their connections with the ruling party-state, political change would similarly threaten their economic advantages. In addition, as the perceived gap between the upper- and lower-level tiers of China's socioeconomic structure has grown, those at the top have enjoyed a lifestyle that has increasingly diverged from that of those at the bottom, leading to a diminished sense of commonality in values across socioeconomic strata that has worked against the wealthy group's potential ideal interest in liberal democratic change.

At the bottom of China's onion dome-shaped socioeconomic structure have been rank-and-file state and private sector workers, self-employed small-scale entrepreneurs, and farmers. Given their relatively poor economic conditions and their majority status, these groups might be expected to find mass political enfranchisement desirable. Yet, as noted above, many in this group do not feel the need to press for systemic political change. Those at the lower level of the onion dome have tended to support socialist economic ideals, including greater equality and strong labor protections. Even as the ruling CCP has promoted economic privatization and marketization, it has retained at least some commitment to socialist economic values. Consequently, without alternatives that do a better job in upholding these economic priorities, those of limited economic means have had little reason to believe that a change in the political status quo will improve their material circumstances. On the contrary, they have had cause to fear that such change would unseat the only entity that appears to have the commitment, power, and economic resources to improve their daily circumstances—the central government. This perception has been strengthened by the widespread belief that socialist economic policies are "right" and moral. Thus, when relatively poor citizens have engaged in protest in the late reform period, rather than calling for an end to CCP rule, they have urged the party to live up to its socialist rhetoric.

Particular segments of China's lower economic group have had further reason to tolerate the political status quo. For most state sector workers—especially those employed in state-owned enterprises (SOEs)—the second phase of the reform era has been jarring. Although in the early 1990s, SOE employees continued to enjoy secure employment and pay, relatively lax working conditions, and high social status, since the mid-1990s SOE workers have been laid off or forced to retire in droves. Subsequently, they have been forced to compete with unskilled rural migrants (whom most city dwellers view as social inferiors) for jobs with low and often delayed pay, extremely long hours, and draconian working conditions. Furthermore, even SOE employees that have retained state-owned enterprise employment typically have faced job insecurity, reduced pay and/or benefits, and more demanding working conditions. At the same time, both current and former SOE workers have remained dependent on the state for their livelihood. Despite their somewhat diminished privileges, those who still are employed by SOEs hold the most desirable jobs available to unskilled workers. They also continue to receive some state-provided benefits, such as subsidized education, medical care, and pensions. Even those who have been laid off are eligible for state-provided privileges that are unavailable to other unemployed workers, including job training, employment assistance, and even small loans.[12] Because the livelihood of current and former SOE workers has rested largely on their continued connection with the party-state and their privileged status relative to other workers, they have had reason to support the existing CCP-led political system and to oppose the political empowerment of those who do not enjoy similar state-provided benefits. Consequently, even when retrenched SOE employees have engaged in public protest, they have evidenced little desire to replace the CCP-led political system with liberal democratic rule. Instead, they have voiced their criticisms from the left, calling for the socioeconomic benefits and protections that they feel that they—as workers—deserve.

Also at the low end of China's socioeconomic hierarchy have been former rural residents who have migrated to the cities in search of employment—most of whom are private sector workers or are engaged in individual enterprises such as street-side sales and services. Just as former SOE workers have done, former rural residents have endured exacting working conditions and received minimal income. Yet unlike retrenched SOE employees, rural migrant workers have been rising in socioeconomic status and have not received special benefits from the party-state. To the contrary, the government often has discriminated against rural migrants. Yet at the same time, China's still nominally socialist regime has ensured the basic survival of these rural migrants by granting them land in their village of origin. Further, because central authorities have made some attempts to address the work-related grievances of rural migrant workers (for example, by requiring that private business owners sign contracts with their employees and provide some job security and workplace protections), these vulnerable laborers have had a diminished interest in unseating the current political leadership.

The final group at the bottom of the socioeconomic structure is farmers, who tend to be poor. Although their income and living standards have progressed much more slowly than that of other groups, farmers have had some incentives to support the central government. Since the late 1980s the ruling CCP has supported local village elections in the countryside as a way to remove corrupt and malevolent local officials. To the extent that these elections have been successful in this aim, rural residents' satisfaction with central authorities has been bolstered. The national government's successful effort to end rural taxes (begun in 2000) has further worked in this direction.[13] Finally, as has been the case with rural migrants, farmers depend on the state for the land on which they rely for their basic needs. On balance, they have shown only tenuous support for the existing political system. As of this writing, they are China's most volatile and politically dissatisfied group.

Overall, in the second phase of the reform era the Chinese people's perceptions of state-led development policies, market forces related to late industrialization, and socialist legacies have engendered a clear popular interest in accepting and even perpetuating CCP rule rather than pursuing systemic political change. This helps to explain why capitalist economic development has failed to breed increased public pressure for liberal democracy in China. Of course, the present constellation of factors is not static and will change. As explained in Chapter 7, the variables that have led to the public's current toleration of an authoritarian government also suggest circumstances under which Chinese citizens may be expected to pursue systemic political transformation.

DO CHINA'S CITIZENS REALLY SUPPORT THE POLITICAL STATUS QUO?

Before examining the social support (or at least acceptance) of China's existing political order, it is necessary to lay out the evidence that such social support (or acceptance) exists. Should one wish to understand only the absence of politically oriented activism between the 1990s and the present, the most obvious explanation is that the public simply fears repression, especially in the wake of the violent crackdown of June 4, 1989. As political scientist Theda Skocpol warns, political passivity should not be confused with political support.[14] The lack of political dissent surely has derived in part from the fact that post-1989 CCP elites have been unusually unified in their views toward economic reform and in their determination to maintain the party's unchallenged power. Without a split in the political leadership, dissidents have had little hope that collective action might result in political reform.[15] To use the language employed by scholars of contentious politics, since 1989, China's "political opportunity structure" has been largely closed.[16]

Even when the "political opportunity structure" has opened slightly in the post-1989 period, few have taken advantage of it. For example, in 1998, when a small group of intellectuals and workers capitalized on U.S. President Bill Clinton's impending visit to China to announce the formation of the China Democracy Party (CDP), central authorities did not take decisive repressive action for roughly four months. CDP activists used this opportunity to expand, yet only a few thousand citizens joined the party nationwide. The vast majority of CDP members were seasoned dissidents who had led earlier political movements (especially the Democracy Wall movement of 1978–80 and the student-led protests of 1989) and had been punished for their political activities. Very few "new" activists joined the CDP's ranks.[17]

Perhaps an even more telling example is the public response to the January 2005 death of former CCP General Secretary Zhao Ziyang, who had been under house arrest since 1989 because of his perceived support for the student demonstrators. In fact, the event that sparked the protests of 1989 was the death of Zhao's mentor, former CCP General Secretary Hu Yaobang, and many anticipated that Zhao's death might spur a similar event. Cognizant of this, ruling CCP elites suppressed the news of Zhao's passing and mounted a substantial security effort to prevent any sort of public "disturbance." Initially, central elites refused to hold any official memorial service, but they later agreed to hold a small public funeral at the official Babaoshan Cemetery, where about fifteen hundred citizens appeared without invitation to pay their respects.[18] Although there is no doubt that the CCP's security efforts prevented many known activists from attending, it is striking that so few common citizens tried. Even in Hong Kong, where through the 1990s massive crowds gathered annually to memorialize June 4, 1989 (and where restrictions on public gatherings have been far more lax), no more than ten thousand gathered to pay their respects to Zhao.[19] Similarly, in November 2005, CCP General Secretary Hu Jintao agreed to hold an official memorial service to mark the ninetieth anniversary of Hu Yaobang's birth. Reportedly, four of the nine members of the Standing Committee of the CCP Politburo argued against holding the memorial, fearing that the event could spark public unrest. Yet, these concerns proved unfounded, and the event passed with nary a public murmur.[20]

Meanwhile, especially since the early 1990s, millions of Chinese citizens have participated in tens of thousands of yearly protests. According to the Chinese Ministry of Public Security, in 2005 there were 87,000 "disturbances to public order," up from 74,000 in 2004, 58,000 in 2003, and 10,000 in 1996.[21] During this time span, the number of yearly participants rose from 730,000 (in 1993) to 3.8 million (in 2004).[22] Protestors' major grievances have revolved around large-scale SOE layoffs, inadequate pensions, unpaid wages, excessive taxes, and land requisitions. Although virtually none of the demonstrations in this period have been explicitly political, their leaders have been subject to official punishment. Yet despite the real likelihood of repression, people have continued to take to the streets. Thus, it cannot be argued that fear of repression has cowed the Chinese public into quiescent submission. Despite the clear risks involved, the populace *has* engaged in many collective acts of public contention in the post-1989 period.

In addition, there is substantial evidence that the popular unrest that has spread since the early 1990s does not denote widespread dissatisfaction with the ruling regime. To the contrary, demonstrators of virtually all stripes have expressed belief in the legitimacy of the overall political system and faith in the willingness of central leaders to address the people's concerns. Simultaneously, protestors generally have not criticized the political system from a Western, liberal perspective. Instead, as noted previously, they generally have called on ruling elites to live up to their socialist claims to legitimacy.

These attitudes have been apparent in each of the major sectors that has participated in the collective "disturbances" that have appeared since the early 1990s. One of the largest such groups has included former state-owned enterprise workers.[23] Within this sector, sociologist Ching Kwan Lee finds that protestors consistently "pledge[] their support for socialism and the central leadership. . . . Conspicuously absent in the vast majority of labor protests is any hint of demands for independent unionism or for democratic rights of political participation, or challenges to regime legitimacy. The most politicized demand to date is removal of specific officials, without questioning the system of communist rule."[24] A second major component of recent "mass disturbances" has been rural migrant workers in the cities, most of whom have found jobs in the private sector. Within this group, Lee shows that explicitly class-based Maoist rhetoric has not been apparent, yet "leftist" rather than "liberal" attitudes have remained predominant. As Lee reports, sociologist Isabelle Thireau and historian Linshan Hua find that aggrieved migrant workers refer to themselves as " 'the people,' 'the workers,' and 'the masses,' appealing to officials as their 'protectors,' identifying them as 'father and mother of the people,' 'protective god,' 'fair judge,' 'uncles,' 'directing comrades,' or 'servants of the people.'"[25] A third major category of protestors has included rural residents.[26] Among them, political attitudes and behavior have exhibited broad similarities with their urban counterparts. As documented by political scientists Kevin O'Brien and Lianjiang Li, a preponderance of aggrieved rural activists have engaged in "rightful resistance" that presses local authorities to live up to what the disgruntled citizens believe to be the righteous claims and legitimate policies of central authorities.[27] These individuals "seldom press for wider civil and political rights to association, expression, and unlicensed participation; nor do they often question the legitimacy of existing laws and policies, not to mention the right of unaccountable leaders at higher levels to make laws and policies."[28] Further, O'Brien and Li state, "there is little evidence that most [rural activists] consider rights to be inherent, natural, or inalienable; nor do most of them break with the common Chinese practice of viewing rights as granted by the state to ensure community well-being rather than to protect an individual's autonomous being."[29]

Public Opinion Survey Results

Surely, the language employed by protestors is in part a tactical decision, designed to minimize the potential ire of political authorities and maximize the possibility that ruling elites will lend a sympathetic ear. Yet the political views expressed by protestors also have been articulated by broad swaths of the populace that have not participated in demonstrations. Indeed, scores of public opinion surveys and interviews conducted in the latter years of the reform period suggest that there is a remarkably high level of popular support for the CCP-led authoritarian political system.[30] Further, this appears to be the case both in urban and rural areas. For example, in a 1995–99 survey of Beijing residents, political scientist Jie Chen found that a "clear majority" expressed "strong support" for the current (authoritarian) political regime, or "considered the current regime legitimate."[31] Similarly, in a 1999 survey of residents in Shanghai, Chongqing, Guangzhou, Shenyang, Wuhan, and Xian, political scientist Wenfang Tang asked respondents whether the CCP-led political system should be changed; 44 percent said "no," and 31 percent responded that they "did not care so long as their lives could be improved."[32] In rural areas, similar statistics emerge. In a 1999–2001 survey of villagers in four counties conducted by political scientist Lianjiang Li, 80 percent expressed a "high" or "very high" level of confidence in the central government, 4 percent reported "low" or "very low" confidence, and the remaining 16 percent stated that their confidence was "so-so."[33] In Li's 2003-5 survey of villagers in Fujian and Zhejiang provinces, 75.7 percent of respondents thought that the "Party Center and the State Council sincerely cared about farmers," and 77.6 percent believed that "the Center welcomed farmers petitioning."[34]

Nationwide surveys have uncovered almost identical public attitudes toward China's current political system. In the 2001 World Values Survey (WVS) and 2002 East Asian Barometer (EAB), respectively, 97 percent and 98 percent of respondents expressed "quite a lot" or "a great deal" of confidence in the national government, while 98 percent (WVS) and 92 percent (EAB) expressed "quite a lot" or "a great deal" of confidence in the CCP.[35] Further, 72.9 percent of WVS respondents reported being "fairly satisfied" (67.1 percent) or "very satisfied" (5.8 percent) with "the people in national office," while only 1.5 percent reported being "very dissatisfied." In addition, 94.8 percent expressed "a great deal" (33.5 percent) or "quite a lot" (61.3 percent) of confidence in China's national legislative body, the National People's Congress.[36] Similarly, a 2008 survey by World Public Opinion found that 83 percent of Chinese believed that they can trust the national government to do the right thing "most of the time" (60 percent) or "just about always" (23 percent). Meanwhile, 65 percent expressed the view that "the country is run for the benefit of the people." Among the nineteen nations (both democratic and not) surveyed in this poll, Chinese citizens displayed the greatest trust in and support for their political system.[37] Further, the Chinese public seems to believe that the existing system is not static or frozen but, rather, open and changing in a positive direction. In the 2001 WVS, 67 percent stated that they were "satisfied" or "very satisfied" with the "way democracy is working" in China, and in the 2002 EAB, 88.5 percent reported being "quite satisfied" or "very satisfied" with the "way democracy is developing" in China.[38]

In rural areas, these views may derive in part from citizens' experiences with local elections. The 1987 Organic Law, which officially sanctioned local rural elections, provided that village committees of three to seven members were to be chosen by all adult registered voters, with all voters eligible to stand as candidates for election.[39] According to the Ministry of Civil Affairs, by

1999, 86 percent of all Chinese villages had elected village committees.[40] In 2003, the Carter Center estimated that in about 40 percent of all villages, elections have been free, fair, and competitive.[41] For some scholars and observers, these elections clearly signify a first step toward higher-level democratization. Most of the research on local elections, however, indicates that this is not the case. In reality, local elections never were seen by ruling elites as a trial run for higher-level democracy; rather, local elections were viewed as a means to strengthen the legitimacy of the ruling regime, remove corrupt local officials, and ease the implementation of unpopular central policies, such as those related to birth control.[42]

More important, in the many cases in which democratic principles have been violated in local rural elections, villagers do not seem to have blamed the central regime. Rather, they often have appealed to central elites to enforce legally mandated electoral procedures. And, in many cases, central authorities have stepped in to do so, even annulling the results of fraudulent or unfair elections.[43] Further, in localities where more truly democratic village elections have occurred, it appears that the goals of the central authorities are being achieved. As documented by political scientists Lianjiang Li and Kevin O'Brien, residents of such villages appear to be willing to comply with unpopular policies.[44] In addition, local activists against corrupt village officials often run in and even win elections for village committees.[45] When the central government does step in to enforce election rules, its legitimacy is strengthened. Overall, then, village elections appear to have increased public support for the central party-state while simultaneously enfolding potential opponents into local government bodies.[46] This may be an important contributor to apparent public satisfaction with the way that democracy is "working" and "developing" in China.

Related to these popular views, social trust appears to be much higher in China than in most countries around the world.[47] In the 2001 WVS, 54.5 percent of Chinese respondents agreed that "most people can be trusted." By comparison, in the United States, 35.8 percent of WVS respondents (in 2000) agreed with this statement.[48] Indeed, if one correlates levels of interpersonal trust and political freedom, China is the biggest outlier in the world, evidencing an almost unheard-of combination of exceptionally high levels of social trust and very low levels of political rights and civil liberties.[49] Interpersonal trust is important because it has a demonstrated connection to political trust. As reported by Jie Chen and Chunlong Lu, "the empirical evidence from the 2000

World Values Surveys show[s] that generalized trust increases people's faith in political and public institutions in all countries surveyed."[50] This finding also is supported by a wide array of studies of "social capital" in Western democracies.[51] Similarly, in China, Tang's six-city survey finds that social trust "promoted individuals' confidence in various national and local public institutions."[52] Tang concludes that "[interpersonal] trust can therefore increase support for the system in democratic as well as non-democratic countries."[53]

Looking at another indicator of popular political views, surveys show that an overwhelming majority of Chinese citizens prioritize social stability and economic prosperity over liberal political freedoms and rights. For example, in Jie Chen's 1995–99 Beijing surveys, "over 90 percent of respondents preferred a stable and orderly society to a freer society that could be prone to disruption."[54] And in Tang's 1999 multicity survey, nearly 60 percent of respondents agreed that "the most important condition for our country's progress is political stability. Democratization under the current conditions would only lead to chaos."[55] Further, when asked to identify their criteria for good government, 48 percent of Tang's respondents chose "economic growth," while only 11 percent selected "democratic elections" and 7 percent "individual freedom."[56] Similarly, in a 1995 Beijing survey undertaken by political scientists Daniel Dowd, Allen Carlson, and Mingming Shen, 56 percent of respondents named "national peace and prosperity" as their most important value, while only 5.8 percent chose "political democracy" and 6.3 percent "individual freedom."[57] In the 2001 WVS, when respondents were presented with four options, 40 percent chose economic development as the top national priority, while only 5 percent chose "seeing people have more say" in their work or community. In another set of four options, 57 percent chose "maintaining order" as their top priority, 26 percent chose "fighting rising prices," 12 percent chose "seeing people have more say in government," and about 5 percent chose "protecting freedom of speech."[58] Additionally, in Tang's 1999 six-city survey, 67 percent of respondents reported being satisfied with their "freedom of speech."[59]

Concurrently, many Chinese citizens have shown a preference for socialist economic benefits and guarantees. For example, in the 2001 WVS, 52.8 percent responded that "government ownership of business should be increased," as compared to 20.2 percent who believed that "private ownership of business should be increased" (18.3 percent fell in between). When asked in the same survey whether society should pursue the more socialist goal of "extensive welfare" or the more neoliberal aim of "lower taxes," 47 percent chose "extensive welfare," and 14 percent "lower taxes"; virtually all of the remainder either leaned toward "extensive welfare" (18 percent) or was undecided (14.8 percent).[60] Similarly, a late 2004 nationwide survey undertaken by Chunping Han and Martin King Whyte finds that "very large majorities . . . would like the government to take measures to alleviate poverty and reduce inequality."[61] Preferences for socialist values are especially apparent among those who feel that their socioeconomic status has declined in the reform era. As Tang finds in his 1999 six-city survey, "the lower social classes were more anti-Western than others and still adhered to revolutionary ideologies" (that is, Marxism-Leninism and Maoism).[62] Such sentiments have been particularly apparent in the rhetoric of former state-owned enterprise workers who have taken to the streets in protest. Overall, recent survey data indicate substantial popular support for the authoritarian ruling regime and weak interest in liberal democratic principles.

Variations in Trends

It is important to recognize the demographic and geographic variations that appear within these general trends. With regard to demographics, age and economic status appear to be particularly influential. Various surveys show a positive correlation between age and general regime support (i.e., the older the respondent, the more supportive). In Jie Chen's 1995–99 Beijing surveys, for example, nearly 100 percent of respondents aged fifty-six or older expressed a "medium" or "high" level of support for the regime. Among respondents aged eighteen to twenty-five, the corresponding figure dropped to 65 to 70 percent. In the groups falling in between, regime support rose in almost stair-step fashion with increased age.[63] Similarly, Tang's 1999 six-city survey finds that younger citizens display more acceptance of liberalization and democratization.[64] Regarding economic status, Chen's surveys show a similar stair-step increase in regime support as a respondent's self-assessed economic status rises.[65] Even so, the gap is not massive; when placed on a scale of 6 to 24 (from low to high regime support) in surveys conducted in 1995, 1997, and 1999, the bottom economic quintile scores an average of 18.6, the middle quintile averages 19.3, and the top quintile averages 19.9.[66] In other demographic measures, variation also exists but is more subtle. Looking at gender, women appear to be slightly less supportive of the regime than are men.[67] With regard to occupation, in Chen's surveys, college students and state-owned enterprise workers report slightly less regime support than do white-collar professionals and private entrepreneurs.[68]

In addition, researchers have documented local variations in political attitudes and behavior. Some of this work seems to support the notion that capitalist economic development and democracy are linked. There is some evidence to suggest that citizens in locations with more thriving and liberalized local economies are more interested in democracy than are those in less well-off areas. For example, in a study of prosperous Wenling City in Zhejiang province from 1999–2004, economists Xuebing Dong and Jinchuan Shi conclude that "in regions with very strong private economies, the local public comes to expect greater democratic rights: with economic power comes political power."[69]

However, a closer look reveals a more complicated reality. Most strikingly, it appears that in more economically prosperous areas, it is not common people who seek and gain greater political rights, but rather the new economic elite. As Dong and Shi note, members of this elite may support democratic processes, but they do so not because they believe in liberal democratic rights for all; rather, they believe that they "are able to use democratic processes to their advantage."[70] Similarly, political scientist Kellee S. Tsai finds that, among private entrepreneurs, only the well-to-do have the necessary resources and leverage to press for greater political inclusion.[71]

In this sense, it may appear that China's capitalists are, in fact, behaving as their counterparts did in the earliest industrialized nations. For example, in England around the time of the Industrial Revolution, private capital holders first sought democratic rights only for themselves; they did so to protect their economic well-being from a predatory authoritarian state.[72] However, research on China's emergent private entrepreneurs finds an important difference from the English case: the authoritarian state is not seen as an enemy that must be weakened but, rather, as an ally that will aid in pursuing and protecting the interests of private capital. Thus, as Tsai shows, even China's most "assertive" entrepreneurs typically "find ways to have their needs met without demanding democratic solutions."[73] Indeed, surveys by Bruce J. Dickson suggest that private entrepreneurs in more prosperous areas are more likely to believe that they can best meet their needs through joining and working within the existing authoritarian party-state.[74]

Other studies further contextualize these findings. In various comparisons of private entrepreneurs in different localities, scholars argue that locational variations in political attitudes and behavior are not fundamentally explained by differences in the level of economic prosperity but, rather, by differences in the orientation of local government officials toward the private economy.[75]

Overall, it appears that when the local village authorities are either support-ive of the private sector, or themselves control the privatization of public enter-prises, private entrepreneurs become more politically integrated in the local party-state and less interested in meaningful local-level democracy.[76] When local officials are unsupportive or indifferent toward the private sector, private entrepreneurs show less interest in working with existing CCP-dominated po-litical institutions and groups and are more likely to support local democracy as a means to press local authorities to be more attentive to the private sector's needs.[77] At the same time, even in these areas, there is little evidence that pri-vate entrepreneurs desire broader democratization of the central political system.

Of course, the political views of the Chinese public are sure to change over time. To begin, because younger citizens appear to be less supportive of the existing regime and more interested in liberal democratic principles, public opinion in China may become more supportive of democratization with gen-erational change. Additionally, in Jie Chen's 1995–99 surveys of Beijing resi-dents, general regime support displayed a gradual decline as time passed.[78] Interestingly, when broken down by economic status, those in the two lowest quintiles registered a slight increase in support for democracy over the course of Chen's surveys, while those in the middle, upper-middle, and upper quin-tiles registered a nominal decrease.[79]

Despite these variations, the overall conclusion of these survey data is clear: Despite nearly three decades of dramatic economic reform and growth in China, as of this writing, popular support for the CCP-led political regime is strong, and public interest in liberal democratic change appears weak. Fur-ther, those at the lower end of China's socioeconomic spectrum display a substantial commitment to socialist economic values. As a result, while public protest has been extensive in the second phase of the post-Mao period, popu-lar pressure for systemic political reform has not emerged.

CAPITALISM AND DEMOCRACY

This reality flies in the face of the pervasive expectation that capitalist eco-nomic development will bring societal pressures for liberal democratic change. In this sense, reform-era China is a crucial case for scholars interested in the relationship between capitalism and democracy. What it illustrates are the circumstances under which the prevailing wisdom does not hold true—namely, in state-led late developers with a socialist past.

Although theorists have contemplated the relationship between capitalist economic growth and democracy since the advent of the Industrial Revolution, the topic's emergence in the modern American social sciences typically is traced to political sociologist Seymour Lipset's attention-grabbing work in the 1950s, which documented a strong correlation between economic development and democracy.[80] Ever since, a constant stream of scholarship—much of which has involved quantitative, multi-country studies—has probed for causal relations. Although differences in design, specification, and measurement have led to some varied findings, the overall conclusion is remarkably consistent: Economic development does indeed increase the probability that a country will become democratic.[81]

Yet within this general consensus, scholars have found that the relationship between economic development and democracy is not fixed; rather, it is stronger under some conditions and weaker under others. Political scientists Ross Burkhart and Michael Lewis-Beck conclude that although "around the world, economic development works to foster democracy," in countries of the "periphery," the "full magnitude" of the relationship is somewhat diminished.[82] In addition, political scientists Adam Przeworski and Fernando Limongi find that economic growth increases the chances of democratic transition, but only to a certain point. Specifically, once a country's per capita income surpasses $6,000 (in 1985 U.S. dollars), "dictatorships become more stable as countries become more affluent."[83] Political scientists Carles Boix and Susan Stokes add that, in real terms, this "income threshold" was much lower before 1950.[84]

Probing this relationship further, scholars have examined *how* and *why* economic development (especially capitalist development) and democracy are linked. The overall consensus is that capitalist economic development gives rise to new socioeconomic classes that struggle for political change to serve their (largely material) interests.[85] For some, the key propeller of democracy is the rising capitalist class as it allies with workers to oppose a feudal and/or authoritarian state that is perceived to be hostile to its interests.[86] Adding to an understanding of the stance of the capitalist class as economic growth proceeds, Boix and Stokes claim that as countries develop, incomes become more equally distributed. As this transpires, capitalists become less fearful that mass democracy will result in the confiscation of private assets. Consequently, Boix and Stokes conclude that "capitalists living in a rich dictatorship are more likely to choose democracy than capitalists in a poor one."[87] In postsocialist states such as China, however, this relationship has not held true.

Other scholars (most notably, political sociologists Dietrich Ruesche-meyer, Evelyne Huber Stephens, and John D. Stephens) argue that the working class is the champion of democratic reform. Even so, Rueschemeyer, Stephens, and Stephens emphasize that the working class needs allies, especially in late-developing countries with smaller and weaker urban working classes. Historically, other sectors whose interests have been harmed by an authoritarian political structure hostile to capitalism and/or economic modernization—especially capitalists and intellectuals—have played this role.[88]

Accepting the broader agreement that pressure from the capitalist class and/or the working class is the key causal linkage between economic development and democracy, political scientist Eva Bellin emphasizes the contingent and variable attitudes of labor and capital, especially among later developers. Specifically, she argues that for the capitalist class, dependence on the state and fear of working class inclusion may breed opposition to democracy, even when the economy is growing and prosperous.[89] Similarly, when organized labor is dependent on the state and enjoys a privileged status relative to unorganized workers, it may oppose democratic change, regardless of the state of the economy.[90] Thus, Bellin finds that overall, the relationship between capitalist economic development and democracy appears stronger in earlier developers than in later developers.

CAPITALISM AND DEMOCRACY IN CHINA

China has been largely left out of these comparative studies. In the past few years, however, scholars increasingly have examined how China's post-Mao experience may inform broader understandings of the relationship between capitalist economic development and democracy. Some observers believe that, although China's progress toward democracy has been slow, its ultimate arrival at a liberal political destination virtually is guaranteed. Among these individuals—who include a few scholars and many prominent Western journalists and government officials—China's aberration from the typical combination of capitalism and democracy is only temporary. In their view the unavoidable reality is that a "modern" free-market capitalist economy simply is incompatible with a Leninist political system. As a result, if the ruling CCP wishes to continue to develop such an economy, it will have no choice but to liberalize the political system.[91] The reason for this has been neatly encapsulated by New York Times columnist Nicholas Kristof, who states that "no middle class is content with more choices of coffees than of candidates on a ballot."[92]

Perhaps the most emphatic articulation of this optimistic position is found in the work of Stanford University business professor and former U.S. cabinet official Henry Rowen, who boldly claims that, should China continue on its current trajectory, "the more than one-sixth of the world's people who live in China will by 2025 be citizens of a country correctly classed as belonging to the Free nations of the earth."[93] Citing Harvard economist Robert Barro's study of more than one hundred countries, Rowen argues that it is common for factors that are "positive for electoral rights" to appear long before they are "expressed" in the political system.[94] According to Rowen, Barro finds that "after about two decades 'the level of democracy is nearly fully determined'" by socioeconomic factors such as levels of income and education.[95] In other words, Rowen argues that what we currently are seeing in China is simply a "lag" between economic and political liberalization.

Rowen's arguments undergird the views expressed by American policy makers across the political spectrum. In the words of former U.S. President Bill Clinton, "just as democracy helps make the world safe for commerce, commerce helps make the world safe for democracy. . . . That's why we have worked so hard to help build free-market institutions in Eastern Europe, Russia, and the former Soviet republics. That's why we have supported commercial liberalization in China."[96] Similarly, former U.S. President George W. Bush argued that "the case for trade is not just monetary, but moral. Economic freedom creates habits of liberty. And habits of liberty create expectations of democracy. . . . Trade freely with China, and time is on our side."[97] Along the same lines, Bush proclaimed that "as China reforms its economy, its leaders are finding that once the door to freedom is opened even a crack, it cannot be closed."[98] Across the Atlantic, former British Prime Minister Tony Blair expressed the same view, asserting, for example, that there is an "unstoppable momentum . . . towards greater political freedom" in China.[99]

Yet, as demonstrated in the survey data and research on popular protests described above, there is little empirical evidence to back this view. As a result, the sanguine ideas of these policy makers and scholars are far from universal. Indeed, most experts have a far less optimistic view when it comes to China's prospects for a liberal democratic future. One of the gloomiest observers is journalist James Mann, who castigates the idea that democracy will arise from free markets as sheer "fantasy." Mann argues that this naïve expectation ignores the CCP's ruthless and successful determination to stifle all political opposition, as well as its stubborn refusal to embrace meaningful political change. In Mann's view, the "soothing scenario" put forth by American policy makers and scholars such as Rowen is based on a fatally flawed logic—what Mann calls the "Starbucks fallacy." In reality, Mann argues, economic and political liberalization are not linked: "Chinese kids can eat pizza and drink Coke, but doing so won't necessarily create a free press or an opposition political party."[100] Indeed, Mann emphasizes that free-market capitalism may in fact be *strengthening* China's existing political system. As he states,

> trade is trade. It is not a magic political potion for democracy. Its benefits and costs are in the economic sphere; trade has not brought an end to political repression or the Chinese Communist Party's monopoly on power, and there is not the slightest reason to think it will do so in the future, either. In fact, it is possible that [America's] trade with China is merely helping its autocratic regime to become richer and more powerful.[101]

Thus, where Rowen finds signs of democratic hope, Mann sees authoritarian fortification.

Most scholars share Mann's general conclusion that liberal democracy is far from being an inevitable consequence of China's capitalist economic reform and growth. Yet, while agreeing that the "fundamentals" of CCP rule remain intact, perhaps a plurality of academics argue that the CCP is much more dynamic, open, and flexible than Mann allows. For these scholars, the CCP's virtually unchallenged political rule since the early 1990s is the result of its adaptation to rapidly changing economic and social circumstances— what these scholars variously call "authoritarian resilience,"[102] "illiberal adaptation,"[103] "nimble authoritarianism,"[104] "Leninist adaptability,"[105] and "adaptive informal institutional change."[106] Just as Mann argues, these scholars argue that China's leaders successfully have embraced and encouraged economic freedom while simultaneously restricting political freedom.[107] However, unlike Mann, they argue that popular political quiescence in contemporary China is not simply the result of fear of repression; rather, ruling elites have embarked on policies that (sometimes even unwittingly) have satisfied the material desires of the public, while simultaneously fragmenting the population to such a degree that organized and sustained political opposition never has the chance to emerge.

Political scientists Bruce Bueno de Mesquita and George Downs, for example, argue that authoritarian regimes such as that in China have become increasingly "sophisticated"; while providing the public goods that the population and the economy need in order to prosper (such as primary education and public transportation), ruling authorities sharply curtail the availability of "co-ordination goods" (such as freedom of press and civil liberties). In so doing, the regime gains increased resources with which to satisfy the population, yet leaves potential political opponents "weak and dispirited."[108] In this way, authoritarian rulers such as those in China not only avoid "the political fallout of economic growth," but actually use economic growth to "increase ... their chances of survival."[109]

In a slight twist on this perspective, political scientist Elizabeth Perry argues that China's ruling regime has survived because it "has proven adept at the art of creating coalitions with, and cleavages among, key social elements."[110] On the one hand, the party-state recruits and rewards members of the elite.[111] On the other hand, "the central leadership ... has adroitly applied techniques of divide and rule."[112] State policies separate different categories of workers and residents, such that the "citizens themselves are often inclined to accept these divisions as a normal part of the political order."[113] And when such groups do show signs of coordination, public security forces work to divide them, meting out differential entreaties, threats, and punishments for each sector.[114]

In a more narrowly focused examination, political scientist Bruce J. Dickson looks at the ways in which these official policies and tactics have played out among private entrepreneurs and college-educated urban residents in the post-Mao era. He finds that, rather than desiring to distance themselves from the political system, these groups are seeking closer connections with the current party-state. They do so because they view the regime as a flexible and relatively open collection of organizations and institutions in which individuals and social groups can expect to find genuine representation of their interests. Thus, Dickson concludes that CCP elites successfully have incorporated individuals and groups that are primarily concerned with economic matters.[115] In a nutshell, the CCP has maintained its power not because the populace fears its repression or is too fragmented to form a coordinated political opposition but because the CCP has adapted its policies and focus in such a way as to attract popular support, at least among critical population sectors.

Reflecting a similar view, other scholars argue that significant administrative reform has resulted in a party-state that is much more institutionalized, meritocratic, and responsive to public sentiments and grievances than it was in the Maoist era.[116] For political scientist Dali Yang, these reforms display a successful adaptive response to problems—such as corruption, a loss of central government control, and increased socioeconomic inequality—that arose from policies undertaken in the first phase of the reform era.[117] In an attempt to address these challenges, in the early 1990s the regime undertook comprehensive tax and fiscal reforms, streamlined and downsized administrative and state institutions, and promoted the codification of laws to limit government behavior. As a result, China's "central state now has *more* fiscal capacity and is *more* capable and effective generally."[118] Consequently, the population has more reason to support it.

Similarly, for political scientist Andrew Nathan, China's contemporary system of rule is characterized by "authoritarian resilience."[119] Although the regime remains fundamentally "authoritarian," it has changed dramatically in the reform era, making substantial moves toward the features that widely are seen as hallmarks of a "modern" state. Specifically, it has "(1) abandon[ed] utopian ideology and charismatic styles of leadership; (2) empower[ed] a technocratic elite; (3) introduce[d] bureaucratic regularization, complexity, and specialization; and (4) reduce[d] control over private speech and action."[120] In addition, "the regime has developed a series of input institutions (that is, institutions that people can use to apprise the state of their concerns) that allow Chinese to believe that they have some influence on policy decisions and personnel choices at the local level."[121] Along with village elections, Nathan points to the relatively new citizens' right to sue the state, as well as an increased willingness to accept and address public complaints among government institutions (such as official "letters and visits" departments [*xinfangju*], people's congresses and people's political consultative conferences, and the media).[122] Nathan concludes that these "institutions for political participation and appeal [have strengthened] the CCP's legitimacy among the public at large."[123] As a result, the Chinese public simply has little reason to push for more systemic political change.

Other scholars, though perhaps a minority, recognize these changes in the party-state but believe that these administrative and political reforms have run into a wall. They stress that the highest priority of the regime is not efficiency and effectiveness but, rather, the maintenance of its unchallenged political power. Former journalist Bruce Gilley, for example, argues that "the CCP has moved . . . from political tumult to an ad hoc peace; but it has gone no further. As a result, the problems traditionally associated with nondemocratic regimes— illegitimacy, misgovernment, corruption, and elite instability—remain legion in China."[124] He cautions readers to heed the example of Suharto's Indonesia, which "fell from power just as it had seemingly bucked the trend [of democratization] and consolidated itself through new forms of institutionalization in the mid-1990s, appearing 'solid and highly efficient.'"[125] Similarly, political scientist Minxin Pei argues that despite substantial movement toward a market economy, China's closed political system has "trapped" China in a "partial reform equilibrium" that will go no further in the direction of capitalism or democracy.[126] For scholars such as Pei and Gilley, the only way out of this "trap" is democracy. Otherwise, China's future will be marked by political decay or collapse.

This book embraces the more mainstream view among China scholars that public acceptance of continued CCP rule derives from the party's successful adaptation to changing economic and social conditions. It departs from existing analyses by providing a coherent and fundamental explanation of *why* the party's adaptive responses have worked. Because most current examinations tend to analyze China as a single case study, they miss the broader factors that underlie the political attitudes and behavior of the various socioeconomic groups that make up Chinese society. By placing China in an explicitly comparative context, this book uncovers the larger forces that have shaped state-society relations in the reform era: state controls over the economy, market forces related to late immersion in the global economy, and socialist legacies.

STATE-LED ECONOMIC DEVELOPMENT AND
LATE INDUSTRIALIZATION

Although conceptually distinct, state-led economic development and late industrialization typically have occurred in tandem, making it difficult to undertake an entirely separate analysis of each. The political consequences of these factors are best understood when viewed in contrast to the experience of the world's first industrializers, particularly that of England. Indeed, to a large extent, the assumed linkage between capitalist economic development and democratic change is informed by the English case.

The First Industrializers

In England, capitalism emerged from a feudal, agrarian economy, where economic inequality was extreme and the state exercised little direct control over the lives of the citizenry. Under these conditions, both capital and labor developed largely independent of the state. Further, the existing state seemed only to constrain the economic, political, and social opportunities of private capital holders. Democracy, then, came to be viewed as a means to wrest power from a backward-looking political regime. However, the version of liberal democracy that initially was embraced by private capitalists in England did not include labor. Rather, in its early form, liberal democracy was viewed as a means to enhance the political power of capital in relation to *both* the existing authoritarian state *and* urban workers. Labor, meanwhile, had little material attachment to the former authoritarian regime and saw the possibility for economic betterment though participation in the emergent democratic polity. Thus, workers played a key role in pushing for the expansion of liberal democratic rights.

In large part, this sequence was made possible by unique global and domestic circumstances that have not been present since the nineteenth century. For England, which in the late eighteenth century was the first country to embark on industrialization, global competition and capital mobility were substantially limited as compared to all "later" industrializers. As the late economic historian Alexander Gerschenkron argues, in England this limited competition meant that capitalists did not need to rely on the state for support and protection. For all subsequent industrializers, increased competition over time has bred a greater need for state involvement with capital accumulation. Thus, even within the first global "wave" of industrialization that occurred in the nineteenth century, in relatively early industrializers (such as England and the United States) private capitalists engaged in business largely independent of the state, while in countries that industrialized later in the century (such as France, Germany, and Japan) state-capital relations were closer.[127]

Further, as Bellin notes, because early formulations of "liberal democracy" did not include labor, in this first "wave" of industrialization, democratization initially did not threaten the material prosperity of the capitalists whose profits derived from low wages and exacting work requirements.[128] Yet at the same time, even in the late nineteenth century, capitalists could choose from among only a small handful of countries with relatively small populations as potential sites for industrial investment. The resultant limitations on capital mobility gave labor sufficient leverage successfully to push for greater political inclusion in countries that industrialized during this period, including England and many of the countries of Western Europe, as well as the United States. Consequently, by the early twentieth century, the idea of "liberal democracy" had been expanded to include those of lower economic status.

Post–World War II Industrialization

Following this first wave of industrialization, there was a lull in the international expansion of industrial development. Beginning in the 1960s, and continuing through the present, industrialization has quickly spread across the globe. For countries undertaking industrial development during this period, the international context has presented greater challenges than those that were faced by industrializing states in the first wave. As Bellin emphasizes, compared to nineteenth-century nations, the post–World War II world has become largely industrialized and commercially integrated and, therefore, highly competitive.[129] Faced with this reality, private capitalists in today's industrializing countries tend to be much more dependent on the state, both for capital investment and for protection from competition against businesses in earlier developers. In comparison to earlier industrializers (especially England), in later developers the state tends to be more supportive of private entrepreneurs, as political leaders quickly come to view industrial development as their only means of ensuring military security and thus maintaining their political power. Bellin notes that in England the state was perceived to be hostile to the interests of capital, but in later developers the state often consciously anticipates the interests of capital.[130] In this context, private entrepreneurs have little reason to oppose the existing regime and indeed have a substantial incentive to support it.

At the same time, for later industrializing countries—especially those, like China, that are in the midst of industrial development today—the greater mobility of capital renders unskilled workers exceedingly vulnerable. With a global surfeit of unskilled labor, workers have little ability to successfully press for improved pay or working conditions; doing so would most likely result in job loss. Further, should the leaders of a presently industrializing state attempt to require potential foreign investors to enforce labor rights and protections, these investors are likely to set up shop elsewhere. According to Bellin, the combined result is that, for countries embarking on industrialization today, a rise in GDP often coincides with a rise in domestic economic inequality. More specifically, economic growth typically is accompanied by the creation of a huge domestic "reserve army" of labor, a rise in poverty, and a decline in working conditions.[131]

When this is true, domestic capitalists have reason to fear the political empowerment of the working class and, thus, reason to oppose the installation of a liberal democratic regime. Should workers gain the right to vote, they likely would support higher wages and improved work conditions, thus diminishing the profits of private capital. Further, as noted above, when economic development coincides with increased economic inequality, the resulting economic structure is shaped like an onion dome, with only a few groups occupying the top and middle layers and the vast majority subsisting at the lowest level. In this context, the vulnerable and often impoverished masses constitute a majority of the population. This, in turn, gives those at the top of the hierarchy reason to fear majoritarian rule.

State Dependence and Political Reform

Comparing the political attitudes and behavior of capitalists in authoritarian states, Bellin shows that, unlike in the earliest developers, in later developers capitalists often are "diffident about democratization."[132] Indeed, private capital holders actually may oppose democratization when two conditions hold: (1) they are dependent on the state for their profitability, and (2) economic growth coincides with widespread poverty and a potentially well-mobilized working class. As elaborated by Bellin, perhaps the clearest examples of this scenario are Tunisia and Indonesia. In both of these countries, capitalists had a symbiotic relationship with the state. In each case, officials doubling as entrepreneurs used their control over allocation of licenses, concessions, and credit to promote their own companies, blurring the boundary between the public and private sectors. Still, the private sector grew and flourished. This made private entrepreneurs wise to nurture cozy relations with state elites. The fact that much of the interaction between entrepreneurs and state officials was shady or corrupt made political transparency (typically associated with democracy) less attractive. Also, the fact that many state officials doubled as entrepreneurs reassured the business community that state elites would anticipate private sector interests when formulating public policy, obviating the need for more formal mechanisms of accountability.

In addition, in both Tunisia and Indonesia, poverty levels were high, and economic development largely derived from the "exploitation of a docile labor force."[133] In this context, the capitalist class had little incentive to push for political reform.[134] In South Korea, Bellin argues, this pattern was replicated from the end of World War II through the early 1980s. By the mid-1980s, however, South Korean businesses had become sufficiently competitive internationally that they no longer needed to rely on state support. Further, as political scientist David Martin Jones points out, the military autocracy was no longer able to guarantee political stability.[135] Consequently, South Korean business owners had less reason to support the authoritarian regime and more cause to support liberal democratic change. In Brazil, Mexico, and Saudi Arabia, Bellin shows that the attitudes of private capital toward the authoritarian state also have waxed and waned in sync with variations in private capital's dependence on the state.[136]

The rising economic inequality that makes capital hesitant to endorse liberal democracy might, at the same time, give workers reason to press for democratic change. However, as Bellin demonstrates, this is not necessarily the case. In reality, the political stance of labor depends on policies undertaken by the leaders of a late-developing authoritarian state. First, as with capital, the political attitudes and behavior of workers hinge on the degree to which they depend on the state. According to Bellin, if the state adopts a "corporate strategy that gives unions financial and organizational support in exchange for political loyalty and self-restraint," organized labor may come to "fear biting the hand that feeds it."[137] Indeed, to the extent that this is true, unionized workers—or, indeed, any workers that enjoy privileged relations with the state—have reason to worry that a change in regime type would jeopardize their existing flow of state benefits.[138] Second, the political stance of workers depends on the "degree to which organized labor is economically privileged relative to the general population."[139] To the extent that unionized workers hold an "aristocratic" position, they are likely to "exhibit 'dissolidarity' with the unorganized masses" and are unlikely to support the political empowerment of their less-advantaged working brethren.[140] Bellin adds that these labor characteristics are more prevalent in later developers than they were in the earliest industrializers. In later developers, workers are in a much weaker position internationally than was the case for those in the first countries to industrialize. As a result, they have no choice but to look to the state for protection. In addition, Bellin argues, the problem of labor surplus in later developers makes unionized workers more prone to jealously guard their "aristocratic" advantages over other workers.

The Rise of Neoliberalism

Although not addressed by Bellin, there is an additional feature of the contemporary world that further serves to push labor into the arms of authoritarian developmental states. In contrast to the first phase of the post–World War II era, when liberal democracy in the industrialized world was wedded to the welfare state, in the past two decades neoliberal economic policies have be-come hegemonic.[141] Although the economic crisis that originated in the United States in 2008 has undermined this consensus to a degree, the leaders of developing countries remain pressured by multinational corporations, in-ternational institutions, and advanced industrial nations to privatize and shrink the public sector, to minimize social spending, to ease trade restric-tions, and to generally diminish governmental "interference" in the function-ing of the free market. As a result, workers in developing countries today are often much more vulnerable than they were in countries undertaking indus-trialization during the first three decades of the post–World War II era. Even so, despite external pressures to do otherwise, the political leaders of develop-ing countries sometimes do increase social welfare spending to ease the "ad-justment costs" of international economic integration. When the authoritar-ian leaders of a developmental state provide their workers with protections against the vicissitudes of global capitalism, labor has incentives to support those leaders.

SOCIALIST LEGACIES

These features of state-led late development are important parts of the broader context that shapes state-society relations in contemporary China. Nonethe-less, China is not simply a state-led late developer; China also is a post-socialist state. As a result, its starting point on the road to capitalist economic develop-ment differs from late developers without a socialist past. Studies of post-communist transitions in Russia and East/Central Europe demonstrate that socialist legacies have a powerful impact on the attitudes of common citizens toward both capitalism and liberal democracy. Overall, these works point to a general lack of excitement about free-market democracy among citizens in postcommunist Russia and East/Central Europe. Although the historical paths of these countries differ in some important ways from that of China, public attitudes in reform-era China exhibit some important similarities to those in those other once-socialist countries that appear related to China's socialist past.

Comprehensive data on the attitudes of contemporary Russian citizens are found in the New Russia Barometer (NRB), a series of surveys conducted by political scientists Richard Rose, William Mishler, and Neil Munro every year since 1992.[142] Among other things, the NRB probes the nature and impact of Russia's socialist legacy on citizens' views, asking respondents to evaluate the pre-perestroika system and tracking the relationship among attitudes toward the past, present, and future. One of the many notable findings of the yearly NRB surveys is a consistently positive assessment of the previous communist system.[143] In 1992, 62 percent expressed favorable views of the pre-perestroika economy; by 2000, remarkably enough, the number had risen to 83 percent, and it has remained between 70 and 81 percent ever since.[144] Further, as Rose, Mishler, and Munro state, "after market mechanisms began to be established, attitudes toward the command economy became more positive."[145] In addition, when asked to rate the pre-perestroika *political* system, sizeable majorities continue to give positive ratings over time (51 to 67 percent from 1992–98 and 65 to 75 percent from 1999–2005).[146] Paradoxically, this is true even though in all NRB surveys, most Russians identify the communist regime as a dictatorship.[147] Further, although a majority of Russians in all survey years believe that the post-reform regimes have been more democratic than the old regime, they still have viewed the old regime more favorably than those that have governed in the post-reform era.[148] Similarly, in a more geographically expansive study based on surveys in the late 1990s and first few years of the 2000s, political scientist Marc Morje Howard finds that citizens of postcommunist Russia and Europe share a profound disappointment with the political and economic status quo.[149]

Howard and Rose, Mishler, and Munro show that over time most citizens of Russia and East/Central Europe continue not to share the values of "Anglo-American free-market democrats."[150] Disappointment with the results of political economic liberalization is deep and endemic. While both Howard and Rose, Mishler, and Munro insist that this does not portend mass political unrest, it does demonstrate that citizens of postcommunist Russia and Europe do not see "more" economic and political liberalization as the solution to their individual and societal ills. As late as the 2005 NRB survey, for example, Rose, Mishler, and Munro report that "only 25 percent said that democracy is always preferable to any other kind of government. The largest group—42 percent—said that under some circumstances an authoritarian government could be better; another 34 percent said it didn't matter to them whether they had a democratic or an authoritarian regime," again a group larger than the one of people who always prefer democracy.[151]

Related to this, for most Russians, the idea "democracy" includes not just the Western liberal values of individual rights and representative political institutions but social and economic welfare as well.[152] Further contextualizing this finding, Howard notes that high unemployment is "particularly excruciating for postcommunist citizens, who lived their lives in a system where everybody had a job, and where the workplace was the cornerstone of social activity."[153] Similarly, looking at Russia in 1999, political scientists Judith Kullberg and William Zimmerman find that common people simply do not "embrace Western liberalism, but rather opt[] for socialism or authoritarian nationalism."[154] This is because, they reason, the "Soviet social structure . . . produced mass publics whose economic interests were tightly interconnected with socialist institutions. Millions are still painfully attached to and dependent on these institutions and the disintegrating state."[155] Recognizing the long-term inability to succeed under the new "structure of economic opportunity" faced by these people, Kullberg and Zimmerman find that the masses are rejecting the new liberal order—including, possibly, even democracy.[156]

Sociologist Linda Fuller's 2000 review of the literature on Eastern and Central European transitions reaches parallel conclusions. She finds that, although workers had complaints about the communist economic system, overall they "spoke with pride about innovations at their workplaces, the new skills they had acquired, the quality of their products, and high productivity levels. . . . [They also] praised job-related benefits such as paid sick/maternity leave, cheap meals, vacation sports, emergency financial assistance, high employment levels, and the availability of affordable and varied public services."[157] In addition, Fuller cites substantial evidence showing "widely held post-socialist preferences for reducing the gap between rich and poor."[158] Consequently, in Eastern Europe and the Soviet Union, ordinary citizens remain disillusioned and skeptical about the transition to liberal capitalist democracy. Not surprisingly, in Russia, the Communist Party (which, unlike the "new" communist parties of East/Central Europe, continued to embrace Soviet-style communism) remained popular through the end of the twentieth century; before 2000 the Communist Party regularly received the highest percentage of the popular vote in legislative elections.[159] Further, a plurality of Russians who adopted a political label (22 percent) endorsed communism, while another 9 percent favored social democracy.[160]

These findings provide a broader context within which to view the economic and political attitudes of contemporary Chinese citizens—especially those at the lower end of the socioeconomic spectrum. Combined with the realities of state-led development and late industrialization, China's socialist legacies have given most Chinese citizens reason to tolerate—and even support—the authoritarian CCP-led political status quo, and disincentives to seek the installation of liberal democracy.

MATERIAL AND IDEAL INCENTIVES

Most fundamentally, the argument proposed herein is economic: Virtually all of China's major socioeconomic sectors have had material incentives to support (or at least accept) the existing political order. Yet, these material incentives have been colored and shaped by ideal interests and incentives—that is, popular beliefs regarding what is right and good.[161] In large part, these beliefs have derived from the Chinese citizenry's lived experience of Maoist and post-Maoist CCP rule. In this sense, China's socialist legacy has had much more than an economic effect on China's population; it has instilled deeply held values and dispositions toward what is moral, just, and legitimate.

Citizens at the bottom of China's socioeconomic hierarchy have not simply had material disincentives to press for an end to CCP rule. Inasmuch as these individuals have espoused "socialist" values such as the right to work (either in industry or on the land) and to decent pay, accommodations, and benefits, they have had ideal incentives to support political leaders who have displayed these values in rhetoric and in deed. As time passes, and younger Chinese who have lived only in the post-Mao period come to dominate these lower-tier socioeconomic sectors, their less "socialist" ideals and values are likely to shape their political proclivities in different ways.

For those at the top of China's socioeconomic structure, ideal interests also have affected perceived material concerns. The CCP's turn from castigating private entrepreneurs, professionals, and intellectuals in the Maoist era to embracing them in the post-Mao period has made the existing governmental system appear more open and fair. Thus, it is not just that these sectors have had material incentives to support the status quo; their ideal desires for social respect and approbation have been addressed by the central regime as well. As a result, democracy as a set of ideas (rather than simply an alternative vehicle for economic allocation) has not been as appealing as one might expect. As with China's lower-level socioeconomic groups, as time passes, the ideal interests of these upper-tier sectors may change in such a way that systemic political change seems not only economically beneficial but also morally desirable.

CONCLUSION

Chapters 2 through 6 explore the ways in which state-led development, market forces associated with late industrialization, and socialist legacies have shaped public perceptions of socioeconomic mobility; economic dependence on the party-state; relative socioeconomic status; and political options. Looking separately at each of China's major socioeconomic sectors, these chapters detail the impact of these factors on each group's (material and ideal) interests and show their connection to popular political attitudes and behavior. Using the categories employed by the Chinese government, as well as by most scholars who study China, the book proceeds by first examining the two socioeconomic groups that occupy the small upper and middle tiers of China's onion dome-shaped socioeconomic structure: private entrepreneurs (Chapter 2), and professionals (Chapter 3). Next, the book turns to the major strata that make up the massive lower level of the onion dome: rank-and-file state sector workers (Chapter 4), rank-and-file private sector workers (Chapter 5), and farmers (Chapter 6). Taking each group in turn, these chapters trace the ways in which temporal changes in state-led development policies, market forces related to late industrialization, and socialist legacies have affected perceptions of socioeconomic mobility; economic dependence on the party-state; relative socioeconomic status; and perceived political options. As evidence, these chapters cite general economic statistics, party-state pronouncements and policies, and qualitative and quantitative studies of daily living conditions. Linking these factors to each group's political attitudes and behavior in the reform period, these chapters present public opinion survey data, statistics on membership in the CCP and party-state organizations, evidence of participation in local elections, and research on the nature and frequency of contentious popular actions (such as petitioning and protests). In addition, Chapters 2 through 6 examine variations among different subgroups within each stratum, as well as distinct geographic patterns.

Chapter 7, the conclusion, emphasizes that this examination of state-society relations in contemporary China provides a snapshot of the current incentive structure; it does not claim that these motivations will remain in place in perpetuity. Should the domestic and/or international context change, so too may these incentives. Thus, Chapter 7 also discusses the most likely sources of attitudinal change in China and explores what might come next in terms of political transformation. In addition, the final chapter assesses the uniqueness of China's developmental experience, comparing it with that of other state-led developers, later industrializers, post-socialist states, and politically restrictive regimes. In so doing, it examines the possibility that China is forging a new model of political and economic development in contradistinction to that of the West.

2 PRIVATE ENTREPRENEURS

AT THE HIGHEST LEVEL OF CHINA'S socioeconomic hierarchy are private entrepreneurs. Defined officially as the owners of businesses with eight or more employees, this sector is perhaps the most studied of any in the reform era.[1] Although private entrepreneurs constitute less than 1 percent of China's population, their political attitudes and actions are widely thought to be key in determining the future stability of the CCP-led political regime.[2] First, as outlined in Chapter 1, some believe that China's emergent "capitalist class"[3] will chafe under authoritarian rule, as its economic liberty inevitably will be restricted by its lack of political freedom and rights. As noted earlier, informing this view is the experience of England around the time of the Industrial Revolution, when private entrepreneurs pressed for political liberalization as a necessary means to break the power of an authoritarian state that limited their economic prosperity and opportunity. Many studies of China's private business owners are motivated by the desire to find out whether or not this chain of events may be repeated in China.

Second, the economic power of China's private entrepreneurs gives them potential leverage over the state. As of 2003, official sources identified 26.57 million private enterprises in China.[4] According to official statistics reported in 2005 and 2007, domestic private businesses accounted for one-third to one-half of China's GDP.[5] In addition, they employed more than 100 million people.[6] Together with foreign-invested private firms, they provided an estimated 75 percent of employment and 71 percent of tax revenues.[7] Privately owned businesses also have been the most dynamic and growing sector of the economy. From 1992–2002, the number of private enterprises grew by 33 percent, while the number of state and collective enterprises declined by −2.73 percent and −7.6 percent, respectively.[8] Over the same time period, the average yearly growth of total registered capital among domestic private enterprises was 60 percent, as compared to 10 percent for state firms and 2 percent for foreign firms.[9] From 1992–2006, private business provided virtually all net urban job growth and nearly all economic growth.[10] It is clear that private capital holders have great power over China's economy. As a result, they hold substantial potential leverage over the country's political leaders, whose legitimacy rests largely on their ability to deliver economic prosperity.

Yet China's private entrepreneurs have not pressed for systemic political change. To the contrary, they have appeared quite willing to tolerate, and even support, the current CCP-led regime. Indeed, there are more CCP members per capita among private entrepreneurs than in any other social sector.[11] In addition, they appear quite willing to join government-sponsored business associations and to work within existing political institutions. Further, private businesspeople show great interest in participating in local elections, as well as in government bodies at the county level and higher.

Thus, at present, there is little evidence that China will repeat the experience of seventeenth- to eighteenth-century England, where private capital holders were at the forefront of democratization. The reason: Unlike in England, China's capitalists are operating within the context of state-led development, late industrialization, and a legacy of socialism. As the reform era has progressed, the confluence of these factors has affected private entrepreneurs' perceptions of socioeconomic mobility; economic dependence on the party-state; socioeconomic polarization; and political options such that a substantial portion of private businesspeople has come to hold a clear stake in the perpetuation of CCP rule. This chapter delineates the ways in which these variables have interacted to affect the political attitudes and behavior of private entrepreneurs as the reform era has progressed. As a whole, private entrepreneurs have evidenced greater acceptance of the existing CCP-led political system over time, confounding any assumption that they will become the agent of liberal democratic political transformation.

THE EARLY REFORM ERA (LATE 1970s TO THE EARLY 1990s)

In the first phase of the post-Mao period, state-led development policies tolerated the rise of small private enterprises but discriminated against their owners.

Meanwhile, China's socialist economy—characterized by a dominant and privileged public sector—remained largely intact. Finally, during this time, few areas in China had been opened to international trade and investment, such that market forces associated with late development generally had little bearing on the financial circumstances of domestic private businesspeople.

Following decades of recurrent repression under the rule of CCP leader Mao Zedong, private entrepreneurs emerged nearly "from scratch" in China's reform era. From the mid-1950s through Mao's death in 1976, despite some fluctuation in official policy, private entrepreneurs were scorned as "capitalist roaders" and faced substantial restrictions and punishment. In this atmosphere, most private businesses ceased.[12] According to one estimate, "on the eve of market reforms, the number of self-employed 'individual laborers' constituted a tiny 0.01 percent of the Chinese population."[13]

When economic liberalization first started in the late 1970s, the CCP began to tolerate the emergence of small-scale private business. According to political scientist Dorothy Solinger, in late 1978 the party "uncritically redefined a large majority of the entire bourgeoisie . . . as having been transformed into people who live by their own labor," thus repealing the notion that private businesspeople engaged in exploitation and were part of the "tail of capitalism." In so doing, the CCP "accepted . . . small traders as socialist . . . an unambiguous title they had not enjoyed since the mid-1950s."[14] Yet, both central and local authorities continued to view "capitalists" as politically suspect. Consequently, in the first decade of the reform era, private entrepreneurs had an attenuated and sometimes strained relationship with the ruling regime.

In this early phase of the post-Mao era, private enterprises were seen by central leaders as a way to "fill up the gaps" left by the public sector in terms of employment as well as consumer goods and services—gaps that were especially apparent in the aftermath of the tumultuous Cultural Revolution of 1966–76.[15] Accordingly, most private business undertakings of this time period were extremely small and mobile and relied on little capital. Among other things, they included street-side fruit stands, shoe repair services, and improvised taxis. The party-state's first legal reference to private business—a State Council text issued in 1981—reflected this official view, as well as the empirical reality of existing private enterprises. In the State Council document, private businesses were referred to as "individual enterprises" (*getihu*) with no more than seven employees. The official statement also emphasized that these businesses were to complement, rather than compete with, public sector enterprises. Formal sanction of the private sector came in 1982, when the Chinese Constitution was revised to state (in Article 11) that "the state protects the lawful rights and interests of the individual economy." At the same time, however, the 1982 Constitution continued to describe the "individual economy" as only "a complement to the socialist public economy." Perhaps more importantly, Article 11 of the 1982 Constitution asserted that "the state guides, helps and supervises the individual economy by exercising administrative control."[16]

Despite these somewhat encouraging rhetorical developments, throughout the 1980s private businesspeople remained vulnerable to various policy shifts and political campaigns. These included economic "rectification" campaigns against smuggling and profiteering in the early 1980s, the "anti-spiritual pollution" campaign of 1983–84, a campaign against "suitcase companies" (*pibao gongsi*) that "exist on paper but lack assets" in 1985–86, and the "anti-bourgeois liberalization" campaign of 1987.[17] Although varying in duration and intensity, the overall result was a political environment in which private businesspeople remained vulnerable to political attacks.

In 1988 the State Council approved an amendment to Article 11 that articulated a more favorable official stance toward private business. Although the earlier version expressed only tolerance of the private sector, the revised Article asserted that "the State *encourages, supports* and guides the development of the non-public sectors of the economy" (italics added). A few months later, the State Council legitimated the existence of "private enterprises" in a document entitled the "Provisional Regulations on Private Enterprises." Along with defining private enterprises as for-profit organizations employing eight or more people, these regulations spelled out the requirements for establishing and dissolving private enterprises as well as terms of employment. Even while acknowledging the legality of medium and large private enterprises, central officials took virtually no action to encourage and support the nonpublic sector.

To the contrary, through the late 1980s private businesses faced discrimination at the hands of local officials, especially when competing with public sector enterprises for resources such as supplies, land, buildings, and access to utilities.[18] Among other things, local state representatives levied exorbitant taxes and imposed fees related to sanitation, urban construction, transport, and weights and measures. At times, these financial burdens were so high that they "amounted to nearly the total of the net profits the firms had taken in."[19] As the 1980s drew to a close, circumstances for many private entrepreneurs became even more precarious. In late 1988 the central party-state announced a policy of "rectification and retrenchment" to address skyrocketing inflation, a growing budget deficit, and widespread government corruption. At this point, economic reform stalled, and the status of private entrepreneurs was thrown into question.

Nonetheless, the party-state's partial privatization of the economy amidst continued government controls in the early reform period opened opportunities for well-connected individuals to gain inside information or market access and thereby reap high profits. Many benefited from the dual-price structure, established in 1985, for consumer products and some industrial products, reaping significant rewards from "buying low and selling high." They were enabled by their privileged backgrounds, including relatively high levels of education and close relations with representatives of the party-state.[20] Similarly, between 1987 and 1992, a massive amount of state-owned land was transferred to the private sector. As historian Zhaohui Hong notes, this did not occur via a fair and open bidding process; to the contrary, those with close relations to party-state officials received the majority of the land at bargain rates.[21] Subsequently, these real-estate entrepreneurs expanded into finance, construction, advertising, and insurance, again benefiting from their close relations with political authorities.

Perceptions of Socioeconomic Mobility, Relative Socioeconomic Status, Material Dependence on the Party-State, and Political Options

In the early reform period, despite an inhospitable political context, many private entrepreneurs were able to make great economic gains, affording them increasingly high economic status and upward socioeconomic mobility. Further, although this group, relative to other sectors, had low social status, in the early post-Mao era its status was far higher than it had been in the Maoist period. Because connections with the party-state enabled private businesspeople to profit from the partially state-controlled and partially privatized economy, their prosperity depended on the ruling regime. However, throughout most of the early post-Mao period the suspect political status of private entrepreneurs restricted their ability to participate overtly in the political system. Those who were party members before their entry into private business typically had to cover their entrepreneurial activities, while non-party members who became successful in business were not welcomed into the party. Indeed, a few months after the regime's brutal suppression of the student-led protests of 1989, central authorities announced an outright ban on the recruitment of private business-people into the party.[22]

Political Attitudes and Behavior

The political attitudes and behavior of private entrepreneurs during the early reform era reflected these realities. At the end of 1988, only 1 percent of private entrepreneurs were party members, and the vast majority of these had joined the party before their entry into business.[23] In spring 1989, when students and city dwellers took to the streets to protest corruption and to call for greater political liberalization, some private entrepreneurs in Beijing made financial contributions to demonstrators. Most notable among these was the founder and CEO of China's largest and most successful private business at the time, Wan Runnan of the Stone Corporation. Still, most private entrepreneurs did not actively support the demonstrations, and many openly disapproved of the movement, believing it to be disruptive of the business environment.[24] Nonetheless, given the regime's restrictions on and sometimes hostile policies toward private entrepreneurs in the first phase of the reform era, it seemed possible that China's emergent capitalists might indeed follow their counterparts in England and press for systemic political change in order to protect and support their interests.

THE LATE REFORM ERA (EARLY 1990 THROUGH THE PRESENT)

Since the early 1990s, however, this possibility has appeared increasingly remote. In the second phase of the post-Mao period, state-led development policies, market forces associated with late industrialization, and socialist legacies have combined to create much more favorable conditions for private entrepreneurs. In early 1992, top CCP leader Deng Xiaoping made his famous "Southern Tour" of special economic zones in Shenzhen and Zhuhai and the cities of Guangdong and Shanghai, all of which had been allowed to experiment with foreign investment and free markets. Deng declared the experiment a great success and called for further economic liberalization. At the Fourteenth Party Congress in late 1992, Deng's appeal was enshrined in official doctrine, which now openly called for the establishment of a "socialist *market* economy" (italics added) and touted economic growth as the country's highest priority. As the clear engine of economic growth, private business gained a much-elevated status. In 1994, China's first Company Law came into effect, allowing for the establishment of limited liability shareholding corporations. Three years later, at the Fifteenth Party Congress in 1997, private enterprise was described as an "important," rather than a "complementary" element of China's economy, and in 1999, the Constitution was modified to reflect this shift in status. Further, party cadres no longer were restrained from engaging in private enterprise.[25]

As a result, the 1990s witnessed a sea change in relations between private entrepreneurs and the party-state—preventing (or, at a minimum, forestalling) the possibility that China's emerging "capitalists" would follow in the footsteps of their English counterparts and press for liberal democratic change. During the 1990s, relations between local officials and private entrepreneurs generally warmed. As Bruce J. Dickson explains, "because promoting economic growth was a key criterion for evaluating the work performance of local officials, many were eager to cooperate with the entrepreneurs who could provide that growth."[26] In this context, many private businesses engaged in the practice of "wearing a red hat"—that is, registering as a local government-controlled collective enterprise. By doing so, private entrepreneurs hoped both to gain a more reputable status and to take advantage of tax breaks granted to new collectives.[27] Rather than attempting to prevent this practice, local authorities encouraged it. As Kellee S. Tsai emphasizes,

> most local cadres knew exactly what they were doing when they accepted, or perhaps extracted, a registration fee from a local entrepreneur to run a collective enterprise . . . cadres in many rural localities had a vested interest in allowing profitable businesses to operate and contribute to local revenues regardless of their true ownership status.[28]

The practice of privately owned business "wearing a red hat" proliferated in the early 1990s, with hundreds of thousands taking part. Along with fueling local economic growth, "wearing a red hat" allowed individuals who were registered as collective enterprise owners, yet were in reality private enterprise owners, to join the party without technically violating the official national ban on membership for private businesspeople. At the same time, a significant number of party officials themselves "entered the sea" of business (xiahai).[29]

By the mid-1990s, tax breaks for new collective enterprises had been eliminated, and many private entrepreneurs sensed that central policy was becoming more favorable toward the private sector.[30] As a result, many opted to remove their "red hats" and register as privately owned businesses. Consequently, the official number of privately owned enterprises skyrocketed. In 2004 private property rights gained constitutional protection. Although the earlier version of the Constitution declared that only *public* property is "sacred and inviolable," the 2004 constitution (in Article 13) added that "the lawful *private* property of citizens" also is "inviolable" (italics added). At the Seventeenth Party Congress in late 2007, representatives amended the party Constitution to place the nonpublic economy on equal footing with the public economy, stating that the party will "unswervingly encourage, support and guide the development of the non-public sector." More concretely, this change gave private businesses access to some areas of the economy that previously were "off-limits" and ended preferential policies toward state-owned enterprises.[31]

Although the tax burden on private entrepreneurs has increased since the mid-1990s, it has remained quite low relative to the private sector's contribution to China's GDP, as well as in relation to the tax share provided by other types of enterprises. From 1996–2000, private enterprises contributed 2.2 percent of total taxes on enterprises. From 2001–5, this portion rose to 7.1 percent. Even with this increase, the portion of taxes provided by private business owners has remained far below their roughly 50 percent share of GDP. By way of comparison, although the tax share of state-owned, collective, and share-holding enterprises[32] dropped from nearly 76 percent in 1996–2000 to almost 63 percent in 2001–5, their contribution has remained far higher than their estimated 37 percent share of GDP. For foreign enterprises, the tax share has risen from 14.5 percent (1996–2000) to 20.5 percent (2001–5), a portion that is higher than their roughly 16 percent share of GDP (in 2006).[33] If anything, state-led development policies in the late reform period have given preferential tax treatment to domestic private enterprises.

With regard to socialist legacies, the alteration of key social and economic policies in the latter portion of the post-Mao era has dramatically improved the business prospects of private entrepreneurs. As the privatization of public sector enterprises became more rapid and extensive beginning in the mid-1990s, new types of private business owners emerged. First, as the lifetime employment system was dismantled, many skilled and savvy state-owned enterprise workers voluntarily left their public sector jobs. Feeling freed rather than threatened by the liberalization of China's economy, these individuals viewed it as an opportunity to use their talents for greater financial benefit than was available to them in the public sector.[34] Accordingly, many such state-owned or collective enterprise managers and employees resigned from their posts and established independent private businesses unrelated to their previous public sector enterprises.[35]

A second type of private entrepreneur to arise from the privatization of the public sector included managers of state-owned enterprises and township and village enterprises who gained the largest shares in their former enterprise when it was transformed into a shareholding company. These individuals thus obtained control of the assets, networks, land, and equipment of the former public sector enterprise. Technically, they were required to employ a majority of the former enterprise workers, who themselves were required to buy shares in the newly privatized company. In reality, however, many former employees were fired, even after being forced to pay for shares as a condition of their continued employment.[36] Other entrepreneurs bought former public sector enterprises outright, often facilitated by their ties to local government officials. These entrepreneurs gained the assets of the enterprise without being responsible for its debt or for employing its former workers. In most cases, a large portion of the previous workforce was retrenched. Further, those workers fortunate enough to remain employed in the privatized firm typically were forced to accept less pay and more exacting working conditions.[37]

Meanwhile, the party-state's dismantling of socialist labor controls and protections provided private business owners with a massive oversupply of unskilled workers during most of the late reform period. First, beginning in the early 1990s, the regime eased the internal migration restrictions that had been strictly enforced throughout the Maoist period and that had loosened only slightly in the first phase of the reform era. The result was a massive movement of rural residents to the cities. The pool of unskilled labor available for private business owners was further increased by the extensive state-owned enterprise reforms that began around 1995, resulting in the unemployment of tens of millions of former state sector employees. These policies provided private business owners with a seemingly unending number of employees willing to work for minimal pay and to endure relentless working conditions.[38]

Finally, the party-state's opening of China's economy to the international capitalist system since the early 1990s has been extremely beneficial to private enterprise owners. With the establishment of special economic zones, free trade zones, and economic and technological development zones, private businesspeople have earned profits through contracts with foreign buyers that have enabled China's private entrepreneurs to capitalize on the domestic surfeit of low-cost workers. Rightly perceived by government leaders as the engine of China's economic growth during the late post-Mao period, central elites generally have turned a blind eye to the exploitative (and often illegal) employment conditions of the unskilled workers who have labored in these highly profitable export-oriented firms.

Also benefiting from the privatization of China's domestic economy and its opening to the global capitalist system are private entrepreneurs who have relied on tech-intensive and creative projects (rather than political connections) to attract venture capital.[39] Most of these individuals are university-educated and have no prior public sector employment experience. Their firms tend to employ more skilled "professional" workers, who enjoy better pay and working conditions than do the unskilled employees in other kinds of private enterprises and who themselves sit within the upper echelon of China's socioeconomic hierarchy.

It is clear that from the early 1990s through the present, state-led development policies have increasingly favored the private sector. Simultaneously, the party has dismantled and transformed the "socialist" attributes of the public sector in a manner working to the benefit of private business owners. Central authorities also have eased the socialist-era labor migration controls that impeded the large-scale movement of rural residents to the cities through the 1980s. When combined with China's opening to global markets, these factors have enabled many private entrepreneurs to reap immense profits.

Perceptions of Socioeconomic Mobility, Relative Socioeconomic Status, Material Dependence on the Party-State, and Political Options

Together, the developments just discussed have affected perceptions of socioeconomic mobility, relative socioeconomic status, dependence on the party-state, and political options among private business owners. The majority of private entrepreneurs in this period have experienced upward socioeconomic mobility. In contrast to the first phase of the reform period, the party-state generally has been viewed as a facilitator of this rise, rather than an impediment. As a result, private entrepreneurs have had diminished reason to desire a change in the political status quo.

Simultaneously, the increase in material inequality that has resulted from state-led development, late opening to the global economy, and socialist legacies has undercut potential desires for mass political enfranchisement among private business owners. As in other late developers, in China economic growth has bred an increasingly polarized socioeconomic structure with a lower "class" that includes the vast majority of society. Private entrepreneurs generally occupy the upper level of this socioeconomic hierarchy, while their employees occupy the bottom. In addition, the profits reaped by many private business owners have derived from the low wages and exacting working conditions of their employees—the very factors that have kept unskilled workers poor.

Because China is a post-socialist state undertaking economic reform from a starting point of notable economic equality, the unskilled former SOE employees who now work in private enterprises have moved down in the socioeconomic hierarchy as a result of reform. Among them, there is substantial bitterness toward the wealthy.[40] These feelings are influenced by decades of socialist indoctrination castigating the well-off as "bloodsuckers" and praising the poor as "heroes." These feelings are reinforced by the widespread (and generally well-founded) perception that wealthy entrepreneurs have gained their wealth illicitly through corrupt connections and shady practices. In addition, as in other post-socialist states, a majority of China's unskilled workers espouse "socialist" economic values. As a result, mass political empowerment likely would lead to demands for higher wages and less exacting working conditions, the satisfaction of which would eat into profits. Consequently, wealthy private entrepreneurs have had cause to fear majoritarian rule.

These considerations have been reinforced by the fact that most private entrepreneurs in the late post-Mao period have owed their economic prosperity to beneficial connections with the party-state. In this regard, a key factor has been the ability of private entrepreneurs to raise capital. Despite the wide-ranging economic reforms that have been undertaken since the early 1990s, China's banks have remained under state control, and they have been notoriously stingy in meting out credit to private businesspeople. In 2000, less than 1 percent of state bank loans were estimated to have gone to China's private businesses.[41] As studies by political scientists Victor Shih and Kellee Tsai show, private entrepreneurs with connections to the party-state (through personal ties, membership in the party or its affiliated organizations, or the establishment of a CCP branch within the enterprise), have been more likely to secure bank loans.[42] In addition to credit, connections with the party-state have facilitated the ability of private entrepreneurs to procure licenses, premises, and access to utilities and also have enabled them to avoid onerous taxes and fees, to gain insider information and market access, and to enjoy protection from market competition.[43] Given this economic dependence on the state, private businesspeople have had a rational interest in embedding themselves in the CCP and disincentives to oppose it.

Private entrepreneurs whose profits have derived from high-tech and creative pursuits rather than political connections have been relatively independent of the party-state for their material livelihood. The economic autonomy of this category of private business owner may engender a potential openness to systemic political change. Yet at the same time, this possibility has been undercut by the fact their economic rise has been facilitated by the party-state. As historian Zhaohui Hong states, "the government policy to support the development of high-tech industries in China and the corresponding eagerness of government officials in encouraging this particular group to invest in high-tech ventures have lessened the bureaucratic obstacles for this group."[44] Further, because private business owners of this type have been part of China's "upper class" minority, they have had cause to fear the political enfranchisement of the poor majority—especially given the socialist ideological tendencies of many who sit at the bottom of the socioeconomic hierarchy.

In terms of political options, scholars emphasize that private businesspeople in the late reform period have had "little to complain about."[45] In the words of political scientist Kellee Tsai, "capitalists have never had better access to the political system in PRC history."[46] In the early post-Mao era, private entrepreneurs expanded their businesses and prospered by ignoring formal institutions that potentially constrained them. As the reform era progressed, rather than opposing this behavior, local and central authorities adapted formal institutions to incorporate and legitimate the informal practices that were developing in the private sector. Political leaders saw that these private sector developments were not posing a threat to the party-state but, rather, were beneficial to it.[47] For example, as party elites recognized that large numbers of so-called collective enterprises actually were private businesses "wearing a red hat," they removed restrictions on the private sector, thus making it "safe" for "red hat" collectives to re-register as private enterprises. Similarly, instead of attempting to enforce the ban on party membership among private entrepreneurs, CCP leader Jiang Zemin proposed in 2001 that "advanced productive forces" (a term that includes private businesspeople) be admitted to the party. In late 2002, the ban formally was ended. Around the same time, the central party school began to offer special classes and programs for private entrepreneurs, and top CCP leaders invited private businesspeople to accompany them on trips abroad.[48] These decisions have derived in part from the central leadership's desire to co-opt private entrepreneurs, but they have derived equally from the recognition that the interests of private business owners largely converge with those of the CCP.[49] Whatever the reason, in the late post-Mao period private entrepreneurs have enjoyed attractive political opportunities to work both with and within the party.

Political Attitudes and Behavior

In the second phase of the reform era, these factors have led most private businesspeople to display little interest in pursuing alternatives to the current political system. To the contrary, a substantial portion has eagerly pursued greater embeddedness in existing party and state entities.[50] Despite the official ban that technically was in place through 2002, since the early 1990s there has been a substantial rise in the percentage of private entrepreneurs who are party members. In a 1991 survey of private entrepreneurs, 7 percent reported being CCP members.[51] By 1993 this proportion had nearly doubled, rising to 13 percent. It continued to grow, reaching 18.1 percent in 1997 and 19.9 percent in 2000.[52] After the turn of the millennium, the numbers continued to climb. In 2002, an estimated 29.9 percent were party members, and another 11.1 percent indicated interest in joining.[53] By 2003, the percentage of private entrepreneurs who were party members had risen to nearly 34 percent. Over the course of the next five years, this percentage remained roughly the same.[54] By way of comparison, as of 2007 only 5.5 percent of the entire population was a CCP member.[55] Indeed, as noted earlier, there are more CCP members per capita among private entrepreneurs than in any other social sector.[56]

Remember that the vast majority of private entrepreneurs who joined the CCP throughout the second phase of the reform era did so before entering into private business. In surveys conducted in the late 1990s, 25 percent of all private entrepreneurs fit into this category. By 2005, this percentage had risen to just over 34 percent.[57] Simultaneously, the number of co-opted private entrepreneurs increased, rising from just over 13 percent of private business owners in 1999 to slightly less than 16 percent in 2005.[58]

Even private entrepreneurs who are not party members have not shown interest in challenging the ruling regime. To the contrary, many have indicated a desire to join it. In Dickson's 2005 survey, for example, nearly 31 percent of private businesspeople without a CCP affiliation had applied to join the party, and more than 50 percent expressed interest in becoming a member.[59] In addition, research suggests that private entrepreneurs who have not sought CCP membership have not been motivated by a desire to distance themselves from the party. Rather, they simply have not felt that it has been worth the effort to join, because CCP membership requires much more than simply signing up. To join the party, an applicant must submit a formal application (supported by two sponsors) and undergo a probationary period of assessment. The applicant then must be approved by various levels of the party hierarchy. Further, on admission, the new member is required to take part regularly in party meetings and activities and to pay party dues. Given these requirements, many private entrepreneurs who already have a close relationship with one or more party members or party-state officials have declined to join the party. With preexisting political connections, they have viewed party membership as more of a bother than a necessity. As David Goodman reports, when asked in the early 2000s about their lack of membership in the CCP, many private business owners responded, "Why should I join the CCP? I have grown up locally and my [father, mother, or some other relative] was the [village head, county party secretary, or some other local position of leadership]."[60] Thus, among private businesspeople who have not attempted to become CCP members, there has been little evidence of antagonism toward the party and clear indications of a desire to have close connections with it.

In addition, even the business owners who have become successful through high-tech and creative efforts that do not rely on political connections have demonstrated little inclination to challenge the political status quo. In one indication of this group's political acquiescence, in 1998 its "dutiful tax payments" "amounted to 2.25 times more than those rendered by all the other private enterprises combined."[61] Although researchers find that these private entrepreneurs "have deliberately kept their distance from [the] power establishment," high-tech and creative business owners have appeared quite willing to cooperate with it.[62] Even so, this group has relatively little reason to actively support CCP and may be the most likely subcategory of private entrepreneurs to some day oppose it.

Along with joining the party, in the second phase of the reform era, private entrepreneurs have embedded themselves in the party-state by joining government-sponsored business associations, such as the Self-Employed Laborers' Association, the Private Enterprises' Association, and the Industrial and Commercial Federation.[63] These quasi-corporatist organizations are designed both to "maintain state control" over private entrepreneurs and to represent their interests.[64] In Dickson's surveys in the late 1990s, nearly 70 percent of private enterprise owners were members of at least one CCP-created business association.[65] Similarly, Alpermann's 2002–4 study of rural private entrepreneurs found that more than 70 percent were members in at least one government-sponsored association. Of those, 63 percent described themselves as "active" participants.[66] In addition, Dickson's late 1990s surveys showed that private enterprise owners did not perceive any incompatibility between the associations' dual functions of state control and member representation. The reason: These businesspeople "[saw] themselves as partners, not adversaries of the state."[67]

In addition, in the latter portion of the reform era, private entrepreneurs have displayed the belief that local village elections provide private business owners with an attractive opportunity for political participation. Thus, their potential desire to seek an alternative political system has been undermined. Research conducted by political scientist Jianjun Zhang in the early 2000s found that in some wealthy areas virtually all candidates for village elections were well-off private entrepreneurs.[68] Similarly, Dickson's surveys in 1999 and 2005 reported that roughly 14 to 16 percent of private enterprise owners had been candidates in village elections.[69] In Dickson's 1999 poll, more than 40 percent of the private enterprise owners who had been successfully recruited by the party had run in village elections.[70] However, private entrepreneurs do not appear to have seen candidacy in village elections as a way to challenge the ruling regime. In Dickson's 1999 survey, nearly 68 percent of private business owners agreed that if a non-CCP member were elected to a village committee, then he or she should join the CCP.[71]

Private entrepreneurs also have displayed substantial interest in joining other state entities, including (1) the Chinese People's Political Consultative Conference (CPPCC) and lower-level Political Consultative Conferences that represent members of the CCP, members of China's other legal political parties (all of which were allied with the CCP during the party's civil war with the Kuomintang, or KMT), and individuals without a party affiliation; and (2) the National People's Congress (NPC) and lower-level People's Committees (PCs) that technically serve as the legislative and administrative arms of the state. As of the late 1990s, an estimated 8,500 private entrepreneurs belonged to Political Consultative Conferences at the county level or higher, and 5,400 private entrepreneurs belonged to People's Committees at the county level or higher.[72] In addition, Dickson's 1999 and 2005 surveys of private entrepreneurs show that approximately 5 percent had served or were serving on local Political Consultative Conferences (nearly 61 percent of whom also were CCP members), and 10 to 11 percent had served or were serving on local People's Committees (close to 78 percent of whom also were CCP members).[73] Citing Chinese media sources, Zhaohui Hong reports that as of 2002 more than 17 percent of private entrepreneurs were members of the NPC, and just over 35 percent were members of the CPPCC at various levels.[74] For example, the Zhejiang delegation to the Fifteenth NPC in 2003 included seventy-eight representatives, of which fourteen (18 percent) were private entrepreneurs.[75] Private entrepreneurs make up less than 1 percent of China's population, so their level of participation in these state entities is quite high. Indeed, a 2005 study concludes that "in some parts of the country, private entrepreneurs already make up a very substantial proportion of the local policy elite."[76] As these statistics suggest, rather than seeking to change the existing political system, beginning in the early 1990s private businesspeople increasingly have chosen to become part of it. In sum, as the reform era has progressed, China's private entrepreneurs generally have become more supportive of, and embedded in, the existing political system.

VARIATIONS BY LOCATION

Within this general context of temporal changes in state-led development policies, market forces associated with late industrialization, and socialist legacies, there has been some variation in different geographical locations. As noted in Chapter 1, a common assumption is that localities with more prosperous and liberalized economies will exhibit more public pressure for democratization. Yet the political attitudes of private entrepreneurs have not correlated uniformly with the level of capitalist economic development in a given location. For example, surveys conducted by Kellee S. Tsai from 1994–2001 show that in some economically developed localities private businesspeople view local party-state actors as predators and thus feel alienated from party-state organizations and institutions.[77] However, Tsai also finds that even politically dissatisfied private entrepreneurs typically do not press for systemic political change. Further, Bruce J. Dickson's surveys of private business owners in the late 1990s suggest that, rather than challenging the existing authoritarian party-state, private entrepreneurs in more prosperous areas generally seek closer connections with it.[78]

Thus, it is not simply the level of economic growth and liberalization in a locality that determines the political attitudes and behavior of private entrepreneurs. More important geographic variations derive from different perceptions of (1) the role of local authorities in hindering or aiding the economic rise of private entrepreneurs; (2) the extent of socioeconomic polarization in the local community; and (3) the degree of economic reliance of private entrepreneurs on local representatives of the party-state. Depending on the stance of party-state representatives in a specific location, private entrepreneurs have evidenced different political attitudes and behavior. When local authorities have been seen as facilitating the material gains of private entrepreneurs, businesspeople have been more supportive of the political status quo. In contrast, when local officials have been viewed as antagonistic toward or harmful to the economic interests of private entrepreneurs, businesspeople have kept their distance from the regime and have shown less support for the existing political system. This contrast is documented in Bjorn Alpermann's comparison of Xiajin county (in Shandong province) and Tianmen city (in Hubei province). In Xiajin, local party-state representatives have been supportive of the private sector. In contrast, in Tianmen city private companies have been "grudgingly tolerated" and often have been subject to heavy fines.[79] Accordingly, private entrepreneurs in Xiajin have been much more likely than those in Tianmen to be CCP members and have been much less inclined than those in Tianmen to participate in party-state-controlled business associations. Based on these findings, Alpermann concludes that "the party-state has been successful in politically integrating rural entrepreneurs where the local state had a more developmental and supportive attitude toward the private sector, but not where local states were more ambivalent and less supportive toward the private economy."[80] Viewed from a broader comparative perspective, in localities where the authorities have been seen as constricting the economic rise of private entrepreneurs, businesspeople have been in a situation roughly analogous to that of their counterparts in seventeenth-century England, when a predatory authoritarian state was viewed as detrimental to the prosperity of private business owners.[81] In areas of China where these circumstances have appeared, private entrepreneurs have been more likely to hold negative views of the ruling regime and have had a greater potential to support a change in the political status quo.

The degree of material polarization and the level of economic dependence of private entrepreneurs in a given locality also are important. Looking at both rural and urban businesspeople in relatively prosperous and privatized local economies in Sunan (the southern portion of Jiangsu province) and Wenzhou (a city in eastern Zhejiang province), sociologist Jianjun Zhang shows that in Sunan, local party-state representatives controlled the privatization of public enterprises, transferring virtually all of them to the former managers of the firms at very low prices. In addition, local authorities ensured a stable social order and an obedient working class.[82] Thus, Sunan's private entrepreneurs have depended on the ruling regime for their material prosperity. In addition, the distribution of wealth in Sunan has become highly unequal, with "only a few people in the rich elite and the majority at the bottom."[83] Further, those at the bottom believe that the wealthy have gained their riches unjustly, by unfairly capitalizing on their political connections. In this context, Sunan's wealthy business owners have viewed the party-state as an essential ally, rather than an antagonist.[84] In this way, Sunan's polarized socioeconomic structure and symbiotic capital-state relations have given its private entrepreneurs strong incentives to perpetuate both the political monopoly of the CCP and the political passivity of common citizens.[85]

Zhang documents an almost entirely different situation in Wenzhou: private entrepreneurs whose profits have not depended on political connections and a fairly equitable distribution of wealth. In Wenzhou, the state sector was small during the Mao era. As economic reform progressed, local officials took a relatively "hands off" approach toward the development of private business. Thus, the private sector grew largely independent of the party-state. Of equal importance, Wenzhou's economic development has featured "a relatively equalized class structure with a large number of rich people."[86] Further, most of Wenzhou's private entrepreneurs came from poor families with limited education and few political connections. Consequently, Zhang states, Wenzhou's entrepreneurs "have no reason to fear democracy. On the contrary, they have an interest in pushing for democratic change, from which they can benefit."[87] In fact, they have established many "bottom-up, grassroots associations" that are "gradually turning into interest and pressure groups, pushing for government reform."[88] They also have come to be the major candidates in village elections.

At the same time, both Alpermann and Zhang find that even in localities where private entrepreneurs have demonstrated an interest in political reform, they have evidenced little desire to politically empower common people and have sought democratization only to the extent that it does not threaten their own socioeconomic standing. In Tianmen, Alpermann emphasizes that although private entrepreneurs have displayed little trust in the party-state, they have shown minimal interest in the political enfranchisement of the masses. Indeed, among the Tianmen private entrepreneurs in Alpermann's study, more than 60 percent believed that rich people were of "higher political quality" than poor people, so "rich people should have more influence in policymaking than poor people."[89] Similarly, Zhang finds that most village elections in Wenzhou have become "contests among the rich," wherein wealthy entrepreneurs use their money to compete for votes through "wining and dining" and vote-buying.[90] Given this, successful businesspeople in Wenzhou feel secure that they can use democracy to their own advantage.

CONCLUSION

When viewed from a broader vantage point, it becomes clear that the political attitudes and behavior evidenced by private entrepreneurs in the post-Mao era do not derive from factors that are unique to China but, rather, reflect the broader characteristics of state-capital relations that appear in many countries undergoing state-led development and late industrialization. Specifically, most private businesspeople (1) have been rising in socioeconomic status with the aid of the government; (2) owe their material prosperity to their dependence on the state; (3) sit atop a highly unequal distribution of wealth, at the bottom of which are the employees on whom their profits depend; and (4) have been welcomed to join the existing regime. An application of Eva Bellin's work shows that these features have been found in late-developing authoritarian states as diverse as those in South Korea, Brazil, Mexico, and Saudi Arabia. In all of these cases, private entrepreneurs were "contingent democrats," whose attitude toward an existing authoritarian regime waxed and waned in conjunction with the private sector's perception of its own socioeconomic mobility, relative level of wealth, material dependence on the state, and options for political participation.

Overlaying these factors in China is a socialist past that colors these realities in two ways. First, in China, capitalism emerged from a socioeconomic structure that was one of the most egalitarian in the world. Second, capitalism developed under the leadership of a political party that for decades had promoted the idea that lower economic classes did not deserve their pre-1949 lowly status but, rather, had it forced on them by unjust and exploitative profit seekers. Consequently, although those at the bottom of the socioeconomic hierarchy in any country rarely are satisfied with their economic conditions, in China many of those at the bottom had, through the early 1990s, sat comfortably in the middle. And a large majority of these downwardly mobile citizens have continued to believe in the socialist economic policies and values that the ruling Communist Party touted for virtually all of their lives.

Putting these factors together, Zhang's comparison of Wenzhou and Sunan may have important implications for the political future of China as a whole. In localities that mimic the experience of Wenzhou—where private entrepreneurs have been largely independent of the state and wealth has been distributed in a relatively equitable fashion—public pressures for local democratization are likely to increase. At present, some of China's southeastern coastal regions exhibit similar patterns. Yet the Sunan pattern of economic polarization and symbiotic relations between economic and political elites characterizes much more of China today.[91] Making a "provocative prediction," Zhang states that "Wenzhou's trajectory resembles that of [seventeenth- to eighteenth-century] England" in terms of "its spontaneous development, its self-made bourgeoisie and low concentration of industrial structure, its gradual increase of class awareness in seeking political inclusion and state protection during which rationalization of bureaucracy and even democratization are pushed forward." In contrast, "Sunan's development is similar to that of Germany before World War II or to the bureaucratic-authoritarianism in South America."[92] If so, then to the degree that China exhibits the basic features found in Sunan, its private entrepreneurs are more likely to move toward a new variant of authoritarian rule—possibly even one with fascist characteristics—than they are to move in the direction of liberal democracy.

Even if the Wenzhou pattern becomes dominant in China, private entrepreneurs likely would endorse a transition to liberal democracy at the national level only if they felt secure that their wealth would be protected. As political scientist Adam Przeworski emphasizes, at the base, democracy requires the acceptance of uncertainty in political outcomes. Historically, in countries around the world, the well-to-do have been willing to accept such uncertainty only when they have felt assured that their own wealth would remain shielded from the dictates of majority rule.[93] In seventeenth- and eighteenth-century England, for example, wealthy landowners and private entrepreneurs pressed for political liberalization only because it was seen as essential to the protection and promotion of their own interests; they staunchly supported restrictions on the political participation of common workers and individuals lacking property. Thus, if the Wenzhou pattern of economically independent private entrepreneurs and evenly distributed wealth spreads, China's private entrepreneurs are likely to support systemic political change only when they do not perceive such a transformation as a threat to their material well-being.

3 PROFESSIONALS

AS DISCUSSED IN CHAPTER 1, China's current socioeconomic structure forms the shape of an onion dome made up of a small and wealthy minority and a large and poor majority. With average yearly incomes more than four times higher than that of an average citizen, most professionals are part of the higher-level minority.[1] Yet because they generally are not among the wealthiest 5 percent of the citizenry that earns more than 500,000 yuan/year, professionals often are viewed as an emergent "middle class" in reform-era China.

To the extent that this is true, the political attitudes and behavior of China's professionals may have a crucial influence on China's political future. Historically, the political leanings of the middle class have had a key impact on the direction of political change. As political scientist Barrington Moore outlined decades ago, if the middle class aligns with the authoritarian state, liberal democracy is unlikely to emerge. Should the middle class join forces with nonagricultural workers, the chances for democratization rise.[2]

However, reform-era China differs from the liberal democratic countries studied by Moore (namely, England and France) at the time of their early industrialization. As political scientist David Goodman emphasizes, post-Mao China is characterized by the restructuring of a partially industrialized, planned economy, rather than the "modernization" of an agrarian, feudal economy.[3] Further, this restructuring has been directed by an authoritarian state that has continued to control key economic resources. In addition, especially in the second phase of the reform period, China's political leaders consciously have recruited and welcomed members of the new "middle class" to become part of the political establishment. This development has been especially striking when compared to the CCP's castigation and punishment of most professionals during the Maoist era. Consequently, surveys document a growing perception among Chinese professionals that their interests converge with those of the state.[4] Thus, unlike in early industrializing Europe, where middle class "independence and distance" from the state engendered pressures for liberal democratic change, in reform-era China "middle class" professionals have had clear incentives to perpetuate the (authoritarian) political status quo.[5]

Although it is tempting to view China's professionals as a new "middle class," in actuality their income is extremely high compared to that of the majority of the populace. As such, their economic interests more closely resemble those of the "rich" than those of the "poor." Further, to the extent that the poor citizens who occupy the wide base of China's socioeconomic structure espouse socialist values such as higher taxes on the wealthy and greater government aid for the economically disadvantaged, professionals have material disincentives to promote mass political enfranchisement. In addition, professionals share a "bourgeois" lifestyle that in their eyes denotes their more civilized and superior quality (*suzhi*) relative to lower-level socioeconomic groups. Accordingly, rather than confronting the existing political establishment and allying with less prosperous socioeconomic groups, China's professionals generally have been content with the political status quo. Only a tiny minority of professionals (mainly with occupations as intellectuals, lawyers, and journalists) has been active in pressing for systemic political change.

Broadly construed, professionals have "specialized secondary or postsecondary educations" and "perform nonroutine white-collar jobs."[6] As such, this stratum includes teachers, intellectuals, medical doctors, lawyers, accountants, engineers, and other technical personnel. Compared to state sector workers and private enterprise owners, who form clear categories in government statistics and policies, professionals do not fall under a single official label. In some documents and pronouncements, professionals are considered state sector workers, but in others professionals are lumped together with private entrepreneurs and categorized as "new social strata." In addition, many "intellectuals" would not place themselves in the same category as accountants and engineers. Because there are few official statistics that single out professionals as a group, an analysis of their experiences and political proclivities presents special challenges.

Despite having different jobs, virtually all professionals share a common feature that generally is not exhibited by the other groups examined in this book: a college education. Given this, an examination of China's college-educated population may provide a window into the minds of current and future professionals. While there is little data on professionals as a general stratum in the reform era, there has been substantial research on college-educated individuals. Thus, although there are many varieties of professionals, they are examined here in a single chapter.

Given the paucity of data on professionals and the plentitude of information on college students and degree-holders, this chapter begins with an analysis of the ways in which China's state-led development, market forces, and socialist legacies have impacted college students' perceptions of socioeconomic mobility, relative socioeconomic status, dependence on the state, and political options over time. Next, the chapter examines existing data on specific professional occupations, with a particular focus on intellectuals, lawyers, and accountants. As with private entrepreneurs, this review uncovers distinct political patterns in the first and second phases of China's post-Mao period. Overall, with the exception of a small minority, the trend among China's professionals has been toward greater acceptance of the CCP-led political status quo.

COLLEGE STUDENTS

Although it commonly is assumed that capitalist economic development inevitably leads to strain between society and an authoritarian regime, this has not been the case with college-educated individuals in China. To the contrary, as the reform era has progressed, those pursuing university degrees have shown less support for political change and a greater interest in embedding themselves in the current system. In the 1980s relations between college-educated youths and the state were increasingly attenuated, at times flaring into outright confrontation. Since the early 1990s, Chinese college students have been remarkably quiescent, and have joined the CCP in growing numbers.

The Early Reform Era (Late 1970s to the Early 1990s)

In the first phase of the reform era, university students became a key focus of the party-state's new developmental policies. Following decades of Maoist rule that privileged individuals with "red" class backgrounds and castigated Western-style intellectual pursuits, the party firmly shifted to policies that promoted and rewarded technical knowledge, seeking to create a new group of "experts" to modernize China's economy. During the Cultural

Revolution of 1966–76, China's universities were shut down almost entirely, with the result that few youths of this generation earned a college degree. Before 1966, primary, secondary, and tertiary education under CCP rule focused on manual labor and the cultivation of ideologically purity. Following the death of Mao and the arrest of the Maoist "Gang of Four" in 1976, the party came to rest in the hands of Deng Xiaoping—a pragmatist committed to China's scientific and technological modernization. To serve this cause, China's universities, which tentatively reopened in 1975, were given a new focus.

In 1978 a unified national entrance exam was reinstituted. Unlike the exam used by the CCP before the Cultural Revolution, the new exam emphasized academic knowledge rather than Maoist ideology.[7] Through the 1980s, access to universities was determined by a student's score on this examination. Admission was extremely limited, and only a tiny portion of all exam takers was able to enter a university. In 1978, 5.7 million youths took the national university examination, but only .3 million (or 4.8 percent) were accepted into a four-year institution.[8] From the late 1970s through the late 1980s, roughly .1 percent of the Chinese citizenry were university students, and just over 1 percent were university graduates.[9]

Reflecting a "socialist" mentality on the part of the political leadership, throughout the early reform era university tuition and fees were extremely low, and financial concerns rarely deterred an admitted student from enrolling. Although wealthier families were able to put more resources into their youngsters' preparation for the national exam, and in some cases students with lower exam scores were allowed to enter college on a self-paying basis,[10] in general, the early-reform-era higher education system was based on merit, not money.

After graduation, most university students of this period were assigned to jobs by the government. Indeed, virtually all "professionals" were employees of the state. Reflecting the party-state's socialist legacy, college-educated workers in the state sector generally were not paid much more than workers who had no postsecondary education. At the same time, as state-led development policies tolerated the development of the private sector, those with college degrees enjoyed more alternative options for employment. Because the number of university graduates was exceedingly small in the early reform era, the employment "demand" for college degree holders outstripped the "supply" by a ratio of 3 to 1, guaranteeing that virtually all would garner an attractive job.[11] Even so, because most university graduates became state sector employees, their incomes and living standards were only marginally higher than those of their uneducated coworkers.[12] Meanwhile, in the private sector, individuals without college degrees increasingly were earning more than university graduates who had state sector jobs.

Perceptions of Socioeconomic Mobility, Relative Socioeconomic Status, Material Dependence on the Party-State, and Political Options   These developments affected college students' perceived socioeconomic mobility, relative socioeconomic status, material dependence on the party-state, and political options in such a way that their interest in becoming part of the party-state declined, and their potential for political dissent increased. In terms of mobility, most university graduates felt somewhat stunted. With the increasing availability of lucrative occupational opportunities that did not require a university education or government assignment, state sector employment did not promise college graduates much in the way of financial gain. Indeed, beginning around 1988, when the party's lifting of price controls resulted in spiraling inflation, material conditions for most college-educated individuals actually declined.

The early reform era had a mixed impact on the relative socioeconomic status of college graduates and their dependence on the party-state. On one hand, the regime's new emphasis on "experts" improved the social standing of those with a postsecondary education, especially when viewed in light of the disdain and repression suffered by "intellectuals" in the Maoist era. On the other hand, to the degree that the newly emergent private sector enabled less educated individuals to take advantage of consumer comforts that educated professionals in the state sector could not afford, the relative economic status of university degree holders declined. At the same time, the greater availability of nonstate employment for college graduates somewhat diminished their economic dependence on the ruling regime.

In terms of political options, CCP leaders in the early reform era displayed somewhat schizophrenic behavior toward college students. As historian Merle Goldman has documented, from the time of Mao's death through the student demonstrations of 1989, central elites swung between policies that ceded greater autonomy and power to university students and administrators, and policies that repressed and constricted their freedom.[13] Whenever the regime relaxed its stance, student and intellectual hopes were raised, but each time, these hopes were crushed. Still, throughout this period, college-educated individuals believed that they held a special social status entitling them to remonstrate ruling elites, and at least some top CCP leaders looked to them for advice.

Political Attitudes and Behavior As a result of these factors, university students in the early post-Mao period displayed decreased interest in joining the party. In the late Mao era, more than 26 percent of university enrollees were CCP members. According to Gang Guo, by 1978—the first year of the reform period—this had dropped to less than 11 percent.[14] Following the institution of exam-based admissions in 1978, CCP membership among college students declined further. By 1982, only 1.9 percent of university students had joined the party. Disconcerted by this turn of events, CCP leaders made a push for greater campus recruitment, and the percentage rose to 4.7 in 1984. During the rest of the decade, the proportion declined yet again—dropping to 2.9 percent in 1988 and less than 1 percent in early 1989.[15] This decrease emanated from a decline in official recruitment efforts in the late 1980s, along with the institution of stricter standards for admission beginning in 1986.[16] At the same time, students displayed little desire to join, and an ever-smaller percentage submitted applications to the party during the late 1980s.[17] Thus, relations between university enrollees and the party-state became increasingly distant in the first phase of the post-Mao era.

Indeed, at times, college students in the early reform period engaged in outright protest directed at the central government. The most notable cases occurred in the winter of 1986–87 and the spring of 1989. In the first half of 1986, party elites such as General Secretary Hu Yaobang expressed the belief that economic modernization required further educational, political, and administrative reform. In both "big-character" wall posters (*dazibao*) and public demonstrations, students responded by airing grievances associated with their stunted socioeconomic mobility, relatively low socioeconomic status, and constrained political options. Demonstrations began in late 1986 at the University of Science and Technology (UST) in Anhui province, where students met to protest their inability to nominate candidates for the local People's Congress. Before long, students on other campuses expressed their support. Students at UST and other schools also complained about their poor living conditions, including relatively high-priced but low-quality cafeteria food. In addition, students expressed indignation at the gap between their "elite" educational status and the low salaries they received after graduation, which was made all the more upsetting by the relative affluence enjoyed by those with lesser academic credentials but greater connections to representatives of the party-state.[18]

Students generally did not challenge the legitimacy of the central regime. As sociologist Julia Kwong notes, "there is little to suggest that they were rejecting communist rule in favor of a multiparty system."[19] Nonetheless, as campus protest activities spread across the country—including roughly 40,000 students at 150 higher education institutions in seventeen cities—some powerful party elites pressed for a clamp-down.[20] Although party General Secretary Hu Yaobang quietly indicated his support of the students, the CCP's most powerful leader—Deng Xiaoping—instructed party elites to bring the movement to an end.[21] At UST, activist vice-president Fang Lizhi (who had voiced a radical cry for "total Westernization") was expelled from the party and dismissed from his university position. Within the top ranks of the party, General Secretary Hu was forced to resign from his post, but he remained in the party's Politburo, and his younger protégé, Zhao Ziyang, became the new general secretary. In official media outlets the protestors' demands were criticized as "bourgeois liberalism," and participants were described as having been led by a "handful of lawbreakers who disguised themselves as students," bent on fomenting nationwide chaos and disrupting stability and unity.[22] Even in this atmosphere, student participants generally were not punished, and central authorities actually responded to some of the protestors' grievances. Perhaps most importantly, authorities announced that candidates for local People's Congresses would now be nominated by the electorate.[23] Still, the underlying causes of the students' dissatisfaction—stunted economic mobility, relatively low economic status, and limits on political expression and participation—remained.

When former General Secretary Hu died on April 15, 1989, spontaneous popular mourning soon developed into renewed activism by college students. Exacerbating the grievances that had not been resolved by the protests of 1986–87, inflation soared into the double digits. By the end of May, student-led protests had spread to virtually every major Chinese city, involving millions of people. Along with street marches and sit-ins, students formed autonomous organizations free from CCP control. As in the campus-based protests of 1986–87, participants drew attention to their poor living conditions, especially in contrast to "corrupt" cadres that used political connections to profit from market reforms. Students also demanded democratic rights, such as freedom of association and speech. Yet, as was the case in 1986–87, protestors in 1989 did not call for an end to the CCP-led political system.

Their collective actions persisted for more than one and a half months, due not only to the determined efforts of the participants but also to a factional battle between more sympathetic party elites (led by General Secretary Zhao Ziyang) and more hardline figures (such as Premier Li Peng). On June 3–4, 1989, when Deng Xiaoping ordered the military to repress the Tiananmen Square demonstrators and violent force was used to remove anyone who stood in the soldiers' way, it was clear to the public who had won.[24] Shortly thereafter, Zhao was dismissed from his post and placed under house arrest. The official verdict in the media was similar to that employed against the student-led protests of 1986–87, but its language was much more vehement: A "small handful" had incited "chaos" and "pandemonium," resulting in a "shocking counter-revolutionary rebellion"—a "struggle involving the life and death of the party and the state."[25]

The Late Reform Era (Early 1990s Through the Present)

The brutal crackdown on the demonstrations of 1989 marked a watershed for college-educated Chinese. Although university students in the 1980s participated in numerous political protests, since 1989 they have been remarkably quiescent. Indeed, rather than challenging the CCP, post-1989 college students have displayed a remarkable interest in joining it. What accounts for this shift? Fear is surely a significant factor, and fear may explain the lack of political activism among university attendees, but it does not adequately address the reasons for college students' increased desire to become embedded in the party-state. To understand this, one must look at key shifts in state-led development policies, market forces, and socialist legacies from the 1990s through the present.

Changes in these contextual factors have resulted in a dramatic transformation of China's college student population since 1989. Most importantly, China's higher education system has been marketized: Increasingly, wealth has determined enrollment, and the party-state no longer determines a graduate's employment fate. As political scientist Stanley Rosen reports, in 1992 universities were allowed to "determine their own fee structures," and in 1993 universities were told to "move gradually from a system under which the government guaranteed education and employment to a system in which students were held responsible for both."[26] Meanwhile, the government contribution to education funding fell—dropping from 82 percent in 1993 to 62 percent in 2002. As of 2005, the regime still paid for more than 75 percent of the total cost for kindergarten through ninth grade. At the high school and university level, government funding dropped to less than 48 percent. The balance has been made up by an increase in tuition and ad hoc fees.[27]

With these changes, the pre-1989 socialist commitment to equal educational opportunity has fallen largely by the wayside. Instead, money has come to play a key role in university enrollment. Rosen finds that "money . . . has become the standard method by which—and often the only way—parents can get children into the [prestigious senior high] schools of their choice."[28] Because attendance at key high schools ensures scores on the national university entrance examination that enable college admission, those who cannot afford to attend an elite high school probably will not receive a university education. In addition, those with money are more likely to attend the leading middle and primary schools that feed prominent high schools. Even if one is accepted to a university, the required tuition and fees have become prohibitive for most families. In 2000 the average annual expense for a college student was estimated at 8,000 to 10,000 yuan, while the average annual per capita income in China was only slightly more than 7,000 yuan.[29] Consequently, since the early 1990s in China, more university students have come from financially privileged families who have benefited from economic reform. Fewer qualified students from average and low-income homes have been admitted, and fewer have had the financial capacity to enroll.[30]

In addition, central authorities have expanded the number of people admitted to colleges. In the early 1990s, the number of university students in China was around 2 million; by 1998 that number had risen to 6.4 million. Following the 1999 announcement of a new plan to dramatically increase enrollments, the number skyrocketed. By 2005, the number admitted to colleges each year had climbed to nearly 5 million, making for a total university student population of 20 million.[31] Consequently, secondary education has become far less exclusive. In the first phase of the reform era, around 4 percent of those who took the national exam gained university admission, but in 2003 this proportion reached 60 percent.[32] Compared to the early reform era, in the later reform era the percentage of the Chinese population with college degrees has more than tripled.[33]

This expansion in university admissions has intensified the competition for jobs among college graduates. Although in the first phase of the post-Mao period, the ratio of the "demand" to the "supply" of university degree holders was 3 to 1, by the early 1990s this ratio had dropped to .9 to 1. Since then, the job market for college graduates has become even more competitive. Further, beginning in 1997, the government ceased to assign jobs to college graduates.[34] As a result, new degree holders no longer have been assured employment. Still, these developments have coincided with China's opening to foreign investment and the boom in the private sector in the latter phase of the reform period. Although employment is no longer guaranteed, those with a college education have enjoyed greatly expanded opportunities for wealth.

Perceptions of Socioeconomic Mobility, Relative Socioeconomic Status, Material Dependence on the Party-State, and Political Options For students entering college after 1989, the factors mentioned earlier have influenced perceptions of socioeconomic mobility, relative socioeconomic status, material dependence on the party-state, and political options in such a way that students generally have eschewed political dissent, seeking instead to become more closely attached to the political establishment. Overall, college graduates in the early reform era experienced stunted socioeconomic mobility and low socioeconomic status relative to their exclusive educational credentials, all of which derived from their dependence on the regime for employment. In the late reform period degree holders have enjoyed upward mobility but also increased financial uncertainty due to the end of government job allocations. No longer required to enter state sector jobs with limited pay, educated individuals have found that the private sector offers opportunities for affluence. Further, because the state sector has had to compete with the private sector to attract university graduates, government-affiliated employers have offered higher pay for skilled positions than was the case under the allocation system in place in the first phase of the post-Mao period. Consequently, in comparison with the early reform era, in the late reform period a college graduate's "return" on education has more than doubled.[35] The overall result is that degree holders have experienced a reduced gap between their educational attainment and their socioeconomic conditions.

Because family wealth is now correlated with education levels, the college-educated stratum includes fewer individuals from families of average or poor financial means. Although the educational system before the early 1990s featured a remarkable openness to students of all economic levels, since that time the educated stratum has become increasingly self-replicating. As noted by Christopher Buckley, the late reform period has featured an ever-higher level of "inheritance" in the professional sector, with most children of educated and affluent parents following in their elders' footsteps and a smaller portion of less-privileged youths entering the pool of college-educated professionals.[36] To a large degree, those who have attended college since the early 1990s have come from families who have been the beneficiaries of China's economic reform, so these individuals have harbored little bitterness toward the ruling regime.

In addition, the late reform period has witnessed a growing sense of distance between youths within the educated and well-off professional stratum and those of lower socioeconomic status. This phenomenon is perhaps best illustrated by a 2002 debate that appeared in the widely read journal *China Youth*. Titled, "Can Friendship Transcend Stratum?" the discussion opened with the story of two childhood friends, one of whom was accepted into a key university and the other who failed the entrance exam and found employment as an ordinary worker. Over time, their divergent lifestyles made it impossible for their friendship to last. In the magazine's twenty-five published responses to this story, more educated and wealthy contributors overwhelmingly agreed that "changing economic and living conditions" made it impossible for friendships to be maintained across strata.[37]

Beyond an inability to enjoy interaction with those of lower socioeconomic status, many economically successful individuals have evidenced disdain for the "unrefined" occupants of the lower level of China's socioeconomic structure—especially those from the countryside. In one striking report, well-off residents of the city of Qingdao allegedly "proposed that a separate section of public transportation be set aside for migrant workers on the grounds that 'neat and tidy' urban residents could not tolerate the smell of these outsiders."[38] It seems unlikely that such attitudes would coincide with support for mass political enfranchisement or a political system based on majority rule.

In terms of political options, compared with university students in the 1980s, students attending college since the early 1990s have viewed connections with the ruling CCP as important means to attain material comfort and high social status. Although in the first phase of the reform period government assignment of jobs in the public sector meant that degree holders would have stable employment yet a rudimentary standard of living, in the latter portion of the post-Mao era, professionals with a secondary education have had to fend for themselves. Those who succeed may enjoy a very comfortable lifestyle, yet success is in no way guaranteed—especially given the increasingly tight economic situation fueled by the expansion of university enrollments. In this context, "party membership has become a decisive edge."[39] When asked in 1996 why they joined the party, 30 percent of college students openly stated that they did so in order to find desirable employment, and 70 percent agreed that "entering the party is a bargaining chip that can increase one's chances in the competition to find a good job."[40] Meanwhile, rather than rejecting college students due to their participation in the protests of 1989, in the second phase of the reform era, the CCP has "concentrate[d] its recruitment efforts on the young and the well educated."[41] In a "dramatic shift toward a 'technocratic' pattern . . . individuals from red households [have been] abandoned in favor of young college graduates."[42]

Political Attitudes and Behavior   In the second phase of the reform period, college-educated Chinese have demonstrated a reduced desire to challenge the political establishment and a heightened interest in joining it. Although there has been a slight decrease in the overall number of young people recruited into the CCP, the number of *college-educated* youths has climbed substantially.[43] As Rosen notes, the percentage of party members under the age of thirty-five declined slightly in the late reform era, from 23.1 in 1998 to 22.3 in 2000.[44] Meanwhile, the portion of university students who are CCP members rose exponentially—from .8 percent in 1990 to nearly 8 percent in 2001.[45] Further, in 2001, an estimated 33 percent of those attending college had applied to join the party.[46] Other surveys circa 2000 have found that "40 percent of students expressed interest in joining the party, with the number increasing to 50 percent for new students."[47] Among graduate students, by 2000, 28.2 percent were party members.[48] In 2007 the official Xinhua news agency proudly proclaimed that between 2002 and 2007, 32.5 percent of new CCP members were college graduates.[49] In addition, rather than seeking jobs that are distant from the party-state, many young people have reported "a strong desire" to be employed as a government or party official.[50]

Conversely, unlike the early reform period, college students in the late reform era have evidenced virtually no public political contentiousness. Although awareness of the brutal crackdown on the demonstrations of 1989 surely has helped to motivate their quiescent behavior, even when opportunities for political dissent have arisen in the post-1989 period, virtually none have indicated any interest. Notably, when the opposition China Democracy Party (CDP) formed in 1998, 41 of its top 151 leaders had a college education, but only 2 of these individuals had entered college in 1990 or later.[51]

Still, post-1989 college students are not committed communists. Numerous surveys show that there is no identifiable difference in the ideological orientation of student CCP members and non-members.[52] For example, "in one survey of over 800 graduating party and CYL [Communist Youth League] members at 16 universities in Beijing . . . only 38 students expressed a belief in communism."[53] More anecdotally, a "political education instructor at Beijing University . . . said that he had never met a student who really believed in communism."[54] To the contrary, many studies indicate that student CCP members in the late reform period have been "even more receptive to privatization and capitalism than ordinary students."[55] This is not surprising, because China's market reforms largely have enabled China's post-1989 college students' education and prosperity.

Overall, since the early 1990s, state-led policies to marketize education and job allocation, coupled with the development of a private sector open to foreign investment and international markets, have given college-educated individuals upward mobility and a high standard of living. Because the party-state has facilitated these improvements, and because it has welcomed rather than rejected university degree holders, these individuals have had cause to support, and even join, the existing political establishment rather than press for liberal democratic transformation.

PROFESSIONALS

As noted earlier, beyond data on college-educated individuals, studies have yet to be undertaken on the political attitudes and behavior of China's contemporary professionals as a group. Even so, existing work on various types of professionals has uncovered patterns that parallel the trends among college students discussed earlier. In the first phase of the reform era, most professionals worked in state sector jobs offering pay and lifestyles roughly equivalent to those of rank-and-file workers. Since the early 1990s, China's professions have been largely privatized. Yet interestingly, rather than leading to a desire for greater distance from the party-state, this development has spurred many professionals to seek closer connections to the political establishment. As with college students, rather than appearing as a constraint on socioeconomic mobility, the existing regime has been viewed as a facilitator of professional success. In the reform era many of China's professional sectors—including medical doctors, engineers, and technical personnel—have received scant scholarly attention. However, a substantial amount of research has been done on intellectuals and lawyers and some on accountants. The sections that follow review these findings, highlighting the ways in which they may be suggestive of general trends among professionals.

Intellectuals

Among China's "professional" occupations, intellectuals have been the subject of the most sustained scholarly research. Unlike other professionals, intellectuals in the early reform era displayed a clear commitment to liberal democratic political reform, although they typically pressed for such change from within the political establishment. In the late reform period, changes in state-led development policies and China's opening to global market forces have transformed the perceptions of intellectuals such that they have become more critical of liberal ideas and more overtly supportive of the CCP-led political regime.

The Early Reform Era (Late 1970s to the Early 1990s)   As with other professional sectors, during the Maoist era, intellectuals were castigated as "rightists," forced to undergo "re-education" in labor camps, and "sent down" to the countryside to engage in manual labor. Following the 1976 death of Mao, virtually all intellectuals were rehabilitated. Indeed, because educated individuals were seen by post-Mao CCP leaders as the key to China's economic modernization, intellectuals were brought into the party-state itself. Reflecting the elevated status of intellectuals under the party's new leadership, in 1978 General Secretary Deng Xiaoping expressed his desire "to serve as the 'director of support services' for China's scientists and technicians so that they could devote themselves wholeheartedly to their work and to China's modernization."[56] Concretely, Goldman relates that under the patronage of reformist party elites such as Hu Yaobang and Zhao Ziyang, intellectuals "assumed the leadership of important government policy-making institutes and think tanks, published in official newspapers and journals, participated in policy deliberations, and were put in charge of professional federations."[57]

Given their recent experience of official repression, many intellectuals were grateful to post-Mao party elites for welcoming them into important positions in the political establishment. To these people, working within the now reform-oriented party was much more appealing than confronting it from the outside. In addition, these intellectuals experienced upward mobility—compared to what their counterparts faced in the late Mao era—as well as high social status relative to other socioeconomic sectors. Still, as state sector workers, their pay and benefits were stable, but their standard of living was not significantly higher than that of rank-and-file government employees.

In terms of political attitudes and behavior, most intellectuals of the early reform era were "establishment intellectuals" who did not reject or attempt to overturn CCP rule.[58] Yet at the same time, many espoused liberal beliefs connected to the values of the European enlightenment. They saw it as their "self-assigned mission" to move the state in this direction, albeit "from within."[59] Given the prominent position of sympathetic CCP leaders such as Hu and Zhao, it seemed plausible that the party might indeed reform itself along more liberal democratic lines.

Meanwhile, a small minority of intellectuals worked outside party-state institutions and employed unsanctioned means to press for political change. Political activism on the part of these individuals crested in the Democracy Wall movement of 1978–80 but also was prominent in the student-led demonstrations of 1989. The Democracy Wall movement arose in the context of the Third Plenum of the Eleventh Central Committee, which was scheduled for December 1978 and was widely expected to usher in a new reformist leadership and policy focus in the party. A few months before the meeting, citizens began to attach posters to a wall located a short distance from Beijing's Tiananmen Square. The posters called for redress of the injustices of the Cultural Revolution and pointedly criticized Mao and the Gang of Four for their role in the campaign. After Deng Xiaoping publicly expressed his support of "Democracy Wall" in November 1978, the number of posters swelled, and thousands came to read them. In addition, some citizens—mostly individuals whose education had been interrupted by the Cultural Revolution—began to distribute "people's periodicals" that called for varying degrees of political reform.[60] As Goldman explains, generally speaking, the editors of these publications expressed views that were the same as those of liberal "establishment" intellectuals: "they were concerned primarily with issues of freedom of speech, publication, association, and rule of law."[61] The difference was that Democracy Wall activists "expressed themselves directly and specifically," and—importantly—in public.[62]

The government officially tolerated the movement for nearly half a year. Following "people's periodical" editor Wei Jingsheng's publication of articles that were explicitly critical of Deng Xiaoping, the party (under Deng's direction) arrested Wei and other prominent activists. Despite remarkably unified opposition to the arrests on the part of the disparate groups that participated in the movement, by early 1980 "Democracy Wall" had been shut down, and most authors of the "people's periodicals" had been jailed. In response to the movement, Deng announced that all citizens must abide by the "four basic principles" of socialism, the dictatorship of the proletariat, the leadership of the Communist Party, and Marxism/Leninism/Maoism. In addition, the party excised the "four big freedoms" (to post big-character wall posters, speak out freely, air views fully, and hold great debates) that Mao had added to the constitution in 1975.[63] Even so, Goldman notes that although most establishment intellectuals "remained silent and chose not to become associated with the Democracy Wall activists," some of the movement's proposals for political reforms "continued to be echoed in the official media in the 1980s by establishment intellectuals connected to reformist party leaders Hu Yaobang and Zhao Ziyang."[64]

Many of the non-establishment intellectuals who were prominent in the Democracy Wall movement remained in jail through the late 1980s. A few, however, were spared imprisonment and attempted to forge an intellectual status that differed more from the regime than the establishment intellectuals. In 1980 some ran as candidates for local People's Congresses. In 1986, a few formed the Beijing Social and Economic Sciences Research Institute (SERI)— what Goldman calls the "first nonofficial social science think tank in Beijing."[65] Along with printing its own journal, SERI published translations of Western works and original pieces by Chinese reformers, established a public opinion polling organization, organized conferences, and funded independent research projects.[66] "By the late 1980s," Goldman reports, SERI "had built a network of independent organizations that attracted hundreds of professors, graduate students, and well-known intellectuals." Indeed, "even intellectuals associated with Hu Yaobang's and Zhao Ziyang's intellectual networks, who had earlier kept their distance," wrote in SERI's journal and participated in the group's workshops.[67]

When the student-led demonstrations of 1989 emerged, many intellectuals—especially those affiliated with SERI—served as advisers to protesting students and workers. Indeed, the protests had been sparked by the death of Hu Yaobang, the sponsor of many liberal establishment intellectuals, and the party's general secretary before his forced resignation in the wake of the campus demonstrations of 1986–87. To the extent that intellectuals were involved in the movement of 1989, they acted as a moderating force. Initially, they attempted to dissuade students and workers from engaging in public protest, and in the later stages of the movement they worked to organize an agreement among student and worker factions to withdraw from the Square. Despite their caution, as well as their lack of a major leadership role in the demonstrations, intellectuals who participated in the protests were severely punished. Following the bloody crackdown of June 3 and 4, SERI's offices were raided, and the institute's most prominent leaders were jailed for their alleged role as "black hands" behind the movement.[68] Others went into hiding or fled the country. Further, having lost the factional struggle that raged in the top ranks of the CCP during the spring of 1989, reformist Party General Secretary and liberal "establishment" intellectual sponsor Zhao Ziyang was removed from his post and placed under house arrest.

The Late Reform Era (Early 1990s Through the Present)   In the months immediately following the brutal suppression of the demonstrations of 1989, most intellectuals were "shocked into silence."[69] To the surprise of many observers, when intellectuals reengaged in public discourse in the early 1990s, "much of the antagonism they had directed toward the state only a few years before had largely dissipated."[70] Scholars who study China's intellectuals maintain that fear is not an adequate explanation of this development. In the words of historian Joseph Fewsmith, "neither political suppression nor exile (voluntary or otherwise) fully account for the change in intellectual atmosphere in the 1990s or for the changed relationship between the state and intellectuals that began to emerge in the years after Tiananmen."[71] The more fundamental cause is the confluence of changes in state-led development policies and China's opening to the global capitalist market since the early 1990s.

In terms of state-led development policies, political scientist Yongnian Zheng reports that, rather than punishing intellectuals as a whole for the role of some in the Democracy Wall movement and the 1989 protests, since the early 1990s, "the government has allocated enormous economic resources to intellectuals, especially top universities."[72] Further, in contrast to the 1980s, since the 1990s the party's leadership has not been split on the issue of capitalist economic reform. Throughout the late reform era, virtually all top CCP elites have agreed that it is both appropriate and necessary. As a result, Fewsmith states, policy makers "no longer need to be given broad advice about whether to reform but instead need highly specific advice . . . about *how* to reform."[73] In addition, most high-ranking party officials in the late reform era themselves have a university education, typically in technical or scientific fields. Thus, the distinction between intellectuals and political leaders has not been as clear as it was in the early post-Mao period. The positive consequence for intellectuals as a whole is that party elites are more likely to see intellectuals as peers and less likely to view them as a threat. Simultaneously, to the extent that issues surrounding reform are now more technical and CCP leaders themselves have a technical background, party elites have had less need for advice from intellectuals—especially generalists with expertise in the social sciences and humanities.[74]

Coinciding with these changes in the orientation and character of the party-state's approach to development, China's greater opening to the global capitalist market since 1992 has resulted in a "commercialization of culture" that has altered the status of intellectuals. In the early post-Mao period intellectuals viewed themselves, and in turn were viewed by the public and by political decision makers, as the conscience of society, charged with "giving wise moral advice to the political leadership." Fewsmith states that since the early 1990s this intellectual role "has largely disappeared."[75] Intellectuals have been "professionalized" and "privatized," such that their work is now judged by the market.

These changes have engendered among intellectuals a perception of a less privileged and respected social status than they were accorded in the early reform era, uncertain socioeconomic mobility, and decreased dependence on the party-state. At the same time, however, intellectuals have been embraced by the party-state. These perceptions have coincided with political views that are skeptical of—and even reject—the liberal values evidenced by intellectuals in the early post-Mao period. Instead, in the late reform period most Chinese intellectuals have espoused versions of "statism" or "neo-conservatism" in the political realm, portraying the party-state as a bulwark against the disorder and moral slide wrought by capitalist economic reform. They have criticized free market capitalism and globalization, expressing leftist/socialist concerns about the rise of materialism and material inequality and the loss of community solidarity.[76]

In terms of political behavior, rather than seeking greater distance from the party as a result of the sour experience of 1989, intellectuals generally have continued to join it. As of 1991, more than 37 percent of college teachers and administrators were CCP members.[77] Further, intellectuals in the late reform era have participated in numerous party-state bodies. As Yongnian Zheng reports, many intellectuals "sit in people's congresses and political consultative conferences, even in the party's committees."[78] In other words, intellectuals are "part of the decision-making body."[79] Overall, Zheng finds that they have been effectively co-opted by the regime.[80]

Even so, a very small group of intellectuals who participated in earlier political movements such as Democracy Wall and the protests of 1989 have continued to actively promote democratic change. For these people, the economic reform period has brought very poor material conditions and prospects, complete economic independence from the party-state, a severe decline in social status, and harsh repression at the hands of the CCP. Identifying these individuals as "disestablished" intellectuals, Goldman notes that they had been on their way to becoming "establishment" intellectuals, but their public acts of dissent prevented this from coming to fruition. As Goldman relates, "when they were released from prison or labor reform camps . . . most members of their generations were going into business (*xiahai*) or were becoming increasingly professionalized. But because of their past political activities, [they] had difficulty entering the professions."[81] In addition, their "blackened" records have made it difficult to borrow money and find desirable employment. Consequently, many have endured bleak economic conditions, with little hope for improvement. Although most college-educated citizens have prospered materially, these "disestablished" intellectuals have eked out a marginal existence. They have not been simply rejected by the ruling CCP but have been harshly repressed by it.

People in this category were key leaders of the opposition China Democracy Party (CDP) that formed in 1998. As noted earlier, 41 of the top 151 CDP leaders had a university education, and 39 of those 41 attended college before 1990. In addition, virtually all of the leaders of the CDP had been punished for engaging in political protest actions *before* their involvement in the CDP. Twelve of the 39 CDP leaders educated before 1990 held leadership positions in the Democracy Wall movement or the 1989 demonstrations. Most of the remaining 27 participated in one or both movements but did not play leadership roles. Overall, 70 to 80 percent of all top CDP leaders had some prior protest experience. As was the case with Democracy Wall and the protests of 1989, these intellectuals were harshly punished for their participation in the CDP, including years of imprisonment, official surveillance and harassment, and permanently marred political records.[82]

Even among this group of highly committed democracy activists, socialist values have been apparent. Like the Worker Autonomous Federations that formed in 1989 (discussed in Chapter 4), the CDP did not seek a return to the communist authoritarian past or a continuation of the capitalist authoritarian present; rather, it espoused a modern form of social democracy. CDP members sought to "end single-party rule," "establish a separation of powers," "establish a constitutional democracy," and "protect freedom and human rights."[83] At the same time, CDP supporters adhered to key socialist values such as "social equality" and "social security."[84] Similarly, they lamented the rampant "social contradictions"[85] that have emerged in the reform period, leaving the "poor and rich at two extremes."[86] CDP members also embraced economic reforms to protect private property and ensure "fair economic competition."[87] Overall, however, these disestablished intellectuals represent only a miniscule portion of China's intellectuals in the late reform era. The vast majority has maintained ties to the political establishment and has evidenced little interest in systemic political change.

Other Professionals

As with intellectuals, other professional occupations did not exist for most of the Maoist period. After they were reestablished, virtually all professions remained within the state sector, offering pay and lifestyles similar to that of rank-and-file workers in state firms. Indeed, most professional firms actually grew out of the state sector. With the acceleration and expansion of state sector reforms beginning in 1996 the need for independent professions rose. For example, after bonus schemes were introduced in state-owned enterprises, independent accountants and quantity surveyors were required to ensure that managers would not manipulate their firms' figures to their advantage.[88] In addition, with China's opening to foreign investment and development of the private sector, the functioning of China's nascent capital markets suffered from a lack of intermediary services, including legal, accounting, surveying, and financial analysis.[89] The Chinese government thus embarked on a policy of disaffiliating the professions from the state sector and essentially privatizing their operations. Yet, as with intellectuals, this development has not led other professions to challenge the political status quo. Indeed, many professionals have sought to embed themselves within it.

Lawyers The development of China's legal profession displays this dynamic most clearly. During the bulk of the Mao era, lawyers were virtually nonexistent.[90] Attorneys reappeared in China in 1979, spurred by the trial of the Maoist "Gang of Four" that was charged with orchestrating the excesses of the Cultural Revolution. That year, the Ministry of Justice was restored, and lawyers were recruited to work for the government as "state legal workers" in "legal advisory offices."[91] Like other public sector employees, they received standardized wages and a wide range of government-provided benefits. As a government worker, a lawyer was not a "private agent of the defendant, but an independent party who must 'act on the basis of facts, take the law as the criterion, and be loyal to the interest of the socialist cause and the people.'"[92]

The Early Reform Era (Late 1970s to the Early 1990s) In the first phase of the reform era, lawyers were recruited mostly from existing personnel in party-state agencies and organizations. Passing a bar exam was not required; anyone with legal training or experience was eligible for official approval to enter the profession.[93] Through the late 1990s, sociologist Ethan Michelson points out that roughly 40 percent of lawyers were either "specially appointed" or "part-time" attorneys.[94] The former were individuals tapped by the state to become lawyers after retiring from long careers in judicial agencies (including judges and procurators) or legal education. At their peak in 1996, specially appointed lawyers accounted for 18 percent of all attorneys.[95] "Part-time" lawyers held regular full-time positions at party-state work units, especially law schools and research units, and (legally) moonlighted in law firms that typically were operated by their university or research institution. Through the late 1990s the remaining 60 percent of China's lawyers had less formal legal work experience and practiced law full-time. Still, even these attorneys were formally tied to the state through their employment in law firms affiliated with the government. Through the late 1980s, there were no private law firms to serve as alternative places of employment.[96]

Despite their official status and close connections to the political establishment, lawyers in the early reform period often were castigated and subject to harassment. One reason was that, through the 1980s, lawyers mainly were occupied with criminal defense—an activity that all too often was seen by state agents as inappropriate *support* for criminals. As sociologist Ethan Michelson reports, "throughout China officials in the Ministry of Justice routinely denounced defense lawyers simply for defending their clients."[97] Indeed, a 1988 report found that criminal defense lawyers frequently were dismissed from their jobs, expelled from the party, and sometimes even driven out of court, handcuffed, shackled, and beaten.[98] Central party elites expressed concern, especially when it appeared that the hostile environment was causing lawyers to resign. Along with providing state employment, national authorities attempted to shore up the status of attorneys by creating a "police-style uniform" for them to wear.[99]

Overall, in the early post-Mao era, lawyers depended on the party-state for employment. Those who managed to avoid sanctions for engaging in criminal defense were financially secure in their state employment, but they were not particularly wealthy relative to the general population. Nor were they upwardly mobile. Although many faced harassment at the hands of local authorities, the central regime worked to protect them. Although we have no data on the political attitudes of lawyers during this era, we also have no evidence of their opposition to the regime. To the contrary, a sizeable portion of lawyers in this period had prior or contemporaneous careers in the party-state and were themselves party members.

The Late Reform Era (Early 1990s Through the Present) In the second phase of the reform period, changes in state-led development policies subjected lawyers to the vicissitudes of market competition, yet the legal system continued to be dominated by the party-state, and negative attitudes toward independent lawyers that were forged in the Maoist era remained pervasive among judges and public security personnel. Moving to privatize lawyers and law firms, in 1993 lawyers' status as "state legal workers" formally was abolished, and government-affiliated law firms were pressed to become independent. By 2004 only 15 percent of all law firms remained state-owned.[100] Privatization has made lawyers responsible for their own profits and losses. Unlike in the early post-Mao period, their income has been highly unstable. In 2000 a survey of Beijing lawyers found that approximately half were paid exclusively on commission.[101] Further, few received any job-related benefits or social security guarantees. As one lawyer reported to Michelson in 2001, "lawyers are *getihu* (individual entrepreneurs), just like those who set up stalls on the side of the road, like *getihu* who sell fruit."[102] Only elite corporate law firms in big cities have offered salaried positions—a tiny minority among all attorneys.[103]

A second major change in the late post-Mao period is that, since 1996, lawyers have been required to pass a national bar exam before entering practice.[104] In 2001 all lawyers who had begun their practice before the institution of this rule were required to pass the bar exam or discontinue their practice.[105] The category of "specially appointed" lawyers was officially dropped, and the ranks of part-time lawyers diminished. By 2004, virtually all lawyers were full-time lawyers without "specially appointed" status.[106]

At the same time, beginning in the early 1990s the number of law firms and lawyers in China began to rise rapidly. Between 1993 and 2004, the total number of lawyers grew by more than 300 percent—from approximately 45,000 to about 145,000.[107] Even so, lawyers remain in short supply. As of 2006, China had roughly 1 lawyer for every 10,800 people, compared with a ratio of 1 to 375 in England.[108]

Altogether, these changes have given lawyers an insecure and volatile socioeconomic status. Although some have become quite wealthy, most cobble together an income that is higher than rank-and-file workers yet is subject to substantial fluctuation. In terms of reliance on the state, lawyers no longer receive their paycheck and benefits from the government; yet even so, their income continues to depend largely on their connections with the regime. Success in the courts requires access to information (such as evidence, witness statements, and charges) that public security officials and the courts do not readily provide. Indeed, lawyers are routinely denied permission to see their detained clients. Further, success often turns on a lawyer's relations with judges, who typically hold negative views of lawyers—especially those engaged in criminal defense. The hostile environment faced by lawyers has intensified in recent years. According to a 2008 Human Rights Watch report, the CCP has tightened its control over the legal profession since 2006, with lawyers (especially those representing clients charged with a political offense) facing great party-state interference in collecting evidence and interviewing defense witnesses. As one lawyer states, "The judicial organs will only give you what they want."[109] To overcome these obstacles, lawyers have needed strong connections to the political establishment.

In this context—characterized by market competition for clients on the one hand, and party-state domination of a secretive and biased legal system on the other—lawyers who have succeeded in the profession have been "precisely [those who have been] most folded into the state and the party."[110] Given this, most have had little reason to seek an end to CCP rule. Indeed, Michelson concludes that, although "under many circumstances [lawyers] are a politically liberal force," "the case of China identifies conditions under which lawyers also, wittingly or unwittingly, *stymie* political change" (italics in original).[111] Indeed, available evidence suggests that, rather than seeking increased distance from the CCP-led political establishment, most lawyers have desired close ties with it. As of 2000, 39 percent of all lawyers were CCP members.[112]

Still, a very small percentage of attorneys has pressed the regime to become more politically liberal. These lawyers typically have been economically independent of the party-state (often having made their money in commercial law) and have defended those accused of political crimes or otherwise taken on human rights cases.[113] Beginning around 2002, lawyers of this type became associated with a growing "rights protection movement" (*weiquan yundong*) that also has included intellectuals and journalists. In addition to their work on politically sensitive cases, these activists have "circulat[ed] articles, maintain[ed] web pages, and mobiliz[ed] internet communities."[114] Even so, they have referred to the Chinese constitution as the basis for their actions and have not overtly questioned the legitimacy of the CCP-led political system. As reported in a 2008 Human Rights Watch report, "the hallmark of the movement has been to keep all activities strictly within the realm of Chinese law."[115] Such efforts have not enabled "rights protection" activists to avoid punishment. To the contrary, since 2006, central party elites have "urged the adoption of 'forceful measures . . . against those who, under the pretext of rights-protection [*weiquan*], carry out sabotage'" and "attack . . . our judicial system."[116] Most well-known participants in the movement have been subject to surveillance, harassment, threats, and physical violence. Many also have been barred from practicing law, and some have been jailed.[117] As a result, the already tiny number of lawyers pressing for greater political liberalization in the late reform era has been dwindling.

Accountants   Though less studied, accountants' experiences have some basic similarities with those of lawyers. As with law, the accountancy profession was privatized starting in the late 1990s. Before 1996, accountancy firms were affiliated mostly with large state firms and accounting rules were issued by the Ministry of Finance and provincial finance departments.[118] In 1996 central authorities ordered China's accounting firms to sever their ties with their sponsoring government units. By the end of 1998, virtually all had been transformed into private practices. The goal was twofold: Private accounting firms would ensure more accuracy and independence in accounting, and the firms rather than the state would be responsible for profits and losses.[119] As a result, accountants became nominally independent of the state.[120]

Because their pay ceased to be dictated by relatively uniform state sector standards, accountants started to experience more upward social mobility. Small in number and much in demand (as of 2006, China had 69,000 licensed accountants and was estimated to need more than 300,000 more), accountants saw rapid salary increases. In 2006 the average salary for Chinese accountants at foreign firms, for instance, was $9,000 (roughly 72,000 yuan), an increase of 30 percent from 2005.[121]

Although research on the political attitudes and behavior of accountants has yet to be undertaken, it is clear that their upward mobility has not been hindered by the government. To the contrary, they have become system beneficiaries. Therefore, despite their increased autonomy from the party-state, they seem unlikely candidates to oppose the present system, and, in fact, face certain commercial and career pressures to further embed themselves within the party.

Professional Contentiousness

An overwhelming majority of educated professionals in the late reform era has displayed a remarkable desire to be part of the political establishment and little interest in opposing it. Even so, professionals have not been entirely quiescent. Throughout the second phase of the post-Mao period, a small segment of defense lawyers, intellectuals, and journalists has criticized the CCP's repression and called for political, economic, legal, and human rights. The most organized and publicized example was the establishment of the China Democracy Party in the late 1990s. Since then, overt domestic political dissent on the part of professionals has been almost nonexistent, yet a small number have not only remained active but also have joined ordinary citizens in protests.[122]

Among professionals more generally, there have been some cases of disruptive collective actions. These acts of contention have focused on threats to the quality of the areas in which professionals live. As local officials have sought to promote development and economic growth (both to increase the government's—and their own—coffers through taxes and kickbacks, and to improve their chances of promotion), they often have approved development projects that impinge on the quality of life and property values of existing homeowners. Notable examples of homeowner-related protests on the part of professionals include collective actions in 2007–8 against the extension of Shanghai's high-speed "mag-lev" train and demonstrations in 2007 in Gulei (Fujian province) and 2008 in Chengdu (Sichuan province) to oppose the construction of petrochemical factories and oil refineries. In addition to these cases, there have been myriad smaller acts regarding the building of roads and the loss of open space in areas in or adjacent to housing developments in which professionals reside.

Yet, rather than indicating growing *political* restiveness, political scientist Yongshun Cai finds that professionals who have engaged in homeowner-related protests have been overwhelmingly "moderate" and—even while criticizing and opposing local officials—have displayed faith in and support for the central regime. In one example of this mentality, demonstrators raised a banner accusing local authorities of "cheating the premier at the top, and cheating the people at the bottom."[123] These protestors also consciously chose strategies and slogans that were legal according to central policy. Although participants stressed that this tactical choice was necessary in order to reduce the likelihood of repression, they also expressed no antagonism toward the ruling regime and no desire for systemic political transformation. Overall, Cai concludes that even when China's professionals engage in collective resistance, they "wish to advance their interests without threatening the political order."[124]

CONCLUSION

Changes in state-led development policies, market forces, and socialist legacies over time have led most of China's professionals to enjoy a comfortable lifestyle and a high socioeconomic status relative to other groups. At the same time, they have become formally independent of the state. Rather than causing professionals to question the legitimacy of single-party rule, these developments have made most skeptical of majority rule and desirous of close connections to the existing authoritarian political establishment. Because professionals are part of the minority that sits at the upper level of China's highly polarized socioeconomic structure, they have had little cause to support the political empowerment of the masses. In addition, inasmuch as the ruling CCP has served as a vehicle for economic success, professionals have had incentives to join it and to work within its structures—both to maintain and to promote their own prosperity.

4 RANK-AND-FILE STATE SECTOR WORKERS

DESPITE THEIR POSITION in the vast lower tier of China's onion dome-shaped socioeconomic hierarchy, rank-and-file state sector workers tend to be better off than common private sector workers and farmers, the two other major groups that make up China's large lower "class." The political attitudes and behavior of rank-and-file state sector workers in the reform period have been much studied. Not only does this sector represent an enormous portion of the population, but it also is the only group that has been clearly harmed by China's neoliberal economic reforms. Through the early 1990s, permanent state-owned enterprise (SOE) employees made up roughly 46 percent of all employed legal urban residents and 42 percent of the total industrial workforce.[1] Yet with the large-scale SOE reforms that began in the mid-1990s, approximately one-third of SOE employees were laid off.[2] Among them, a substantial portion has sunk into poverty, with little hope of financial improvement.[3] Meanwhile, still-employed state sector workers have experienced cuts in pay and benefits, as well as more exacting and undesirable working conditions. This situation has bred great dissatisfaction and, in some very notable cases, has led state sector workers to rise up in protest. These workers formed a major component of the "mass disturbances" that were widespread in China in the late 1990s and first few years of the 2000s. Given the size of this sector, its grievances, and its propensity for public contentiousness, it has seemed possible in the late reform period that this group might pose a challenge to the stability of China's ruling regime.

Yet, as of this writing, this possibility appears remote. Protests by state sector workers seem to have peaked around 2002; since that time, such events have become scarce.[4] Even during the height of state sector worker unrest, fewer than one in ten laid-off SOE workers participated in public demonstrations. In addition, almost none of the protesting state sector workers sought to challenge the legitimacy of the central party-state. Further, SOE employees who have retained their jobs generally have not participated in contentious collective actions at all.

As detailed below, the political attitudes and behavior of China's rank-and-file state sector workers have derived from their perceived direction of socioeconomic mobility, relative socioeconomic status, dependence on the state, and political options. In turn, these views have been shaped by the confluence of state-led development, market forces associated with late opening to the global capitalist system, and socialist legacies in post-Mao China. In the first and second phases of the reform period, these factors have combined in different ways, engendering temporal variations in state sector workers' political views and actions. In addition, geographic differences in the context faced by state sector employees have engendered locational variations in political attitudes and behavior. Nonetheless, both current and former rank-and-file workers in China's state sector have evidenced little public criticism of the central party-state and minimal interest in liberal democratic change, and these trends have become more pronounced over time.

THE EARLY REFORM ERA (LATE 1970s TO THE EARLY 1990s)

In the early reform period, China's state-led development policies left the basic state sector system of the Maoist era intact. Thus, the socialist economic and social guarantees and privileges of the pre-reform period remained in place. Because virtually all unskilled workers in state sector jobs continued to enjoy guaranteed employment, most remained sheltered from the market forces that appeared in the emergent private sector. Only those state sector workers that believed that they would benefit from work outside the public sector left their state-provided jobs. Those that did were mostly skilled and educated, characteristics that enabled them to succeed in the private sector as professionals and private entrepreneurs. For the unskilled workers that remained employed in the state sector, the effect of China's economic liberalization and opening to the global economy in the early reform era was only positive: These developments increased the availability of consumer goods to state sector workers without reducing their pay or job security and without any negative impact on their work conditions.

The state-controlled employment system that remained in place throughout the early post-Mao period was characterized by very limited labor mobility. Key to this labor regime was the household registration system that gave each individual a registration card (*hukou*) designating his or her residential status. Through 1984, only those with an urban *hukou* could live in the city legally. Beginning the following year, those with rural *hukou* were permitted to move to urban areas but remained ineligible for most of the state-provided benefits enjoyed by those with urban registration cards (such as education, health care, subsidized transportation, and subsidized basic foodstuffs).

During the 1980s, three categories of jobs were available to city dwellers: permanent work in SOEs, temporary employment in SOEs, and somewhat secure employment in urban collectives.[5] According to Andrew Walder, permanent SOE workers represented the largest share, numbering 32.1 million in 1981. In the same year, 14.9 million were employed in urban collectives, and an estimated 4 million worked as temporary SOE workers.[6] An individual was assigned by the party-state to a job in one of these three categories and typically remained in that position until his or her retirement.

Walder writes that those placed in permanent SOE positions were the most fortunate. The chances of receiving such an assignment were higher for those with more formal education (with a preference for college graduates, followed by those with a vocational-technical degree, and, finally, high school graduates). In addition, priority was given to the children of individuals already employed by a particular SOE.[7] Along with lifetime job security, SOE workers were afforded privileges known collectively as the "iron rice bowl." First, their wages were markedly higher than those of other workers. In 1981, for example, the average annual wage of permanent SOE employees was 864 yuan, compared to 622 yuan for urban collective workers and 420 yuan for temporary SOE employees.[8] Second, permanent SOE workers enjoyed a wide range of valuable state-provided benefits and services that were less available to other kinds of urban laborers. Among other things, SOE work units provided subsidized meals in on-site cafeterias, ration coupons for consumer goods and daily necessities (including cloth and coal), housing with monthly rents rarely amounting to more than one or two days' pay, medical care, child care, and a complimentary set of work clothes and shoes each year (worth about a month's wages). In addition, workers received guaranteed labor insurance and pensions and were eligible for state-provided loans. Further, many larger SOEs maintained plots of land that provided additional produce to workers, either free of charge or through enterprise meal halls.[9] Altogether, at the beginning of the reform period, these benefits and services were estimated to reach a monthly value of roughly 527 yuan per worker.[10] Even this figure does not adequately capture the importance of these provisions, as many of the goods and services distributed by SOEs were simply unavailable by other means.[11] As a result, although permanent SOE workers legally were allowed to resign from their positions, few did. They knew well that "quitting a state sector job . . . invariably mean[t] a drop in living standards and damage to future life chances—not to mention one's children's chances of gaining state employment."[12]

According to Walder, differences existed in wages, benefits, and services among SOEs, and even among permanent SOE workers in the same enterprise. Yet as a whole, permanent SOE workers had a distinctly higher position than other types of urban workers.[13] On average, employees of urban collectives received less than three-fourths the wages of permanent SOE employees. In terms of benefits, urban collectives exhibited extremely wide variations, but few provided the services and subsidies that were provided by SOEs.[14] Although urban collectives were not as stable as SOEs, by the late 1970s urban collectives had "developed permanent business connections with state agencies and enterprises," such that employment in those collectives had become fairly secure.[15] Temporary SOE workers had much more tenuous terms of employment. They also faced a large range of working conditions. Further, they received much lower pay, and few, if any, job-related benefits and services.[16] Nonetheless, as legal city residents, both temporary SOE workers and urban collective employees were eligible for subsidized foodstuffs, transportation, and medical care. As a result, as of 1982, "only 5.2 percent of the average urban Chinese family budget was spent on the necessities that comprise[d] 45 percent of the American family's expenditures and 21 percent of the Japanese family's."[17]

Beginning in 1984, new SOE workers were hired without guarantees of lifetime employment or "iron rice bowl" benefits. These younger workers had no experience or expectation of receiving "iron rice bowl" provisions, so they displayed little discontent with the terms of their employment. To the contrary, many younger workers welcomed the increased job flexibility. In addition, when small and medium-sized SOEs first were encouraged to engage in marketizing reforms in the early 1990s, most did little to reduce the benefits and job security of those who had been hired before the mid-1980s.[18] Thus, longtime state sector workers experienced few, if any, negative changes in their employment.

Indeed, during the first phase of the reform period, state sector wages, benefits, and services improved. As Walder notes, after being "virtually frozen from 1963 to 1976 . . . nominal wages were raised for almost one-half of the [state sector] workforce on three separate occasions from 1977 to 1984." As a result, "nominal wages in state industry increased by 37 percent, real wages by 18 percent."[19] Further, bonus pay was restored and expanded for SOE workers, such that by 1982, they received bonuses worth more than two months' average salary.[20] At the same time, "state expenditures on housing construction increased almost fivefold, from the 1958 to 1977 average of 5.5 percent of the national construction budget to 25 percent in 1981 and 1982."[21] As a result, "more new urban housing was built from 1978 to 1984 than in the first three decades of the people's republic," and "state expenditures on benefits financed through the state labor insurance system increased by 170 percent from 1978 to 1983, while the number of state employees grew by only 18 percent."[22] Party-state representatives worked to improve workers' living and working conditions, including funds for housing renovation; improved variety and quality of produce from the factory's farmland; employment for more workers' children; expanded daycare and kindergartens; new repair services for workers and their families; the purchase and delivery of coal for apartment and dorm residents; and even matchmaking services.[23]

At the same time, the party-state's toleration of the emergence of limited free markets dramatically increased the number and quality of goods and services available to urban consumers. Perhaps most importantly, the establishment of the rural "household responsibility system" that gave peasants greater freedom in terms of crop production and sale led to increased agricultural productivity and greater variety in produce. As the urban ration card system for most basic goods was abolished and rural residents were allowed to travel to the cities to peddle their wares and offer small-scale consumer services, urban residents enjoyed an exponential increase in the number of available points of sale and acquisition.[24] Reflecting these changes, between 1978 and 1981 the total amount of per capita purchases of consumer goods in urban areas rose by 26 percent.[25] Overall, in the early reform era state sector workers received the benefits of privatization and liberalization without being subjected to the harmful effects that such developments often have on unskilled labor.

Perceptions of Socioeconomic Mobility, Relative
Socioeconomic Status, Material Dependence
on the Party-State, and Political Options

Although the changes just discussed generally improved the living and work-ing conditions of state sector workers, those changes did not translate into a feeling of upward socioeconomic mobility relative to other groups. The eco-nomic reforms of the early post-Mao period also led to a dramatic increase in socioeconomic inequality. As noted in Chapter 1, between 1978 and 1988, the level of economic inequality in China more than doubled—moving from a Gini coefficient of 0.15 that ranked China among the most egalitarian coun-tries in the world to a score of 0.386 that almost matched the degree of eco-nomic polarization found in the United States at that time.[26] Consequently, although most state sector workers experienced a rise in income and enjoyed more consumer goods, their gains paled in comparison to those made by others—especially new private entrepreneurs with close party-state connec-tions. This reality was especially jarring to SOE workers, who, during the Mao era, had enjoyed a place near the top of China's socioeconomic structure. For them, the early reform period brought lower relative socioeconomic status. Indeed, surveys conducted in 1986 and 1991–92 show that roughly 57 percent of SOE workers thought that their social status had declined since the initia-tion of economic reform.[27]

In addition, state sector workers' perceived opportunities for upward eco-nomic mobility diminished. During the Mao era, many moved from manual labor into white-collar positions. In that period, "technicians and managers were often promoted directly from among the workers," and one's level of ed-ucation had little relation to opportunities for promotion.[28] In contrast, as the early reform period progressed, "upward social mobility increasingly was cre-dentialized, including a greater role for exams and education level." As a result, there were "even fewer opportunities for manual workers to be promoted from below."[29]

In terms of economic dependence on the state, most permanent SOE workers continued to enjoy state-provided benefits and privileges. At the same time, the greater availability of consumer goods and services in the open marketplace decreased SOE workers' economic reliance on their work units. Further, private enterprise offered alternatives to state sector employment. As a result, SOEs were no longer the only means for urban residents to garner a comfortable livelihood. Thus, although SOE workers continued to rely on the party-state, their level of dependence declined in the first phase of the post-Mao period.

During this time, state sector workers had few political options and increasingly were shunned by the CCP. As Bruce J. Dickson relates, in late 1978 the party "decreed that the period of class struggle was over, and that the CCP would begin to concentrate on economic modernization as its key task. This change in the party's main mission brought about changes in its priorities for recruiting new members and appointing key personnel."[30] Specifically, CCP cadres sought to attract younger, more educated, and more technically oriented individuals to join the party. Coupled with SOE workers' growing economic independence from the party-state and lowered position in an ever-more-polarized socioeconomic structure, their diminished ability to join the party gave them greater potential interest in political reform.

Political Attitudes and Behavior

During the first phase of the post-Mao era, these developments led to a relatively distant relationship between rank-and-file state sector workers and the ruling CCP. As reported in a 1986 survey, SOE workers believed that party recruitment favored intellectuals over workers. Further, respondents complained that whereas "under the old system, workers were the 'masters,' managers and cadres were the 'servants' of the socialist firm . . . during reform the 'servants' were penalizing the 'masters.'"[31] As economic reform decreased SOE workers' reliance on the ruling regime, they had less cause to desire greater involvement in it. As a result, the portion of nonmanagerial SOE employees who were party members declined dramatically—dropping from 17.9 percent in 1982 to 8.3 percent in 1990.[32]

Even so, throughout the majority of the early reform period, the generally rising material standard of living among state sector workers bred political quiescence. The major exception occurred in the spring of 1989. Since the mid-1980s, China's increasingly polarized socioeconomic structure—in which a small segment of urban residents closely related to the party-state enjoyed a life of luxury while average urban residents struggled to buy basic goods—had aroused a sense of injustice among state sector workers. This was especially the case for SOE employees, who were accustomed to occupying a privileged socioeconomic position. As inflation flared into the double digits in the late 1980s, the resulting decline in financial well-being for SOE workers (and other common city dwellers) engendered greater dissatisfaction with the political status quo. When university students raised the possibility of political change in the spring of 1989, some SOE workers joined the demonstrations.[33]

The student protests of 1989 began in mid-April and continued until the party's violent crackdown on June 3–4.[34] Approximately four weeks after the student-led demonstrations had begun, SOE workers began to form their own dissident organizations. By early June, some 20,000 SOE workers had joined non-party "Worker Autonomous Federations" (WAFs) in more than twenty major Chinese cities.[35] The demands and rhetoric of WAF participants showed the imprint of China's socialist legacy. Along with a clear commitment to socialist values of economic justice and worker rights, their words articulated a deep sense of indignation regarding the socioeconomic polarization that emerged in the early reform era, and that diminished their relative socioeconomic standing. For example, one handbill stated that "we have calculated carefully, based on Marx's *Capital*, the rate of exploitation of workers. We discovered that the 'servants of the people' swallow all the surplus value produced by the people's blood and sweat."[36] Other documents reported that the goal of the WAFs was to guarantee "that the workers become the real masters of the enterprise."[37] At the same time, WAF statements showed an awareness of, and attraction to, political values such as democracy, freedom of association, and the rule of law. Some also linked China's socioeconomic inequality to the corrupt and "dictatorial" nature of the regime.[38] Connecting their cause to that of the French revolution, WAF documents called on workers to "storm the Bastille of the 1980s" and to save China from leaders who "murder democracy, and trample human rights."[39] Similarly, the "guiding principles" of the Beijing WAF stated that the "organization should be an entirely independent, autonomous organization, built up by the workers on a voluntary basis, through democratic processes."[40] Overall, sociologists Andrew Walder and Xiaoxia Gong conclude that WAF rhetoric "fused together the idea of working class struggle with the language of democratic opposition to political oligarchy."[41] In other words, their political preference was not free-market liberal democracy but, rather, a form of social democratic governance.

The WAFs did not develop beyond a very preliminary stage. As the regime resolved to crush the various organizations that had formed in the spring of 1989, all major worker leaders of the WAFs were detained and arrested. Further, only a miniscule percentage of China's roughly forty million SOE workers had joined the WAFs before their suppression. Even so, the participation of some SOE workers in these protests emanated from frustration with their decline in material conditions as a result of inflation, as well as their feeling of injustice that their socioeconomic status was being lowered while well-connected and corrupt cadres prospered. At the same time, their willingness to take on the party-state was enhanced by their decreased economic dependence on the ruling regime.

THE LATE REFORM ERA (EARLY 1990s THROUGH THE PRESENT)

Although worker outrage at the harsh punishment of WAF leaders might have been expected to cause further agitation for political reform, this did not transpire. Rather, in the second phase of the reform era, SOE workers have evidenced a curious mix of increased public contentiousness toward *local* officials and managers, and support for the *central* regime. This seemingly paradoxical behavior has emanated from changes in China's state-led development policies, market forces related to China's late opening to the global capitalist system, and socialist legacies in the late post-Mao period. Because these contextual changes have caused laid-off state sector employees to experience downward economic mobility and a further decline in socioeconomic status relative to other groups, former state sector workers of this period have been highly dissatisfied, leading hundreds of thousands to take to the streets to express their grievances. At the same time, the party-state's special treatment of current and former SOE employees has maintained among retrenched SOE workers some degree of economic dependence on the ruling regime. Because the party-state has not extended these policies to other poor city dwellers (in particular, rural migrants), unemployed SOE workers have enjoyed a privileged status within the general unemployed population. SOE workers have continued to believe that they are morally entitled to these special government provisions. As a result, when former SOE employees have risen up to protest their diminished livelihood and status, rather than opposing the central party-state, they have clung to it, begging existing leaders to better fulfill the socialist promises that the party has made to SOE workers. Further, retrenched SOE employees have not shown a desire to unite with other economically depressed groups.

Overall, in the second phase of the post-Mao period, the economic position of state sector workers has diminished dramatically. This has resulted from a momentous change in the government's economic development policy: In 1995 the central party-state announced its intention to "keep the large [SOEs] and let the small go" (*zhuada fangxiao*). Supporting this decision was the fact that, as of the mid-1990s, China's "500 largest state firms held 37 percent of the state's industrial assets, contributed 46 percent of all taxes collected from state firms, and totaled 63 percent of the state sector's profits."[42] Meanwhile, more than 72 percent of small firms owned by local governments were unprofitable.[43] In 1997 the Fifteenth Party Congress introduced a plan to privatize SOEs. By the end of the following year, more than 80 percent of state and collective firms at the county level or lower had experienced some form of privatization.[44]

For the following decade, the main method of privatization was employee shareholding (*gufenhua*), whereby firms required existing enterprise workers to purchase shares as a condition of continued employment.[45] Although touted as a way to enable workers to become "owners," in reality this allowed enterprise managers to raise capital from their relatively poor employees and to shift responsibility for firm debts to enterprise workers/shareholders. Even more troubling to SOE employees was that following *gufenhua*, many firms went under and/or the enterprise managers disappeared with the funds—in either situation leaving the employees/shareholders worse off than they were before privatization.[46] A second method of privatization was the open sale of shares to enterprise insiders and outsiders. Alternatively, some SOEs formed joint ventures, merging with domestic or foreign firms. When an enterprise was sold outright via one of these methods, the buyer was required to sign an agreement with the government concerning firm debts as well as the "redeployment" of the employees.[47] In exchange for retaining workers, buyers often were given a discount, allowed to acquire the firm for free, or provided with subsidies.[48]

Even after negotiations with government officials, most agreements allowed for a substantial number of layoffs. Indeed, in 1998 when the party announced that all SOEs would have three years to become profitable, central elites accepted that layoffs would be required. Further, in many cases, new enterprise owners found ways around their contracts and proceeded with more extensive employee downsizing than the agreement allowed.[49] As a result, beginning in the late 1990s, tens of millions of middle-aged and older SOE employees were laid off. In 2001 alone, the official number of SOE jobs lost totaled 15 percent of urban unemployment.[50] Along with layoffs, SOEs reduced their workforce by forcing employees into early retirement. As a result, between 1995 and 2002 the number of retirees was estimated to have grown from thirty-one million to forty million.[51] In fact, in interviews conducted circa 2000, political scientist William Hurst found that "normal" retirement ages had dropped to ages forty-five to fifty for women and fifty to fifty-five for men.[52]

When an SOE worker has been laid off or required to retire early, the state has made some attempt to provide assistance. In the case of layoffs, if the firm remains solvent, the former employee may retain a nominal connection with the enterprise, with the idea that he or she may resume work should the firm's circumstances improve. Such individuals are said to have "stepped down from their position" (xiagang) and are not counted among the technically unemployed. A former SOE worker is considered officially unemployed if he or she has had xiagang status for three years but has not obtained formal work or if the firm has gone bankrupt.[53] In a 1999–2000 survey conducted by China's National Bureau of Statistics (NBS), 53 percent of laid-off SOE workers remained unemployed, indicating that most had experienced at least four years without formal work.[54] By 2002, the situation had worsened: Nearly 74 percent of former SOE workers reported that they lacked formal employment.[55]

At the national level, since the late 1990s, xiagang individuals have been eligible for government-provided "basic living expenses." Through 2003, these former SOE employees also were required to register at Re-employment Service Centers that were responsible for "economic assistance, social security related services, training, and vocational guidance."[56] For officially "unemployed" former SOE workers, central policies have required the provision of unemployment payments.[57] In reality, these benefits and services have been woefully inadequate, and in many cases they have been entirely unavailable due to a lack of sufficient government funds. In the 1999–2000 NBS survey referenced earlier, only 56 percent of laid-off SOE employees reported receiving any kind of government-provided unemployment benefit.[58] Further, even among those who have garnered some government assistance, the payment has been quite small. As of 2000, the average benefit amounted to 210 yuan/month, as compared with an average monthly wage of 544 yuan/month for reemployed former SOE workers.[59]

Retirees, meanwhile, have been entitled to fairly generous pensions paid in part by the central and local government and in part by the enterprise. In the early 1990s, before large-scale SOE reform, the portion of legal pension relative to pre-retirement compensation reached 90 percent for those with top SOE assignments. Following the major SOE reforms of the mid-1990s, the portion declined to 75 to 80 percent for SOE workers but remained high in comparison to the international average of 40 to 60 percent.[60] Since the mid-1990s, however, pension payments—like unemployment benefits—often have not been made in full. To a large extent, this has been due to a lack of funds. Whereas in 1978 there were only 2.1 million pensioners, by 2005 their ranks had grown to roughly 100 million.[61] When a firm becomes insolvent, it is unable to pay its portion of retiree pensions, but even among enterprises that have remained in business, a sizeable number have failed to make full payments. As of 2000, this was true of roughly 25 percent of work units nationwide, affecting approximately four million retirees.[62]

In this climate, central authorities have demonstrated some commitment to their promises to retrenched SOE employees, repeatedly demanding "that local governments guarantee payment of retirement pensions and subsistence subsidies to laid-off [SOE] workers."[63] As a result, after the late 1990s, provincial and city governments used their power to issue licenses, engage in inspections, approve applications to retire and/or lay off workers, and publicize enterprise arrears in official media outlets to force firms to pay their share of these benefits.[64] There has been some evidence of improvement. Nationally, the number of individuals covered by minimum standard-of-living protections has risen steadily— from 1.84 million in 1998 to 2.67 million in 1999, 4.02 million in 2000, 11.7 million in 2001, and 20.6 million in 2002.[65] The portion of urban workers covered by a pension fund reportedly grew from 46 percent in 2004 to 76 percent in 2006.[66] Government authorities also have claimed that the pension fund rose between 2005 and 2007 and have declared that it will be raised again by a higher margin between 2008 and 2010.[67]

Some local governments have implemented policies giving preferential reemployment opportunities to laid-off SOE employees.[68] For example, cities have enacted rules that reserve some unskilled jobs for former SOE workers, denying access to their potential competitors within the rural migrant population.[69] In 1997 the municipal government of Beijing declared that thirty-five types of work were prohibited to non-local labor. The following year in Wuhan, local authorities decreed that twenty-four kinds of businesses could not use migrant labor and that such individuals should be laid off if they already had been hired.[70] Further, many localities have offered tax breaks to new enterprises that hire retrenched SOE employees.[71]

Similarly, government officials have provided tax incentives and other forms of assistance to laid-off SOE workers who go into private business. For example, in early 2003 the central government made available to laid-off state-owned enterprise workers special business start-up loans of 20,000 yuan (roughly US$2,500), to be guaranteed by municipal and provincial governments.[72] Another program, begun in 2004, has provided approximately fifty thousand laid-off state-owned enterprise workers with private business training, technical assistance, and loans.[73] The government's Labor and Social Protection Bureaus also have established various programs to provide credit to laid-off SOE workers seeking to start their own enterprises.[74] In some cases, when a state-owned enterprise has been shut down, the employees have been allowed to take tools and machines or to use the premises for business purposes. In one such instance, workers took the delivery vehicles of their former enterprise, which they subsequently used to start an independent delivery service.[75] Many laid-off state-owned enterprise workers also have set up shop in their state-subsidized homes.[76] In addition, anecdotal evidence suggests that—in marked contrast to the often hostile treatment of migrants from the countryside—local authorities generally have not hindered the attempts of former state-owned enterprise workers to start a private business. To the contrary, local officials—along with party-state organizations such as the official labor union and the Women's Federation—sometimes have actively supported such efforts, making available low-rent or rent-free premises, furniture, and utility services.[77]

Market forces related to China's economic liberalization have also affected workers' lives. Beginning in the early 1990s, China's political leaders opened the domestic economy much more widely to the international capitalist system. From that time through the present, foreign direct investment has flooded the mainland. As political scientist Mary Gallagher documents, from 1990 through the first few years of the 2000s, China attracted $430 billion in foreign direct investment—more than any other developing country in the world.[78] Consequently, Gallagher notes, when extensive SOE reform began in the second half of the 1990s, foreign-invested enterprises already had become both established and highly successful. The stunning economic performance of foreign-invested enterprises pressured domestic firms (both private and public) to institute the labor practices that were proving successful in foreign-invested enterprises. For example, after foreign-invested enterprises introduced employment contracts, this practice gradually spread to workers in SOEs.[79] In addition, huge numbers of small and medium-sized SOEs were sold to foreign-invested enterprises, and the former SOE workers became subject to the stringent capitalist practices of the foreign-invested enterprises.[80]

According to Gallagher, the result has been that capitalist labor practices have come to permeate all Chinese firms.[81] The overall effect has been a loss of employment security for SOE workers. If the firm does not do well, or they themselves are evaluated poorly, workers have been subject to pay cuts and even layoffs. In many cases, unskilled SOE employees have been told that if they wish to continue to work for the firm, they will have to do more work (often including less desirable tasks than previously had been required of them) and accept reductions in pay and/or benefits. Thus, after the mid-1990s, even SOE workers who have not been laid off or forced to retire have faced a substantial decline in income and working conditions. Meanwhile, former state sector employees have had to look for work in the private sector, where the surfeit of unskilled laborers through most of the first decade of the 2000s made pay and work expectations even worse.

At the same time, China's socialist past has continued to impact urban SOE workers in the latter phase of the reform era. Sociologist Ching Kwan Lee writes that China's "lingering 'socialist' entitlements" in the second phase of the reform era have served as "buffers" against economic distress.[82] Along with the state-provided benefits and services outlined earlier, most current and former state-sector workers have taken advantage of the government's "near universal provision" of urban housing.[83] As Lee notes, "between 1949 and 1990, rent in most Chinese cities accounted for only two to three percent of total household income, with monthly rent for a typical flat costing less than a packet of good cigarettes."[84] In the 1990s, most of this housing was sold to urban residents at far-below-market prices. In the "rustbelt" city of Shenyang, for example, housing units were purchased at roughly 60 percent below market values.[85] Similarly, in Beijing in 2000, the average market price for housing was 7,300 yuan per square meter, yet state sector workers paid only 1,480 yuan.[86] In many cases, the amount was so low that the buyer did not need a loan. According to official data from 2001, roughly 58 percent of Beijing residents had purchased property "from or through their work-units."[87] Nationwide, by 2003, 70 percent of households with urban residence registration owned their own homes.[88]

These socialist housing legacies have enabled current and former public sector employees to become part of the "propertied class."[89] In areas such as Beijing, where "the gap between housing prices and income" is large, these policies have allowed many state sector workers to "carve out lifestyles well beyond their means."[90] Their subsidized housing has created an effective increase in income as compared with non-state workers, who not only have had to pay higher prices for property but also typically have had to take out loans and pay interest in order to do so. Indeed, the high expense has made property ownership impossible for many private sector workers. Some have rented housing from more privileged state sector workers who have acquired units on the cheap.[91] Meanwhile, "even in the worst-hit areas in [China's] rustbelt," although state policies have made joblessness "ubiquitous," "there [has been] no sign of homelessness."[92] Thus, benefits provided to current and former state sector workers have constituted a minimal safety net that has prevented most from falling into extreme poverty.[93]

Perceptions of Socioeconomic Mobility, Relative Socioeconomic Status, Material Dependence on the Party-State, and Political Options

In the second phase of the reform era, state-led development policies, market forces related to China's nearly wholesale immersion in the global capitalist system, and socialist legacies have caused most rank-and-file state sector workers to experience downward socioeconomic mobility, lower relative socioeconomic status, continued reliance on the state for their livelihood, and fewer political options. Former rank-and-file state sector workers—especially those previously employed in large SOEs—have been the most "downwardly-mobile" sector in the late reform era.[94] As Dorothy Solinger notes, "this is a group of mainly unskilled workers who, summarily dismissed from the plants where they had toiled for decades, have had to discover new modes of livelihood from scratch in the midst of middle age."[95] Consequently, their material conditions and prospects have been bleak. Indeed, economists Shi Li and Hiroshi Sato have characterized unemployed and *xiagang* SOE workers as China's "new urban poor."[96] In a 1999 survey of laid-off workers conducted by political scientist Yongshun Cai, 90 percent reported dissatisfaction with their economic and employment status.[97] Similarly, a 1998 survey of laid-off workers in Hunan "found that over 97 percent felt depressed and worried after being laid off, and about 74 percent were pessimistic and felt hopeless."[98] As one former SOE employee related, "After I received the layoff notification, I lay in bed for a few days, eating almost nothing. We were in a difficult time and even had no money for fresh vegetables, not to mention meat. For days, my daughter could only eat the rice mixed with salted vegetables."[99] To survive, most have found informal, temporary work that is not considered "real" employment, including urban sanitation, community service, secondary production services, and personal service.[100]

Even unskilled SOE workers who have retained their jobs have had little sense of upward economic mobility. In a 1996–97 survey of such workers in Guangzhou, for example, sociologists Ka-ho Mok and Cai He found that 64 percent of those surveyed did not think that their income level had improved, and 61 percent felt that their welfare conditions had been declining.[101] A 1999 survey found that 20.5 percent of SOE employees believed that their standard of living was improving, while 46.6 percent felt that it had deteriorated.[102] Further, many have lived in constant (and well-founded) fear that they, too, will be retrenched. In addition, many have faced increased work expectations and more harsh workplace discipline. As sociologist Martin King Whyte reports,

> systems of fines and pay deductions have been implemented regarding a whole range of worker behavior, including matters ranging far and wide beyond production output and quality. In some reported cases issues such as attendance at political meetings, cleanliness of a worker's locker, and compliance with rules about what can be carried in lunch bags are counted in determining compensation.[103]

Thus, despite their continued SOE employment, many still-employed state sector workers have felt that they have been "losers in the reform process."[104]

Linked with this perceived downward mobility has been a loss of relative socioeconomic status. Once heralded as society's "heroes" and "masters" and praised for building China's productive capacity, they have been forced to compete against migrant laborers, whom former SOE workers view as social inferiors.[105] Indeed, Solinger relates that "the current collapse of status hierarchies" has gone so far that laid-off SOE workers have been called *mingong*, a term connoting the low status of casual laborers that previously was used only to refer to migrant workers from rural areas.[106] Reflecting SOE workers' sense of relative loss of status, a 2004 survey showed that most urban residents believed that the main beneficiaries of economic reform were party-state cadres and private entrepreneurs, followed by artists, individual entrepreneurs, SOE managers, and specialists and technicians. Very few of those surveyed thought that SOE workers had enjoyed any gains.[107] Similarly, the still-employed

Guangzhou state sector workers surveyed by Mok and He in 1996–97 reported that "the 'master' status which they enjoyed in the Mao period has gone and that they are in fact degenerating into an 'underclass' in the new market setting."[108] Mok and He conclude that state sector workers, "originally an 'aristocratic' class," have become "a relatively deprived group."[109]

Yet state policies have led state sector workers and migrant workers to see themselves as separate groups with distinct identities and interests. As Ching Kwan Lee states, "a clear boundary is maintained between these two segments of the working class, which have never shown any inclination to join forces or form an alliance. They perceive their interests, life conditions, and social status as worlds apart from each other."[110] Overall, both current and former SOE workers view themselves—and are viewed by migrant workers—as holding a superior and privileged status relative to migrant workers. Indeed, Lee reports that even migrant workers "who have worked in urban factories for more than a decade and have known no other form of waged employment . . . still consider themselves 'peasants' rather than 'real' workers (*gongren*), a title reserved for those with an urban residence card and public sector employment."[111] And this "peasant" status denotes a lower social, economic, and political position. As one migrant worker states, "as a peasant, I just feel naturally inferior."[112]

These perceptions have been reinforced by the fact that current and former state sector employees have retained at least remnants of their earlier official privilege. In addition, they have remained at least somewhat dependent on the CCP-led regime to provide them with a modicum of succor in the face of their overall decline and a small degree of protection from free market forces that have worked to the disadvantage of most unskilled laborers. As outlined earlier, the regime has provided benefits to current and former state sector workers that have been denied to non-state workers.[113] Simultaneously, government authorities regularly have harassed and mistreated the migrant laborers who have competed against laid-off state sector workers for jobs.[114]

Among former state sector employees, preferential treatment for certain groups has been apparent. In particular, pensioners have occupied a privileged position.[115] State workers that have been forced into early retirement have been viewed as a priority among both national and local government officials.[116] As a result, unemployment and even wage payments for still-employed workers often have taken a back seat to pension commitments.[117] Overall, this hierarchy of official status and economic dependence on the party-state has given those in higher positions reason to cling to the regime that provides them with special privileges and to fear the political empowerment of those who sit below them in the eyes of the ruling regime.

Politically, state sector workers—aside from a small number of WAF leaders who were severely punished in the protests of 1989—have had other reasons to tolerate the CCP's rule. Since 1989, the ruling party has shown more interest in recruiting "workers at the forefront of production."[118] Meanwhile, as the second phase of the reform era has progressed, disgruntled SOE workers have been presented with virtually no attractive alternatives to CCP rule. As Gallagher points out, since the mid-1990s, the public has been inundated with the notion that capitalist labor reforms are simply unavoidable if China wishes to compete in the global economic marketplace.[119] Intertwined with this perspective, Gallagher notes, has been the Anglo-American liberal notion that individual merit is the basis of economic success. Official propaganda has inculcated the notion that the market is infallible and does not fail the worker; rather, the worker fails the market. Workers have been criticized for "waiting, relying, and demanding" (deng, kao, yao) and have been told to take individual responsibility for their fate.[120] As one party paper stated in 1997,

> the market economy doesn't pity the weak. Facing up to unemployment, what should Chinese workers do? Straighten up one's back, become one of the strong! As long as one is willing to endure hardship, the ground will be beneath your feet. As long as you use your head, work isn't hard to find.[121]

Thus, Gallagher claims that, by emphasizing the necessity of capitalist labor reforms that make the market the final arbiter of economic success, the party effectively has avoided taking responsibility for the economic dislocation that SOE workers have faced in the post-Mao era. Even if laid-off SOE workers generally have not "bought" official propaganda that blames workers for their plight and asserts the necessity of large-scale layoffs, most have assumed that capitalist reforms are necessary and that any political leadership would be forced to take similar steps.[122] In the 1996–97 survey of Guangzhou workers, for example, more than 70 percent of respondents agreed that market reform was "the only alternative for future economic development in China."[123]

Yet the CCP has not completely abandoned former SOE workers to the vicissitudes of the market. As Dickson notes, even while pressing for and touting the inevitability of economic privatization and marketization, the party has continued its "rhetorical reference to [socialist] party traditions."[124] In 1999, for example, top CCP leader Jiang Zemin proclaimed that workers are the ruling class of our country and are the fundamental force promoting social stability. The party committee and government at each level must take great care of the lives of laid-off workers and their reemployment. This is a serious political task and should be done by all means.[125]

Similarly, in the latter half of the 1990s, party leaders frequently expressed concern for the circumstances of the "weak and disadvantaged" (*ruoshi qunti*), including among them unemployed, *xiagang*, and retired SOE workers.[126] This language has been amplified by Jiang's successor, Hu Jintao, who was appointed to the party's highest post in 2002. Indeed, Hu has defined his major priority as the amelioration of socioeconomic inequality. This emphasis was reiterated at the party's 2007 Congress. As reported in the *South China Morning Post*, the language employed at this meeting was "heavy with Communist rhetoric, with numerous references to 'holding high the great banner of socialism with Chinese characteristics.'"[127] In his keynote speech, Hu stressed the importance of "reversing the growing income disparity" in China, asserting that "vigorous efforts will be made to raise the income of low-income groups."[128] In addition, the socialist rhetoric of party leaders has not been empty talk. As described earlier, the ruling regime has continued to provide laid-off SOE workers with privileges and benefits and has worked to address the economic displacement and polarization that have resulted from China's market reforms. In this way, the party's embrace of both capitalism and socialism has given current and former SOE workers reason to tolerate continued CCP rule; with market reform appearing unavoidable, the party has appeared at least somewhat committed to ameliorating the negative effects of China's capitalist transition.

At the same time, many former state sector workers have had little incentive to participate in public protests. As long as a firm has remained solvent, laid-off workers have had an interest in maintaining conciliatory relations with the enterprise, because management has continued to control the resources (such as severance and pension pay) that the workers need in order to survive.[129] In addition, some former employees have been told that if they protest, they will be unable to return to the factory if its situation improves.[130] Due to their economic dependence on the party-state, most current and former state sector employees have felt that they have had few desirable options and that their best course of action is to hope that the party-state and its enterprises will regain sufficient funds to attend to their needs. When a firm has gone completely bankrupt, workers generally have not believed that the enterprise could be rejuvenated such that they could retain their jobs or that the government has the financial means to keep the failed firm afloat.[131]

Disgruntled state sector workers have had legal ways to express their grievances within the system. Most important among these have been: (1) Letters and Visits Offices (*xinfangke*), which have accepted citizen complaints since the early 1950s but have been much more extensively available and widely used since the early 1980s; (2) arbitration committees (*zhongcai weiyuanhui*), which were established in 1993 to formally adjudicate disputes between employers and employees; and (3) courts, which before the first few years of the 2000s could be used only to contest an arbitrator's decision but since that time have been made directly accessible to plaintiffs.[132] As a result, labor dissatisfaction often has been channeled through the existing political system rather than turned against it.[133] To the extent that they perceive legal processes to have been effective, former state employees have had much more incentive to work within the system than to challenge it.

However, for some laid-off workers, protest has been a practical and appealing option, for the most part because central authorities have maintained a pro-worker stance in terms of both rhetoric and law. Because the managers of state-owned firms depend on central authorities for their continued livelihood and career advancement, workers have been able to use the threat of disruption to pressure concessions from managers and/or local officials.[134] When management and local authorities have flouted welfare and labor laws that have been established by the central government, many workers have believed that higher-level authorities will respond in a favorable manner.[135] As a result, laid-off workers sometimes have felt that collective protest is a practical option. This belief has derived from the party-state's cultivation of a pro-worker reputation that has instilled in workers a faith in the willingness and ability of central authorities to address their grievances.

Political Attitudes and Behavior

The somewhat different experiences and interests among still-employed, laid-off, and retired rank-and-file state sector workers have worked against any possibility that they might form a unified bloc that would challenge CCP rule.[136] In addition, across all subsets of current and former state sector workers, attitudes toward the central party-state generally have been positive (or at least tolerant) since the mid-1990s. This has occurred even as interactions between state sector workers and local authorities and managers have soured.

In terms of general political attitudes, the combined influence of perceptions deriving from China's state-led development policies, market forces related to China's opening to the global capitalist system, and socialist legacies is clear. Recounting interviews with dozens of laid-off SOE employees in the first few years of the 2000s, Ching Kwan Lee states that "conversations with workers about protests and survival today inevitably returned to 'the past,' that is 'in the time of Chairman Mao' or 'under the planned economy.' Rarely could my interviewees articulate and describe the present without invoking the past."[137]

Overall, SOE workers' firsthand experience of the Maoist planned economy has bred somewhat ambivalent attitudes toward the post-Mao economic reforms. Both current and former state sector workers have appeared to recognize the inefficiencies and general limitation on economic opportunities that existed under Mao. Most seem to believe that economic reform has brought a higher material standard of living.[138] Yet numerous analyses show that former SOE workers have lamented deeply the loss of economic security and employment satisfaction that was present in the Maoist era and believe that they have been "wronged" by the economic reforms enacted since the mid-1990s that have taken these things away.[139] As reported by Lee, in the first few years of the 2000s, "the most oft-mentioned characteristic of lived experience under Mao was livelihood and job security."[140] Overall, despite having a lower material standard of living in the Maoist era, former SOE workers stated that "psychologically we felt better."[141] Rather than viewing the planned economy as being unproductive and rife with waste, workers expressed "occupational pride based on skills acquired in the factory . . . [and] emphasize[d] workers' contribution and dedication to national development."[142] They also stressed that they worked hard under the planned economy.[143] Elaborating, one interviewee noted that "every Monday, Wednesday, and Friday we stayed in the factory after work to learn systematically different skills."[144] Indeed, some SOE workers argued that economic reform had caused a *decline* in the quality of labor. One claimed that in the wake of SOE reform, "no one feels responsible for their work." As a result, she stated, "it's natural that we are producing many rejected goods."[145] Further, former SOE employees have decried the marked decline in economic and social security resulting from the economic reforms of the late post-Mao era. Under the planned economy, one reported, "as long as I worked hard, I did not have to worry. The work unit took care of my housing, children's employment and pension. I was very content."[146] Another stated that before SOE reform, "I always felt that life had a natural rhythm: I worked, collected wages, retired, and then my children would inherit my post. Now there is no guarantee of pension, children's education, or employment."[147] Similarly, one of Lee's interviewees stated, "in the days of Mao, no matter how poor, the factory could not ignore you when you got sick. Now, without money, you just wait for death when you get sick."[148]

In addition, Lee reports, because "the official ideology of 'workers as masters of the enterprise' was a lived experience under Mao," former SOE workers have expressed a "'class-based' sense of entitlement, rights, and dignity."[149] For example, Feng Chen found that as of the first few years of the 2000s, laid-off SOE employees maintained the socialist belief that workers have "legitimate rights to factory property."[150] Workers interviewed in Chen's study asserted that "the simple fact that they had contributed their entire working life to the factory justified their share in factory property, while privatization amounted to a deprivation of their share without compensation."[151] Similarly, Chen's review of SOE-related protests in the late 1990s and early years of the first decade of the 2000s concludes that "because most workers spent all their working lives at a state enterprise and contributed to the accumulation of state assets through low wages, they felt strongly that the factory was not simply 'theirs' (the managers') but also 'ours.'"[152] Expressing the same belief, one of Lee's interviewees states that "every inch of grass and every piece of steel in the factory belonged to us workers. They were our sweat and labor."[153]

Relatedly, most current and former urban state sector employees have continued in the late post-Mao period to believe that the government has a responsibility to ensure their livelihood. In a survey of workers undertaken in 1999 by the CCP Central Committee's Ministry of Organization, "only 5.5 reported that laid-off workers or the unemployed should be held responsible for their own subsistence and employment."[154] Similarly, in a 2000 survey of Beijing residents conducted by Martin King Whyte, 95 percent agreed that "it was the responsibility of the government to provide jobs to everyone wanting to work and that the government should guarantee a minimum standard of living for everyone."[155] Many also have expressed support for higher taxes on the rich. For example, a Chinese Academy of Social Sciences study circa 2000 found that more than 84 percent of current and former industrial workers in the city of Hefei (Anhui province) supported an increased income tax on the wealthy to fund more extensive welfare benefits for the poor.[156]

Overall, in the second phase of the reform era, China's socialist legacy has shaped current and former SOE employees' political perceptions in two ways. First the remnants of Mao-era policies that privilege urban state sector workers make them simultaneously yearn for the more economically secure times of the past and cling to the CCP for aid. Second, SOE workers' personal experience of the Maoist planned economy has given them an appreciation for the material improvements that reform has brought, yet also has engendered a firm commitment to an extensive social welfare state that attends to the needs of the working class.

As discussed in Chapter 1, and as will be elaborated in Chapter 7, these attitudes are not unique to China but, rather, are characteristic of working-class citizens across many post-socialist states. In the countries of the former Soviet Union and Eastern and Central Europe, dissatisfaction regarding the demise of the old socialist economic system has been particularly apparent among former state sector workers. In these countries, this nostalgia has led many to support former communist political parties in popular elections. Similarly, in China, laid-off SOE employees have displayed little desire to end CCP rule; rather, they have wanted the party to govern in a more truly socialist fashion. Further, given the experience of countries in the former Soviet Union and in Eastern and Central Europe, China's state sector workers have had reason to believe that, should the CCP fall, the regime that replaces it may be even less committed to socialism than the CCP has been.

Still-Employed State Sector Workers   Due to state-led development policies and socialist legacies, rank-and-file state sector workers who have retained their jobs in the second phase of the post-Mao era have remained dependent on the party-state, leading to a general warming of their political attitudes to the ruling regime. Because their livelihood has rested on the continued economic strength of the ruling CCP, still-employed state sector employees generally have not sought an end to its rule. In addition, they have had cause to fear the political enfranchisement of those who sit below them in the socioeconomic hierarchy—namely, unemployed state sector workers, employed and unemployed unskilled private sector workers, and farmers. Such a development likely would only more thinly redistribute the scarce benefits on which unskilled public sector employees have continued to rely.

These developments have led to a reversal of the decline in CCP membership among still-employed SOE workers that was evident in the early reform
era. As noted earlier, in 1982 the portion of SOE workers who were party
members stood at 17.9 percent. By the end of the first phase of the reform era,
this ratio had declined to 8.3 percent. Since the start of the second phase of the
post-Mao period, this proportion has risen. Due in part to the CCP's renewed
focus on "front line" worker recruitment in the early 1990s, by 2004, 15.6 percent of SOE employees were party members.[157] They also constituted 11
percent CCP members nationwide. Among new recruits in 2004, 8.2 percent
were SOE employees.[158] In 2005 this portion rose to 9.1 percent.[159] Further at-
testing to the improvement in relations between SOE workers and the state,
SOE employees who have retained their jobs have been almost entirely absent
from the ranks of the hundreds of thousands of urban workers who have
taken part in protests during the second phase of the reform era. Although
relations between current SOE workers and the regime have shown some improvement over the first phase of the reform era, they are not particularly
cozy. Despite the rise in the percentage of SOE employees who are party members, this portion still has not returned to levels that were apparent at the start
of the post-Mao period.

Laid-off State Sector Workers   In the second phase of the reform era, SOE
workers who have been laid off or forced into early retirement have shown
much greater public contentiousness and even some interest in democratic
change. This is the result of the extremely negative impact that state-led development policies and China's late opening to the global capitalist system
have had on this group since the mid-1990s. At the same time, the dissatisfaction of former SOE employees is fueled by their experience of socialism.
These factors have led to perceptions of severe downward mobility, a great
loss of social status, decreased dependence on the party-state, and a narrow-
ing of attractive political options. Unlike their still-employed former coworkers, laid-off SOE workers have been largely ignored by party recruiters.
Yet given the perceived necessity of market reform and the party's appearance of concern, former state sector employees have had few alternatives to
CCP rule.

The combination of these factors has made laid-off SOE workers highly
restive but also has bred acceptance of the political status quo. As testament
to their level of dissatisfaction, former rank-and-file state sector workers

have been a major component of the tens of thousands of reported yearly protest incidents in China since the mid-1990s.[160] In addition, demonstrations by this group typically have been the largest. In 2002, for example, two protests in the northeastern industrial cities of Daqing and Liaoyang drew tens of thousands of laid-off workers from state-owned oil plants. Between the late 1990s and the first few years of the 2000s, at least ten of China's twenty-three provinces witnessed similar large-scale and protracted protests by former SOE employees.[161]

In some cases, these discontented individuals have voiced support for democratic reform. As Dorothy Solinger explains,

> In the twenty-odd years before the restructuring of the economy began in the late 1970s, urban Chinese workers, especially those on the payroll of state-owned firms, could count implicitly on a kind of covenant with the state that employed them, to provide for the bulk of their basic needs. With the coming of the capitalist market order, that connection workers used to draw between their jobs and their government has now led some to blame the state—which they view as having thrown them aside—for their current jobless plight.[162]

Reflecting this viewpoint, in 2002 one laid-off worker said to Solinger, "[the government] should take responsibility for our situation, but from the center to the localities all the governments are problematic. The Communist Party, as just one party, can't find a solution. . . . What we need is a political solution: our leaders should be elected as they are in the United States."[163]

However, most former state sector employees who have taken to the streets in the late post-Mao era have not advocated for democratic transformation. To the contrary, disgruntled laid-off SOE workers have aimed their protests at local party-state representatives and have looked to central elites for protection. As Ching Kwan Lee states, former SOE workers have exhibited a "bifurcation of regime legitimacy": They have accepted and supported central authorities yet have disparaged and risen up in protest against local officials.[164]

Even the most extensive, lengthy, and conflict-ridden protests by former SOE employees have not featured calls for an end to CCP rule. Rather, most have appealed to central party elites to make good on their socialist promises to the working class. For example, leaders of the 2002 Liaoyang protests "used highly respectful language that in no way challenged the dominance of the

Communist Party. Instead, they represented themselves as allies of Party central and as guardians of socialism."[165] As the protest leaders wrote in a letter to Jiang Zemin, "Respected and beloved Secretary General Jiang, we do not oppose the leadership of the party or the socialist system. . . . [O]ur efforts [are] aimed to help the country and eliminate all the corrupt worms boring away at and ruining our socialist economic system."[166]

It may be that the respectful language of these protestors has been simply a self-protective tactic designed to obscure their true political desires. Yet extensive interviews with disgruntled SOE workers clearly show that even if these individuals are deeply cynical about CCP rule, their desired outcome has not been the demise of the party but, rather, its re-commitment to the social guarantees, equality, and values of the past. As Ching Kwan Lee reports, the central party-state has been viewed by laid-off SOE workers as "the source of omnipotent power and paternal authority from which flows protection for workers."[167] When these laborers have risen up in protest, they have done so because market reform has "assaulted [their] prevailing sense of justice, worthiness and humanity," standards that in turn are "defined by socialist ideology and institutions . . . and the [national] Labor Law."[168] At the same time, they have been enraged by the violation of their previous "master" status.[169] Further, Lee explains that because the "the central government affirms its moral responsibility for protecting [the weak and disadvantaged]," workers have criticized local officials and managers who have failed to do so and have seen national leaders as workers' only possible saviors.[170]

Another factor that has undercut the desire of China's former SOE employees to end CCP dominance has been the fact that, despite their diminished economic situation, laid-off SOE workers have continued to hold something of a privileged status.[171] In addition, they have remained at least somewhat dependent on the state for their material well-being. As described earlier, even as large-scale SOE reforms proceeded in the late 1990s, top CCP leaders began to undertake a variety of policies designed to ease the economic plight of former SOE employees and thus maintain the allegiance of this restive sector.[172] Despite their inadequacies, these policies have helped to ameliorate the economic hardship of at least some laid-off SOE employees.[173] In addition, inasmuch as these benefits have been available only to this sector, former SOE workers have enjoyed a higher official position than the general unemployed population. Given these realities, pro-CCP rhetoric among protesting former SOE employees may also indicate a hesitancy to endorse political reforms that would empower those who currently are ineligible for the small, but often essential, measures of government support that have been given to laid-off SOE employees.

Further, state sector workers have appeared to believe that official processes and institutions have some degree of legitimacy. For example, two surveys undertaken in 1999 found that most dissatisfied state sector workers who took action outside of the workplace appealed to bodies that represent the party-state.[174] Analyzing the language used by the individuals who filed complaints with government offices, sociologists Isabelle Thireau and Linshan Hua found characteristics that parallel those displayed in worker protests. First, the complainants have acknowledged the legitimacy of the central state, expressing the belief that "rulers and ruled share the same understanding of right and wrong, just and unjust."[175] Second, aggrieved laborers have criticized local authorities.[176] Indeed, Thireau and Hua write that appeals to representatives of the central party-state "often depict[ed] two types of victims . . . both the workers and the state whose decisions [were] not obeyed . . . letters contain[ed] expressions stating that 'workers' legal rights and interests should be protected as well as the state's dignity."[177] Third, disgruntled workers felt that their status as SOE employees rightly entitled them to special treatment by the regime. As Thireau and Hua state, workers who have submitted appeals to government offices "try to characterize themselves as members of social categories that enjoyed a privileged status under the Maoist era—at least ideologically speaking—and whose legitimacy has not been explicitly denied after the reforms."[178] Similarly, complainants have employed socialist language to underscore the legitimacy of their grievances. Thireau and Hua report that state sector workers frequently "resort[ed] to expressions that had been used by the Party to denounce the pre-1949 situation: 'exploitation,' 'capitalists,' 'surplus value,' 'slaves,' 'buffaloes,' 'running dogs,' and 'proletarians.'" In this way, disgruntled workers have emphasized that the kinds of abuses found in the present were condemned by the CCP in the past.[179]

Pensioners Similarly, retired SOE employees—especially those forced to end their employment before their expected retirement age—have exhibited contentious behavior, yet also relative satisfaction with the central party-state. In the late 1990s, there was a rapid nationwide increase in protests by pensioners.[180] Indeed, a plurality of the SOE-related demonstrations that emerged in the late 1990s and first few years of the 2000s appear to have involved retirees.[181] Yet as with laid-off SOE worker disputes, disgruntled pensioners have criticized local officials and enterprise managers and expressed faith in the willingness of central authorities to come to their aid.[182] In articulating their demands, aggrieved retirees have invoked Mao's authority as well as the promises of current top party leaders that pensions will be paid on time and in full.[183]

Related to their support for the party center, aggrieved retirees have displayed socialist beliefs and values. As political scientists William Hurst and Kevin O'Brien relate, "workers devoted their lives to building socialism in exchange for subsistence guarantees while they worked and a decent standard of living in old age. Though they toiled long hours for low wages during their working years, their health and livelihood after they retired were assured."[184] Employing "impeccable Marxist terms," retirees from one factory stated that "pensions represent the work accumulation of past decades and constitute part of the surplus value created by one's labour."[185] Further, as with other SOE workers, retirees have evidenced nostalgia for China's socialist past. In interviews that Hurst undertook with pensioners in the northeastern "rustbelt" cities of Benxi and Datong, for example, he found that "virtually all . . . expressed open hostility towards market reforms, claimed that they and the country had been better off before reform began, and expressed varying degrees of desire to restore large parts of the Maoist social order."[186] Inasmuch as the CCP has been their only hope of retaining something of the old way of life, SOE pensioners have lacked incentives to press for its demise.

Overall, state sector workers of all types have exhibited a remarkable adherence to socialist norms and practices. In addition, they have expressed the belief that the ruling CCP is the best (or only) possible provider of the social welfare benefits and privileges on which most current and former state sector employees have continued to rely. As a result, although market reform has led many to engage in public protest, it simultaneously has caused most state sector workers to look to the still nominally socialist ruling regime for protection. Meanwhile, state policies that "accord different, albeit miniscule, entitlements and compensations to workers in different industries, cohorts, or forms of unemployment" have created "bewildering variations of . . . interests" among current and former state sector employees.[187] Thus, when protests have arisen, they have tended to be cellular workplace-based actions that have been separated from those of other aggrieved laborers.

Variations by Location   Along with differences among various kinds of rank-and-file state sector workers, the political attitudes and behavior of current and former state employees have differed according to location. One such geographic difference has involved the degree to which the private sector has developed in a given area. In regions where private enterprises have been numerous and vibrant, SOE workers have had more economic options than they have had in places where the state sector has remained the dominant source of livelihood. As a result, SOE employees in locations with more thriving private economies may evidence a more positive view of market reform and less antagonism toward local authorities and public enterprise managers.[188] William Hurst notes that in China's more economically "flush" areas, protests by aggrieved former SOE workers have been quickly and effectively dispersed when local officials have provided the monetary compensation that protestors demanded. Conversely, in economically strapped localities lacking the means to "buy off" unemployed SOE workers, confrontations have been much more tense.[189]

These findings suggest that in more prosperous areas where the private sector is relatively advanced, current and former state sector workers have had less cause to feel aggrieved and, thus, diminished reason to challenge the ruling regime. In more impoverished locations with fewer private sector opportunities, public sector workers have been understandably upset with their circumstances, engendering a greater potential for public contentiousness. Yet at the same time, the lack of economic options in these areas has made current and former SOE workers all the more dependent on the party-state, thus undercutting their possible desire to alter the CCP-led political status quo.

CONCLUSION

Overall, the confluence of state-led development policies, market forces, and socialist legacies has given rank-and-file state sector workers little interest in pursuing systemic political change—especially in the late reform period. If economic growth and private sector development expand to China's poorer areas, the number of disgruntled state sector workers may be expected to decline. In addition, as the population ages, the percentage of unskilled state sector workers with positive memories of Maoist-era job security and benefits will decrease. Indeed, the large wave of protests that followed the extensive SOE reforms of the mid-1990s seems to have crested; in the latter years of the first decade of the

2000s, reports of unrest on the part of former state sector workers have been relatively scarce.[190] Thus, as of the time of this writing, there are few indications that this potentially volatile sector will press for liberal democratic regime change.

The Chinese case contributes to existing comparative findings regarding the potential role of the working class in pressing for liberal democratic reform. First, it suggests that when an authoritarian state provides the urban working class with social welfare protections and benefits, the potential for labor activism directed toward the central regime will be low. In this sense, the situation of Chinese state sector workers in the reform era contrasts with that of industrial workers in England around the time of the Industrial Revolution. In the English case, many argue, workers' efforts to press for their political enfranchisement derived from their desire to force the state to provide labor protections.[191] In the Chinese case, the state's provision of labor protections seems to have undercut potential worker efforts to push for liberal democratic change. Indeed, China's reform era appears to be an interesting variation on working-class politics in the United States, where the potential for political militancy on the part of the urban working class was undermined by the fact that universal white male suffrage rights were in place before industrialization.[192] As political scientist Ira Katznelson argues, because white male workers in the United States did not have to struggle collectively for the right to vote, the state never was defined as a target of protest. Instead, workers around the time of America's industrialization focused their protests on the workplace.[193] In China, urban state sector workers also have focused their ire on their employers rather than the central state. Yet, unlike in the United States, the reason for this has not been that these workers already have suffrage rights but, rather, that they already have been granted special economic and social protections by the state.

In addition, the Chinese case buttresses Eva Bellin's finding that workers who are economically dependent on the state and hold a privileged position relative to other unskilled laborers will display low enthusiasm for liberal democratic reform.[194] In the case of Tunisia (the focus of Bellin's study), this was true for organized labor; in China, this has been the case for urban state sector workers, particularly those in SOEs. In countries where the working class has been at the forefront of democratization, such as South Korea in 1960 and the 1980s, labor has been in a very different position. Along with being excluded and repressed by the central state, in South Korea no subset of urban workers held an "aristocratic" position relative to other subsets of workers; rather, all workers were subject to similarly poor working conditions and low pay.[195] Until and unless these factors appear in China, rank-and file-state sector workers should not be expected to call for liberal democratic regime change.

5 RANK-AND-FILE PRIVATE SECTOR WORKERS

A SECOND MAJOR GROUP within China's vast lower socioeconomic tier includes rank-and-file private sector workers. A stratum that is both large and critical to China's continued economic growth, its political proclivities are likely to shape China's future trajectory. As of the middle of the first decade of the 2000s, domestic private businesses accounted for one-third to one-half of China's GDP, employed more than 100 million people, and, together with foreign-invested private firms, provided an estimated 75 percent of employment and 71 percent of Chinese tax revenues.[1] Much credit for China's economic success goes to the manual laborers that have constituted the vast majority of private sector employees. Among these workers, an extremely high proportion has included migrants from the countryside who hold a rural residential registration card but have moved to China's towns and cities (both legally and illegally) in search of wage employment. In the middle of the first decade of the 2000s, China's estimated 131 million rural migrants made up 70 to 80 percent of China's textile, garment, and construction workers and 37 percent of service sector employees.[2] Thus, any study of China's rank-and-file private sector employees is simultaneously a study of China's rural migrants.

Unskilled private sector workers have benefited from the party-state's development policies in the reform era, yet many have been limited by lingering Mao-era regulations privileging those with urban residence registration. At the same time, because China opened its market to the global capitalist system in an age characterized by fierce competition, a surplus of unskilled labor, and great capital mobility, rank-and-file laborers in the private sector have faced brutal and insecure employment conditions. As a result, China's non-professional private sector workers have remained poor. Along with rank-and-file state sector workers and farmers, they have occupied the wide bottom level of China's onion dome-shaped economic hierarchy that has emerged in the post-Mao period. Within this lower tier, rank-and-file private sector workers generally have experienced material conditions that are better than those of farmers, yet worse than those of their counterparts in the state sector. Even so, unskilled private sector workers have been rising in socioeconomic status relative to the pre-reform era and have pursued their livelihoods independently of the state. At the same time, they have not been presented with viable or preferable political alternatives to CCP rule.

Together, these circumstances have bred attenuated relations between rank-and-file private sector workers and the ruling regime. Compared to state sector employees and successful private entrepreneurs, the relative economic independence of unskilled laborers in the private sector may give them a greater potential openness to systemic political transformation. As long as they remain upwardly mobile, their political attitudes and behavior hinge largely on their perception of the central regime's attitude toward and effect on their lives. On one hand, private sector workers who view the party-state as inhibiting their economic rise may chafe at its leadership. On the other hand, workers who see the political system as attentive to their concerns, and as facilitating their material prosperity, have little reason to press for an alternative to CCP rule—especially when they lack political options that promise better policies toward labor. As long as the central state behaves in such a way that it is perceived as a benevolent protector of workers against rapacious and corrupt private sector employers, private sector workers will have both ideal and material reasons to accept continued CCP rule. As of this writing, this scenario generally holds true. Still, this sector's support for the existing political system is tenuous at best.

THE EARLY REFORM ERA (LATE 1970s TO THE EARLY 1990s)

As China's state-led development policies, level of openness to the global capitalist system, and socialist legacies have shifted, the experiences and attitudes of rank-and-file private sector workers—like those of other sectors—have changed as well. However, unlike the other groups discussed thus far, nonprofessional laborers in the private sector have not experienced dramatic alterations in living and working conditions over the course of the reform era. Rather, these workers have encountered a very gradual movement toward greater job opportunities and better employment circumstances and movement away from official discrimination. Given these conditions, this group's political views and behavior have undergone a slow evolution.

In the first phase of the reform era, state-led development policies that focused on economic modernization via economic liberalization made possible the emergence of private enterprises. Simultaneously, continued socialist policies from the Maoist period limited the private sector's expansion. With the socialist urban employment system largely intact through the early 1990s, unskilled state sector workers had little incentive to forsake the "iron rice bowl" and seek out private sector employment. Further, as outlined in Chapter 2, through the early 1990s the party-state tolerated private businesses only grudgingly, so private sector employment opportunities were not extensive.

In addition, from 1962 through the early 1980s, rural residents were forbidden to move to the cities in search of employment; only those chosen by commune leaders to engage in temporary work in state-owned enterprises were allowed to reside in a city legally. In the late 1970s and early 1980s, some individuals with rural residence registration moved to urban areas without official sanction, but with few jobs available, most did not find formal employment. Rather, they eked out a living doing odd jobs (*dagong*) and engaging in street-side sales and services. Their lack of urban registration prevented them from receiving government-provided goods, services, and subsidies, and as a result, they were entirely self-reliant. Still, the central regime's tolerance of the emergence of markets for food and other basic supplies enabled them to survive.[3]

Following the decollectivization of agriculture, nearly all rural households took advantage of new party-state policies granting them the right to operate plots of land through long-term contracts. This new system freed those with rural residence registration cards (*hukou*)[4] from the need to do agricultural work and enabled members of households with "extra" labor to seek alternative employment. At the same time, the party-state's guarantee of land rights to those with rural residence registration provided a safety net for those who ventured into the cities.

In the mid- to late 1980s, the party-state eased restrictions on the geographic mobility of peasants, further sanctioning and facilitating the already existent movement of rural residents to the cities. In 1984 and 1985, central authorities created new residential statuses that enabled peasants to reside in urban areas legally as long as they could supply their own food and/or could show that they had jobs that required city residence for more than three months.[5] In 1986 government approval of the sale of grain to rural migrants with urban employment eased their ability to remain in the city. Two years later, migration to the cities was given further state approval when central organs recommended that "provinces with impoverished populations 'export' their labor."[6] Overall, in the first phase of the reform era, the state gradually "acquiesced in the right of ruralites to make at least a temporary home in the cities," "but it took no responsibility for [their] material or physical well-being" while away from their home village.[7]

Indeed, party-state representatives in most localities made the lives of rural migrants extremely difficult. Those without "legal certificates, proper professions, or fixed living conditions" were taken into custody and often forced to do hard labor until they were sent back to their place of origin. Denied the ability to legally rent state-owned housing (and with little private housing available), most lived in makeshift shelters, which local authorities often demolished.[8] Migrants also were forced to pay a variety of taxes (both legal and illegal), and those seeking legal registration typically faced subjective official treatment and arbitrary charges.[9] Further, many migrants suffered "delayed payments and denial of wages, harassment, physical aggression, and petty theft" at the hands of employers and other city residents, yet received no sympathy or aid from local authorities. To the contrary, public security cadres themselves often were complicit in the mistreatment of rural migrants.[10] In this context, the number of rural migrants remained relatively small throughout the first phase of the reform period. In 1987 (the first year for which survey data on migration is available), rural migrants numbered 15.2 million, or about 1.5 percent of the population. By 1990, this figure had risen to 30 million.[11]

Although the ranks of private sector workers grew in this period, their total number remained low relative to the size of China's population. In 1981, official figures reported 2.3 million workers in "individual enterprises" with fewer than eight workers (at the time, larger "private enterprises" were not legally sanctioned). By 1989 (the first year for which statistics were made available on "private enterprise" and "foreign-invested enterprise" employment), the number of "individual enterprise" employees had grown to 19 million, while 1.6 million labored in domestic "private enterprises" with eight or more employees and .5 million worked in foreign-invested private businesses.[12]

Thus, by the end of the first phase of the post-Mao era, less than 2 percent of China's 1.13 billion citizens worked in the private sector.

Among them, some were "individual entrepreneurs"—mainly former farmers who started a business only because they lacked better options, or individuals who were unable to find employment in the Maoist era due to their stigmatized "capitalist" or "intellectual" family backgrounds.[13] These individuals set up roadside food, retail, and service stands and offered pedicab and improvised taxi services. Others were employed in two general occupational categories: (1) manufacturing, crafts, services, and garment processing; and (2) construction. In the former most laborers were women, and in the latter virtually all were men. In part because the bulk of new jobs in the 1980s were in construction, an estimated 60 to 90 percent of private sector workers in the early reform era were men.[14]

THE LATE REFORM ERA (EARLY 1990s THROUGH THE PRESENT)

After the early 1990s, the party's encouragement of wider opening to foreign investment and further development of the private sector led to a boom in private enterprise. As discussed in Chapter 2, following CCP leader Deng Xiaoping's 1992 "Southern Tour," the party decisively embraced experimentation with free markets and expanded the special economic zones within which domestic and foreign-invested private businesses increasingly thrived. Further, the large-scale SOE layoffs of the mid-1990s forced many former state sector workers to seek employment in private businesses. Simultaneously, many SOEs themselves were privatized. In addition, as noted in Chapter 2, many private enterprises that had "worn a red hat" and masked themselves as state collectives in the 1980s registered as private businesses in the 1990s.

As a result of these factors, the second phase of the reform period witnessed an exponential rise in the number of private sector employees. Myriad types of new firms appeared, many of which were not clearly "private" or "public," but rather some sort of mix, making an analysis of "private sector employees" somewhat difficult. Simultaneously, yearly official statistics vary in their categorization of enterprise types, with the result that temporal comparisons are not readily apparent. Perhaps the best such estimation can be made by comparing government figures for 1989 and 2002, the first and last years for which the categories of "individual enterprise," "private enterprise," and "foreign-invested enterprise" are available. Reflecting the growth of the private sector in the second phase of the post-Mao period, during this span of time, the total number of private sector workers in China rose by more than 400 percent, from nearly 22 million in 1989 to more than 89 million in 2002.[15] Since 2003, government-provided reports place statistics in categories that are vague and convoluted, making it difficult to make comparisons with earlier reports. By all measures, however, the number of private sector workers has continued to rise. In 2006 the All-China Federation of Industry and Commerce cited more than 200 million employees in individual and private enterprises, while the National Bureau of Statistics reported 449 million "non-state" enterprise workers.[16]

Within the general category of private sector laborers, some changes in composition were apparent in the late reform era. Perhaps the most notable was the dramatic increase in the ranks of workers in "private enterprises" with eight or more workers. Between 1989 and 2002, while the number of individual enterprise workers grew by more than 150 percent (to 47 million) and foreign-invested enterprise workers by roughly 80 percent (to 7 million), the number of private enterprise employees rose by more than 2,000 percent (to 34 million).[17] Although since the mid-1990s increasing numbers of former SOE workers have taken private sector employment or because of the privatization of their firms have become private sector employees, in the late reform period the vast majority of unskilled laborers in private businesses are rural migrants.[18] Indeed, among workers entering the private sector since the early 1990s, perhaps the largest portion has been young, unskilled women from rural inland regions who have taken jobs in manufacturing, textile, and garment firms in coastal areas. Consequently, by 2006 the portion of female private sector workers had risen to roughly 50 percent.[19]

While the expansion of capitalism in China provided rank-and-file private sector workers with new employment opportunities, market forces left them vulnerable to abuse. From 1978 through most of the first decade of the 2000s, the huge surplus of unskilled workers relative to jobs resulted in intense competition, forcing private sector laborers to accept work with low pay, no benefits, long hours, exacting work regimens, and little to no employment security. In surveys conducted in the middle of the first decade of the 2000s, only about one-third to one-half of private enterprise workers had signed job contracts, and a substantial portion had never heard of a job contract. In addition, even those who had signed contracts often were not allowed to see the terms stipulated in the document.[20] Further, the surfeit of unskilled labor allowed employers to extract every last ounce of productivity out of their workers. For example, a 2001 survey of migrant workers in Guangdong province (within which roughly one-third of all industrial migrant workers were employed at the time) found that 80 percent worked more than 10 hours per day, and more than 50 percent worked 12 to 14 hours. Nearly half rarely had a day off.[21] In two extreme cases that occurred in 2006, a twenty-five-year-old employee at a Shenzhen factory "collapsed and died from multiple organ failure . . . after working repeated overtime shifts for an entire month," and a thirty-five-year-old employee of a Guangzhou clothing factory died after working 54 hours and 25 minutes (22 hours overtime) in the span of four days.[22]

Unskilled private sector workers in the manufacturing, garment, and textile industries also have faced stringent workplace regulations, the violation of which results in steep fines. At one Shenzhen company, for example, two hundred workers "had just one temporary pass between them to leave their post. Workers had to carry such a pass to use the bathroom or drink water; otherwise they would be deemed to be skipping work and would be fined 10 to 20 yuan."[23] As of the middle of the first decade of the 2000s, an estimated 75 to 80 percent lived in crowded dorms (the average room measuring 26 square meters, shared by roughly twelve people) and ate at canteens that were provided by their employers, with the cost deducted from the employee's wages.[24] These facilities usually were located within the (typically gated and locked) factory compound and often were attached to the shop floor. In these circumstances, fires have become particularly deadly. To name one example, in 1993, nearly two hundred young women burned to death in a fire at the Zhili toy factory in Shenzhen because the steel-mesh doors of their dormitory had been sealed.[25] On the rare occasions when employees have been allowed to leave the factory grounds, they commonly have been searched by security guards carrying handcuffs and electric batons.[26]

Throughout the late reform period, employers have regularly withheld worker pay for long periods, have not paid extra for overtime, and/or have failed to provide wages at previously stipulated rates. According to a 2003 survey conducted by the official Chinese news agency, more than 72 percent of migrants reported wage defaults.[27] Similarly, a 2006 survey by the National Bureau of Statistics found that more than 50 percent of migrant laborers worked overtime with no overtime compensation.[28] As long as the supply of jobs has been smaller than the supply of labor, these workers have had little leverage to improve their terms of employment.

Still, within this general context, pay and working conditions have varied in different kinds of firms. In foreign-invested enterprises, researchers have found that workers have been treated best in companies established with European and American capital; quite a bit worse in those invested with capital from Japan; and dramatically worse in those funded by investors from Taiwan, Hong Kong, and South Korea.[29] In domestically funded private enterprises, the treatment of rank-and-file workers also has varied but generally has been on par with the worst foreign-invested enterprises.[30]

For construction workers—most of whom have been young men with rural residence registration—employment has been much more haphazard.[31] Most have lacked regular jobs with the same employer and instead have been hired on for specific projects. Their on-the-job treatment has varied according to the temperament and proclivities of their boss for a particular project, but generally, non-state sector construction workers have been expected to work extremely hard in very dangerous and dirty conditions. As one urban resident said of jobs such as drilling waterways or repairing roads and bridges, "city people [i.e., urban *hukou* holders] would rather do nothing than this."[32] Further, as has been the case in privately owned factories, most construction supervisors have treated their workers harshly. As Dorothy Solinger relates, "my few encounters with [construction bosses] convinced me they were an arrogant and peremptory lot, wielding enormous arbitrary and fearsome command over their underlings."[33] Also, like the young women with private sector employment, construction workers have put in long hours, and their pay often has been deferred. Yet unlike private factory workers, most private sector construction workers have been on their own when it comes to food and shelter. When employed, many have slept in makeshift shelters on or near the job site. Because they have not had steady work, their income has fluctuated more dramatically than that of factory laborers.

At the same time, their detachment from a fixed workplace and consistent supervision has given construction workers much more freedom in their daily lives than has been the case for unskilled private sector workers with more formal employment. As one states, "we work when there are projects for us to do, but play when there is none. We're not under any constraint [to work every day]."[34] Another relates that "I pretty much played the whole time during the first month [after my arrival to the city]. About thirty to forty of us lived in this place, but ten of us did not have any work to do. So we played poker and slept. For a whole month, I bore a very heavy burden on my mind. I felt rather depressed."[35] As expressed in the latter quote, most construction workers wish to work as much as possible and thus do not welcome their down time. Even so, they have had a measure of freedom that most other unskilled workers have not.

Despite the generally harsh and exploitative treatment that unskilled private sector workers have faced in the post-Mao period, in the early 1990s changes in state-led development policies and Mao-era practices provided at least some potential for improvements in the living and working conditions of nonprofessional laborers in the private sector. As local city authorities increasingly recognized the economic benefits of migration, the incidence of bullying on the part of public security and other party-state officials declined.[36] In addition, by 1993 the system of foodstuff rations and coupons for those with urban residence registration had been abolished, such that this form of institutionalized discrimination against rural migrants ended.[37] The regime also attempted to regulate the employment conditions of those in the private sector in ways that—at least on paper—offered them protection and aid. In 1994 the new Labor Law stipulated that laborers in state, private, and foreign enterprises were subject to the same employment standards in terms of hours, rest periods, overtime, and minimum pay. Simultaneously, the law required that private sector workers sign contracts delineating their terms of employment and job termination.[38] Further, beginning in the late 1990s, the central regime became more willing to pressure foreign-invested firms to comply with Chinese labor laws.[39]

In the first decade of the 2000s, government rhetoric and policies more explicitly addressed the economic grievances of nonprofessional laborers in the private sector. In 2003, for example, a new national regulation prohibited local officials from detaining vagrants and beggars by force and also allowed transients to apply for government support.[40] In the same year, central authorities demanded that migrant workers be paid more regularly. In 2004, city government officials in Beijing guaranteed legal rights to timely pay and improved working conditions for migrant workers.[41] Also in 2004, the Party Central Committee voiced a new and sympathetic assessment of worker protests, acknowledging that they "were not necessarily anti-government or politically motivated," but rather occurred because "the masses believe their rights have been violated."[42] In 2005, central authorities demanded that employers pay their workers "fully and on time," and instructed local governments to set aside contingency funds to prevent wage arrears.[43] The following year, the

State Council issued a document calling for "'fair and equal treatment without discrimination' for migrant workers" and outlining "specific solutions to the problems of low wages, wages in arrears, long work days, poor safety conditions, lack of social security, high rates of work-related illness and accidents, and the need for employment training, housing as well as schooling for the children of migrant workers."[44] Finally, the Labor Contract Law of 2008 stipulated that workers completing two short-term contracts be granted full-time status and permanent benefits, empowered workers to bargain collectively with employers (through official union branches or employee representative committees), and required that dismissed workers be given one month's severance pay for each year worked.[45]

Like plans to ease the economic plight of unemployed state-owned enterprise workers, these policies remain woefully underrealized at the time of this writing. Nevertheless, they have indicated growing government concern with the plight of rank-and-file private sector workers and in at least some cases have helped to resolve their grievances. Further, to the degree that the party-state has guaranteed land rights to rural migrants, they have had a fallback option when their city lives have become intolerable.

At the same time, competition among rural *hukou* holders has risen as official constraints on internal migration have diminished. In the new and old special economic zones, the number of migrants from the countryside swelled throughout most of the late post-Mao period. In the mid-1990s the party-state's abandonment of large numbers of SOE workers only further increased competition among unskilled laborers. Through the early part of the first decade of the 2000s, although employment opportunities in designated development zones expanded, the number of job seekers grew even more rapidly, resulting in low (and often unpaid) wages and exploitative employment conditions for those fortunate enough to find work. In the middle part of the first decade of the 2000s this trend began to abate, as unskilled labor shortages appeared in some coastal provinces. The result was a slight improvement in wages and working conditions in these areas, yet also a movement of factories to more inland areas where labor is less expensive and more pliable. In the fall of 2008, as China's economy slowed in response to the recession in the United States, many private factories shut down, and unskilled labor surpluses again appeared.

Overall, reform-era state-led development policies and market pressures related to China's opening to the global capitalist system have both expanded employment opportunities for unskilled workers and left them vulnerable to exploitation. Meanwhile, for the large portion of manual laborers who have held rural residence registration cards, the easing of Mao-era restrictions on geographic mobility has opened new possibilities for economic advancement, while the continued existence of the residential registration system has continued to limit their ability to improve their socioeconomic status.

Perceptions of Socioeconomic Mobility, Relative Socioeconomic Status, Material Dependence on the Party-State, and Political Options

These contextual developments have shaped private sector laborers' perceptions of their socioeconomic mobility, relative socioeconomic status, material dependence on the party-state, and political options. For the large portion of unskilled private sector workers that are rural migrants, the reform era has brought improved material prosperity and general upward socioeconomic mobility, especially relative to their counterparts who are still residing in rural villages. As Solinger summarizes, these "marginal and/or denigrated people . . . have been relegated to the least desirable and most unstable work available. No matter how bitter, however, their lives have generally improved significantly in material terms."[46] Indeed, most have been willing to work longer hours when doing so allows them to increase their pay. Especially among rural migrants, overtime generally has not been seen as a burden to be avoided but, rather, "an opportunity to make more money."[47]

These perceptions have derived in large part from migrant laborers' experience of socialism. Unlike state sector workers, most migrant workers in the private sector have evidenced little nostalgia for the pre-reform period and thus little sense that China's "socialist" past was preferable to its "capitalist" present. For most rural migrants—as opposed to urban SOE workers, for whom the Maoist era was a time of relative socioeconomic security—this period is remembered as a time of abject poverty.[48] This has produced among migrants "an overall narrative of relative 'progress'" in the reform era that "overshadow[s] or dilut[es] the brunt of present-day urban and rural misery."[49] When migrant workers have sent their earnings from the city back to the countryside, allowing their families to build new homes and generally improve their quality of life, this feeling of upward mobility has been reinforced. Further, the ability of migrant workers to endure hardship in the cities has been eased because central policies have assured rural migrants a tract of land in their home village. As Ching Kwan Lee emphasizes, this land has served as a "safety valve for city survival," while simultaneously "dampen[ing] worker resilience in sustained labor struggles."[50]

Private sector workers who have seen the current regime as facilitating their current socioeconomic progress have had reason to accept the political status quo. The party-state's lifting of Mao-era geographic limitations and encouragement of the private sector in the late reform period have encouraged this tendency. To the degree that the surplus of unskilled private sector workers has left them vulnerable to mistreatment, the still somewhat socialist bent of the party-state also has made it appear as a potential protector of workers.

As a whole, unskilled private sector workers make up a major component of the vast lower tier of China's onion dome-shaped economic hierarchy. Compared to nonprofessional public sector employees, they have received very low wages and virtually no benefits.[51] Even so, because rank-and-file private sector workers work far more hours than do their state sector counterparts, the total income of the former has been roughly equivalent to that of the latter.

Further factors have come into play for the majority of unskilled private sector laborers with rural household registration status. As noted in Chapter 4, in reaction to the large-scale SOE layoffs of the mid-1990s, some cities enacted prohibitions against hiring migrant workers for certain kinds of jobs, generally leaving them eligible only for work that urban *hukou* holders did not desire. As discussed in Chapter 4, at a deeper level lingering socialist-era mentalities have led both rural migrants and urban *hukou* holders to view those with rural residential registration as socioeconomic inferiors. For example, the common appellation for unskilled female private factory workers has been *dagongmei*—a combination of the terms *dagong*, denoting "working for the boss" or "selling labor," and *mei*, for "little sister."[52] Within the workplace, *dagongmei* have been reminded continually of their inferior status. As anthropologist Pun Ngai reports, factory supervisors regularly have criticized their migrant workers for having "rough hands, rough feet" (*cushou, sujiao*) and for being backward "country girls" (*xiangxiamei*).[53] Even further distinctions have been made between those from more- or less-developed rural regions, with the latter viewed as the most coarse and low quality.[54] Urban *hukou* holders have viewed male construction workers with rural residence registration even more negatively. Often lacking regular housing or access to showers and toilets, they have had an unseemly, and even dangerous, reputation. As one migrant worker states, "in the city, some people basically don't consider us to be people. They treat us as a thing."[55]

Overall, these views have undermined any potential solidarity among the various segments of China's extensive lower "class." Among private sector manual laborers with rural residence registration, there has been little sympathy for the complaints and grievances of unskilled workers with a city *hukou*. In the words of one rural migrant, city residents

> are generally not as eager to work as the outsiders. . . . They are also no match to the latter when it comes to work efforts, the ability to absorb hard labor and perseverance . . . I don't care what their living conditions are like, but they still live a better life than the villagers . . . There is no work that migrants can do but the laid-off [SOE] workers cannot.[56]

These views also have influenced the attitudes of migrant workers toward the existing political system. Viewing the central regime as providing preferential treatment for urban *hukou* holders, migrant workers have expressed little support for the political status quo. Yet to the degree that central policies since the early years of the 2000s have led those with a rural *hukou* to believe that national leaders are attempting to force local officials and city residents to treat rural migrants equally, migrants have had increased reason to accept— and even support—the central regime.

At the same time, although the socioeconomic status of unskilled migrants laboring in the private sector has been inferior to that of longtime urban-dwellers, it has been higher than that of those who have remained in the countryside. And in general, it is to the latter group that China's rural migrants have compared themselves, not the former. To begin, private sector workers who have migrated from their home villages typically have not come from the ranks of the poorest and least educated within the countryside; rather, they tend to have a middling level of education and resources relative to their rural compatriots.[57] The cost of transportation and initial sustenance outside of the village alone often prevent the most destitute rural *hukou*-holders from seeking outside employment. Further, off-farm employment widely has been viewed as more attractive than farming, both in terms of income and satisfaction. Indeed, most have held agriculture "in such low esteem that villagers would not even consider it proper 'work.' "[58] The resultant sense of socioeconomic superiority on the part of rural migrants has given them reason to be satisfied with their socioeconomic conditions and has diminished their sense of common cause with rural farmers, thus making it unlikely that rural migrants will find it in their interest to press for systemic political change or majority rule.

In terms of material reliance on the party-state, as a whole, unskilled private sector workers—again, the vast majority of whom have been rural migrants—have been almost entirely independent. With regard to basic needs, through the mid-1990s, those with rural residence registration were ineligible for "any medical, housing, educational, welfare, or services of any sort in the cities."[59] Unable to rely on government support, those without formal employment got by on their own wits, gathering with others from their "native places" to buy dilapidated dwellings or erect shantytowns.[60] In some cases, such as Beijing's much-studied "Zhejiang village," rural migrants created almost entirely self-sufficient "urban 'villages,'" replete with their own medical facilities, schools, restaurants, and markets staffed entirely by those from their place of rural origin.[61] In these areas, Solinger relates, "a coordinated division of labor prevailed . . . totally disconnected from state commercial channels."[62] Meanwhile, for those with formal private sector jobs—mainly the young women in the manufacturing, textile, and garment industries—it has been the employer, and not the party-state, that has attended to their basic needs.

Within the realm of work, most unskilled private sector workers have been ignored by representatives of the party-state. As political scientist Lei Guang relates, "until the time when officials decide to mount a campaign" toward a particular type of private business "or are compelled to pay attention due to a disaster or accident, the state's attention . . . is transient or simply negligible."[63] In the words of one local official, "coming [to the city] without a license is illegal, but nursemaids, helpers in restaurants, and helpers at stalls don't need it. Carpenters, laborers, and shoe repairpeople can do without it . . . it's hard for us to control. There's no way to force them."[64] Contributing to this reality in the early reform era was the fact that urban party-state structures were entirely unprepared for the influx of rural migrants; in most cities, agencies specifically devoted to migrant workers and non-state sector employees did not exist until the early 1990s.[65] Since then, the hands-off attitude of local party-state representatives toward private sector workers has been fueled by official recognition of the contribution that private enterprises make to local economic growth (which, as discussed in Chapter 2, fattens local government coffers and thereby improves local officials' chances of promotion).

Even so, within the general category of rank-and-file private sector workers, individuals in some lines of work have had more economic connections with the party-state than others. Many "private sector" construction workers have been hired through subcontracts from state-owned firms, and even construction teams with no relation to state entities have been ranked and supervised by local authorities. Similarly, some who work as nursemaids (*baomu*) have contracts arranged for them by state agencies. Still, many operate entirely independently, finding their own work and determining for themselves their pay and hours.[66] In addition, unskilled private sector workers who are rural migrants remain economically tied to the party-state by the government's guarantee of land rights to those with rural residence registration. Further, since the early part of the first decade of the 2000s, some of the policy changes discussed earlier have allowed a modicum of increased access to state services for rural migrants to the cities.[67]

In terms of political options, unskilled private sector workers have not been presented with alternatives to CCP rule that will better attend to their needs. In addition, as the reform era has progressed, central authorities have appeared to become more, rather than less, responsive to these workers' concerns. As discussed in Chapter 4, the regime has provided legal mechanisms through which disgruntled workers may seek redress. At the same time, the lack of resources and many divisions among unskilled private sector workers have given them little ability to successfully challenge the central regime. Through the time of this writing, they have had virtually no job security and have been vulnerable to arbitrary layoffs—especially in areas where there has been a surfeit of unskilled labor. Thus, as has been the case for rank-and-file state sector employees, the real fear of job loss has worked against the emergence of potential protest leaders. Similarly, because unskilled private sector workers have lacked social, economic, and political power, they have had little sense of efficacy.

Political Attitudes and Behavior

These perceptions have bred among unskilled private sectors a general political quiescence and only limited contentiousness. To be sure, labor-related grievances have been widespread. They have centered on wage arrears, unwarranted pay reductions, hazardous working and living conditions, and inhumane management practices. Yet, most aggrieved private sector workers have not seen the central regime as an antagonist. Rather, the focus of their ire has been the employer. In a 1996 survey of migrant workers in Shenzhen, 39 percent had expressed their problem directly with their employer, 23 percent had begun a mediation process within the enterprise, 5 percent had quit the enterprise, and 26 percent had given up on resolving the problem.[68] Further, those who have expressed their complaints in the workplace and have been dissatisfied with the employer's response have not challenged the central government. Rather, most have worked through centrally sponsored legal channels to seek redress, seeing the central government as their protector. In the 1996 Shenzhen study referenced earlier, 4 percent had gone to arbitration committees, Letter and Visits Offices, or the courts; another 1.5 percent had contacted the local media.[69] By all accounts, the number of workers seeking adjudication through official channels has grown dramatically from the mid-1990s onward, as laborers have become aware of the more favorable and protective central policies that have been promulgated in the late reform era.[70] In most cases, both the employee and employer have been placated, such that even when aggrieved workers have remained somewhat dissatisfied, their grievances have been ameliorated.[71]

While collective contention outside of official channels has been relatively rare among unskilled private sector workers, public protests have occurred. Beginning in the mid-1980s, work stoppages and strikes on the part of rank-and-file private sector workers appeared in coastal special economic zones, rising to more than a hundred per year by the early 1990s.[72] In 2005–6, when a shortage of unskilled labor appeared in Guangdong province, the proportion and number of private sector (mainly migrant) worker protests grew further.[73] Almost universally, however, collective protests have focused on economic and not political matters. Most often, they have raised demands related to pay arrears and deductions—problems that have been especially prevalent among migrant laborers.[74] To give just one notable example, in spring 2004, approximately four thousand workers at two shoe factories owned by the Taiwanese firm Stella International publicly protested. Along with delays in wage payments and forced and uncompensated overtime, employees claimed that deductions for rent and food left them with virtually no income.[75]

Like disgruntled former state-owned enterprise employees, when aggrieved private enterprise workers such as those at Stella have voiced their complaints, they have shown a notable belief in the legitimacy and good intentions of the CCP-led regime. As noted in Chapter 1, private sector employees submitting complaints to Letters and Visits Offices have referred to central party-state representatives as "comrades," "servants of the people," "uncles," "fair judge," "protective god," and "father and mother of the people." Although such language clearly has reflected a tactical strategy to enhance the chances of a favorable response, most disgruntled private sector workers have viewed the central government as an ally. As sociologists Isabelle Thireau and Linshan Hua state, complainants generally have assumed that "the government and members of society share similar perspectives on what is just and unjust."[76] For example, most unskilled private sector workers have expressed the belief that the regime's minimum wage standards and rates of compensation for injury and loss are reasonable.[77] And although few have displayed a detailed understanding of specific legal provisions, most have referred to national laws to buttress their case, stressing "the distance between what is legal and supposed to be fair and the lived reality" of the aggrieved.[78] Indeed, complaints to Letters and Visits Offices "often depict two types of . . . legal violations: both the workers and the state whose decisions are not obeyed . . . letters contain expressions stating that 'workers' legal rights and interests should be protected as well as the state's dignity.'" Like aggrieved state sector workers, many also have charged that local officials have not been properly implementing national laws.[79] These views have been widely shared among the migrant workers who have constituted the majority of unskilled private sector workers. In extensive interviews, Ching Kwan Lee finds that, as with SOE workers, migrant laborers have had a "bifurcated view of the state," wherein a "righteous and legalistic center" is "far removed from corrupt and predatory local agents."[80]

Further, rather than rejecting the legitimacy of the party-state, in many cases protesting private sector workers have called for greater integration within it—backing Bruce Dickson's assertion that citizens generally want to be more embedded within the system, rather than autonomous from it. For example, in many public demonstrations, private enterprise employees have voiced the desire to form a factory-level branch of the CCP-affiliated All-China Federation of Trade Unions (ACFTU).[81] Similarly, protesting private enterprise workers often have demanded the same protections that the regime affords to those in the state sector.

Still, unskilled private sector workers have evinced more indifference toward the CCP-led regime than has been the case for private enterprise owners and state sector workers. This has been seen perhaps most prominently in their attitudes toward membership in the CCP. Although the party has shown little interest in recruiting unskilled rural migrants, a number of these individuals were party members before they moved to the city. Bruce Dickson notes that, as of the late 1990s, 2 to 3 percent of the migrant population were CCP members, and in more economically developed areas, this percentage reached nearly 10 percent.[82] Yet, it appears that once a formerly rural party member goes mobile, his or her political relationship with the party becomes quite attenuated. As Dickson relates, most of these individuals decline to register with the party branch in their new urban neighborhood or workplace, as doing so requires attendance at meetings and study sessions, as well as the payment of dues.[83] Consequently, rural migrants who are CCP members generally are so in name only, and lack any meaningful political relationship—positive or negative—with the party.

CONCLUSION

As a result of state-led development policies that have opened up new opportunities for unskilled workers, Chinese citizens with rural *hukou* have experienced upward economic mobility in the reform era. When viewed against memories of poverty and economic constraint in the Maoist period, these individuals have tended to be hopeful about their future and accepting of the regime that has made possible their economic advance. Because their vulnerability to global market forces has been assuaged by the still somewhat socialist policies of the CCP-led government—such as land rights and laws that purport to protect private sector worker rights—rank-and-file laborers in the private sector have had further reason to tolerate the authoritarian political status quo. Conversely, because many migrant workers see the ruling regime's perpetuation of the *hukou* system as inhibiting their economic advancement, these workers in the private sector have had cause for political dissatisfaction. In this sense, recent moves by China's central leadership to reduce the discriminatory effects of this system, and to address more generally the concerns of unskilled private sector workers, may be important. If the new policies are viewed as sincere and effective, political dissatisfaction within this sector may diminish. Yet, because their material prosperity has not derived from privileged ties to the party-state, rank-and-file private sector workers have been less tied to the CCP-led regime than have state sector workers and private entrepreneurs.

This constellation of factors surely is subject to change. One major variable is the future development of market forces related to China's opening to the global capitalist system. Key in this regard is the ratio of unskilled labor to jobs. As discussed earlier, as long as China has a surplus of unskilled workers, these laborers will be vulnerable to mistreatment and willing to tolerate an authoritarian political leadership that guarantees their basic sustenance and demonstrates concern with their conditions. Conversely, the appearance of unskilled labor shortages could change the political views and behavior of rank-and-file private sector workers.

The unskilled labor shortage that appeared around 2007–8 in China's southeastern coastal areas is instructive in this regard. During this time period, China witnessed a rise in labor disputes within the private sector. Along with their increased leverage, unskilled private sector workers displayed a growing awareness of their new legal rights.[84] Even so, most aggrieved laborers voiced their concerns in the workplace or through legal channels established by the party-state—in other words, they chose to work within the existing system. When they did so, their view of the ruling regime was subject to change. Those who had a positive experience with official procedures became more supportive of the status quo. In the words of a construction worker whose employer was told by Beijing authorities to pay more than five million yuan in unpaid wages, "it's such an honor for us that the government pays attention to our case; no matter if we can get the money back, the most important thing is that the authorities side with us."[85] However, for most aggrieved private sector workers seeking remediation through official channels, the experience has been much less positive. When these workers have become frustrated with their lack of progress, they have started to question the legitimacy of the central party-state. As one such worker states, "newspapers spent their time reporting that migrants' salaries have to reach minimum wage, the government also says supervision should be reinforced to check illegal practices such as back pay or overtime, but . . . the government doesn't stick to its words."[86] Overall, this suggests that support for continued CCP rule among rank-and-file private sector workers is tenuous at best.

A second major variable that will affect the future political attitudes and behavior of this sector concerns the continuation of socialist guarantees of land rights to unskilled private sector workers with rural residence registration. As discussed above, the government's guarantee of plots of land to those with rural *hukou* has given them a place of respite when working conditions become intolerable in the city. In turn, this land guarantee has diminished the resilience of migrant workers who have become involved in sustained labor struggles in the city.[87] Yet, as will be discussed more fully in Chapter 6, in recent years large numbers of rural residents have been subject to local officials confiscating their land for industrial development or other uses. As a result, by 2006 some fifty million rural *hukou* holders were landless.[88] The short-term result has been a sharp rise in rural unrest. Further, when rural migrants to the cities lose their rights to rural land, they lose the safety net that has sapped their persistence in pursuing labor disputes with their urban employers. In addition, they lose their only meaningful economic tie with the party-state, such that they may be more likely to support regime change. Alarmed by the rise in rural "disturbances," central elites have pledged to stop illegal land requisitions. If they succeed in doing so, China's economic growth is likely to slow, and the socioeconomic mobility of unskilled private sector workers is likely to decline. Though the political repercussions of such a development are uncertain, the current constellation of factors that has led unskilled private sector workers to accept the CCP-led political status quo could be shattered.

6 FARMERS

FARMERS SIT AT THE BOTTOM of the lower tier of China's onion dome-shaped economic structure. As the largest socioeconomic sector in China, farmers have great potential political influence. Despite extensive urbanization and migration, as of the end of 2006, 737 million (56 percent) of China's 1.3 billion residents resided in the countryside.[1] Although this marks a dramatic decline in comparison with the early 1990s, China's farming population is expected to drop to no lower than 40 percent by 2030.[2] Rural residents earn income from a variety of sources, but virtually all are engaged in agriculture. As of 2000, 70 percent did not earn regular incomes from nonfarm wage labor, and only 2.5 percent had registered individual family enterprises.[3]

In the history of political change around the globe, the relationship between rural farmers and liberal democracy has been weak. In most countries that have experienced social pressures for democratization, it has not been peasants, but rather private capital holders, urban factory workers, and intellectuals that have led the charge for democratic change. Yet in China, the possible political role of farmers cannot be discounted. Along with playing a major role in supporting the revolutionary ascension of the CCP, China's peasants were politically engaged and active during the Maoist era. Further, in the reform period, farmers have been extremely restive. As noted in Chapter 1, farmer protests have constituted a major portion of the tens of thousands of yearly "mass disturbances" that have appeared since the early 1990s. Peasants also have submitted hundreds of thousands of collective petitions to government authorities.

Despite their activism in the late post-Mao era, China's peasants have shown little interest in challenging the existing CCP-led political system. As with former SOE employees and rank-and-file private sector workers, farmers have sometimes shown great disdain for local officials, but they have displayed remarkable trust in the central government. When they have engaged in protest, they have appealed to national leaders to enforce what in the peasants' view are benevolent and well-intentioned laws. Even so, there have been signs that peasant support for the central regime may be declining. Further, relative to other socioeconomic sectors, farmers have appeared more open to fundamental political change.

The political attitudes and proclivities of China's peasants have been influenced by their perceptions of socioeconomic mobility, relative socioeconomic status, dependence on the party-state, and political options. In turn, these perceptions have been shaped by state-led development policies, market forces, and socialist legacies. As with other socioeconomic sectors, these variables have not been static but, rather, have changed over time. Yet overall, these factors have led peasants to be restless and only tenuously tolerant of the political status quo.

THE EARLY REFORM ERA (LATE 1970s TO THE EARLY 1990s)

The early and late phases of the reform era have presented farmers with somewhat distinct problems and opportunities. The most important change in the early reform period was a fundamental shift in the party-state's rural development policy. Although the government retained key powers over rural land, the entirely state-controlled socialist system of the past was dismantled, and market forces were allowed to shape peasants' economic decisions and outcomes. During the Mao era, rural land was collectivized, with the governmental structure in the countryside consisting of three levels: the commune (including roughly 2,000 to 3,000 households), the brigade (200 to 250 households), and the production team (25 to 35 households).[4] All produce was bought and sold through supply and marketing cooperatives that were owned and operated by the party-state. Quotas were set for grain and other produce, with a low price paid for quota items and a slightly higher rate for above-quota items. A substantial portion of the quota grain went into the government-run urban food system, which provided basic foodstuffs to city residents with ration cards at highly subsidized rates. In rural areas, peasants were assured basic sustenance, with any additional resources allocated to individuals based on the number of work points that they had accrued through their labor during the year. In most cases, very little was left after the basic needs of the collective were met. As a result, the work point system provided peasants with little incentive to put great effort into their agricultural labor.[5]

Even before the central regime announced any major changes to this system, some localities experimented with allocating plots of land to individual households.[6] These practices spread in the late 1970s and early 1980s, and in 1983 a new "household responsibility system" (*tudi chengbao zerenzhi*) was made national policy. By the following year, virtually all former production teams had adopted the new system. According to official guidelines, the state leased plots to farm families for fifteen-year periods, with the allotment based on household size and labor supply.[7] Among the various plot types sanctioned by central regulations, grain ration land (*kouliang tian*) was supposed to fulfill the basic consumption needs of the household. The party-state made no claim to the produce of these plots. Responsibility land (*zeren tian*) was granted in exchange for a fixed payment of grain or other agricultural items at a below-market price. Any additional produce from the plot could be used or sold as the household pleased. Similarly, contract land (*chengbao tian*) was allocated in return for a fixed cash payment, which was tantamount to rent. In addition, peasants could be granted small private plots (*ziliu di*), over which they had nearly complete control. Reclaimed land (*kaihuang di*) also was available, typically with few constraints. Often, land was granted in a two-field system (*liangtian zhi*) that combined responsibility and grain ration plots or a three-field system that included contract land as well. In surveys undertaken between the mid-1980s and mid-1990s, roughly 78 to 85 percent of all farmland was responsibility land, 8 to 9 percent was grain ration land, 6 percent was private land, 5 percent was contract land, and less than 1 percent was reclaimed land.[8] Because village officials made efforts to distribute good- and bad-quality village land in an equitable fashion, most household plots were not contiguous but, rather, small and scattered.[9]

In terms of socialist legacies, the household responsibility system retained some key elements of the Maoist system: party-state ownership of all land, a relatively equitable distribution of land based on household size, and assured basic sustenance for all rural residents. The result was a blend of socialized assets and a market economy.[10] In addition, as discussed in Chapter 5, the basic features of the Mao-era *hukou* system remained in place through the end of the early reform period. As a result, it was difficult for rural residents to move to the cities in search of nonagricultural work. Consequently, early in the post-Mao period most peasants remained in their villages, engaged primarily in agricultural pursuits.

The interplay of state direction and market forces both encouraged and stifled farmers' ability to advance economically. With higher state procurement prices, the ability to sell excess grain on the open market, and the allocation of plots to individual households, farmers had greater incentive to work the land more productively. The initial results were stunning: Between 1979 and 1984, grain production increased by nearly 5 percent per year, and the real gross value of agricultural output rose by 7.6 percent per year.[11] Yet this increased productivity soon was undercut. Concerned that peasants were producing too much, the state announced in 1985 that it would no longer pay a higher price for over-quota goods. Meanwhile, increased production made the price of agricultural inputs (such as fertilizer) soar and the price of agricultural products decline.[12] As a result, between 1985 and 1994, grain production increased by less than 1 percent per year.[13]

These developments made it clear to both peasants and government officials that agriculture—at least under the "socialist" state-directed strictures embedded in the household responsibility system—was not sufficient to bring economic prosperity to China's farmers. The solution was to have local governments develop township and village enterprises (TVEs), which, reflecting a continued socialist emphasis on state ownership and collective labor, were collectively owned by the village or township. In the early post-Mao period, TVEs were extremely successful: Between 1978 and 1990, the number of TVE employees rose from fewer than 30 million to more than 80 million, and their total output grew from approximately 50 billion to roughly 545 billion yuan per year.[14] Indeed, much of China's phenomenal economic growth during this time span was attributed to TVEs. In township enterprises, where most employees were peasants who came to town only to work, employment conditions typically were harsh. In village enterprises, the situation was different, as both peasants and village leaders exhibited the socialist belief that local residents had a right to employment. With little fear of job loss, workers in village-owned firms felt little pressure at work. As one village leader lamented, peasants "[saw] themselves as owners of the collective firm, a status that accordingly [gave] them the inherent right to be employed; poor work attitude and performance, in other words, [could not] therefore be a cause for dismissal as long as these enterprises [were] owned by the village."[15] Because the household responsibility system stipulated that land rights could be maintained only if

the household met the state's agricultural quotas, all village enterprise employees and most township enterprise employees worked in the firm only part time
and remained engaged in farming. In some cases, TVEs closed down entirely
during harvest season, so that the peasant-workers could work full time in
the fields.[16]

The success of TVEs was made possible by China's opening to the global
capitalist economy via the establishment of special economic zones (SEZs),
which in 1980 were created in a few southeastern coastal cities in Guangdong
and Fujian provinces and the entire island province of Hainan. In 1984–85
fourteen more coastal cities and their environs (in both the north and the
south) were declared SEZs.[17] In villages located within or nearby such zones,
access to supplies and markets was eased, and new opportunities arose to fulfill labor-intensive and low-tech needs within the production process. Consequently, although most villages tried to establish TVEs, these enterprises were
most prominent and successful in coastal provinces and much less so in central and western areas. At the end of the early reform period, nonagricultural
production represented more than 80 percent of total rural output in eastern
regions but only 19 percent in western areas and 15.5 percent in central zones.[18]
Further, within provinces, rural areas that were closer to big cities had more
success with TVEs than did more remote localities.

The introduction of new forms of landholding and wage labor in the mid-
1980s forced the regime to alter the nature and form of China's rural governance. With the decollectivization of land, the commune, brigade, and production team leadership had no function or purpose, and their power dissolved.
Faced with the prospect of having virtually no rural government, central elites
created more than thirty thousand township (*xiang*) and town (*zhen*) governments (with the former typically less urbanized and industrialized than the
latter).[19] Below this level, each town/township contained approximately eighteen villages.[20] Through most of the early reform era, township officials were
appointed by the county (the next higher governmental level). At the village
level, Village Committees were appointed by the township, and village-level
party branches were headed by a Village Party Secretary selected by higher-level
party cadres. Along with maintaining and developing local infrastructure and
education, township authorities were charged with collecting taxes and fees
mandated by the central government, as well as enforcing birth control regulations and mandatory cremation requirements.[21] Village officials were responsible for implementing these township requirements at the grassroots level.

However, the central party-state did not provide adequate funds to pay the salaries of local cadres or foot the bill for local infrastructure, education, or state-mandated projects. Rather, township and village officials had to collect sufficient funds on their own.[22] According to national policy, township and village taxes could not exceed 5 percent of the prior year's net per capita township income.[23] Yet in most cases, this did not bring in enough money to pay cadre salaries and provide government benefits and services. This problem became more serious in the second half of the 1980s, as the number of township employees grew. In part, this resulted from continued socialist practices that forced townships to employ new college graduates and demobilized soldiers assigned to them through the central job allocation system.[24] In addition, as was the case for SOE managers in the early reform era, there was a great reluctance among township and county officials to fire existing employees.[25]

In coastal localities with more abundant market opportunities and less need to rely on state-constrained agricultural pursuits, budget problems were solved by developing TVEs and other forms of enterprise. In these townships and villages, enterprise-driven revenues (such as taxes, rents, and license fees) allowed for light or even nonexistent taxes on individual peasant households. Indeed, some villages in eastern provinces not only paid cadre salaries but also built schools, housing, movie theaters, and community centers and provided free utilities, child care subsidies, and scholarships.[26]

In areas that were more distant from SEZs, and thus less able to establish successful nonagricultural enterprises, the situation was entirely different. In some cases, the local political structure collapsed entirely. In these localities, cadres made little attempt to collect taxes. Local government revenue was so low that virtually nothing was spent on government services and cadre salaries were paid only in part, if at all.[27] Existing political cadres were extremely demoralized, and few younger residents showed interest in becoming government officials. In some areas, traditional groups such as clans and temple associations began to fill the vacated government role, even collecting funds and providing services that had been abandoned by official institutions. In other localities, the public infrastructure crumbled.[28]

In some poor regions, township and village officials remained determined to collect adequate funds—at least revenue sufficient to pay cadre salaries. To do so, they added to legally sanctioned taxes various supplemental fees, assessments, fines, and forced contributions. Peasants were forced to pay for government services such as licenses and birth registration and were penalized for both minor and major infractions—including fines of up to 5,000 yuan (more than the average peasant's yearly income) for having a second child within five years of the first. In addition, compulsory assessments were exacted for school and road construction, water projects, power station building and maintenance, medical facilities, and public security.[29] When peasants resisted making payments, officials sometimes used force against them. According to central accounts, local authorities "ransack[ed] homes, taking grain, furniture or livestock," and bullied and beat peasants— sometimes seriously injuring them or even causing their death.[30] Reflecting the prevalence of increased rural government exactions, nationwide, township and village taxes took nearly 8 percent of average per capita rural income in 1991. When added to various extra-legal levies and fees, as of the early 1990s, up to 40 percent of villager incomes went to the government in some localities.[31] The tax and fee burden within villages also was regressive, with poorer households paying a larger portion of their income than more wealthy households.[32]

To address the deteriorating political situation in the countryside, central authorities took steps to democratize and enhance the power of local Village Committees (VCs). In doing so, party elites did not wish to diminish the party's ability to direct the political system and the economy but, rather, hoped to strengthen the party's ability to implement its policies at the local level and ensure social stability.[33] In late 1987, an Organic Law gave village residents the right to nominate and elect VC members, who would serve three-year terms. In turn, VCs were made answerable to Village Assemblies made up of all adult residents.[34] The law did not subject VCs to the leadership or control of party or state organs but rather stated that the party-state would provide "guidance, support and assistance." At the same time, central authorities made it clear that VCs were expected to maintain public order and to convince residents to "fulfill their legal obligations and respect public property."[35] Beginning in 1988, the Ministry of Civil Affairs worked to implement the new law, establishing province-level guidelines and organizing publicity campaigns, election work, and training classes. By 1990, "rudimentary" VCs had been established in virtually every Chinese village.[36] Yet, only about 15 percent of all VCs were estimated to be operating "reasonably well" in accordance with the standards outlined in the Organic Law.[37]

Perceptions of Socioeconomic Mobility, Relative
Socioeconomic Status, Material Dependence
on the Party-State, and Political Options

These broad contextual developments impacted peasant perceptions of socioeconomic mobility, relative socioeconomic status, material dependence on the party-state, and political options in such a way that peasants became quite testy toward local officials but generally accepted the overall political system. Overall, changes in state-led development policies and increased openness to the global capitalist economy in the first phase of the reform era brought substantial material advancement to China's peasants—especially compared to the pre-reform period. Unlike urban SOE workers, most farmers remembered the Mao era as a time of penury and ignorance. In particular, rural residents voiced strong aversion to the pre-reform collective agriculture system, associating it with individual and collective poverty. As a result, peasants evidenced little nostalgia for China's Maoist past and viewed the early reform period as a time of relative plenty and upward socioeconomic mobility.[38]

Even so, within the first phase of the post-Mao era, the material advance of farmers was not steady. Between 1978 and 1983, real per capita agricultural income rose by around 100 percent. If one includes all forms of rural income, real per capita income increased by approximately 200 percent.[39] Yet in the latter half of the 1980s, agricultural output leveled off, and local government taxes and fees multiplied in most central and western provinces. Nationwide, real peasant income dropped slightly, rural per capita consumption flattened, and rural poverty rates worsened.[40]

In terms of relative socioeconomic status, between the late 1970s and the mid-1980s the disparity in living standards between rural residents and city dwellers narrowed for perhaps the first time in Chinese history. Whereas in 1978, the urban-rural income ratio was nearly 2.4 to 1, by 1985 it had shrunk to roughly 1.7 to 1. This trend was reversed during the remainder of the 1980s, with the result that in 1990 the gap stood at 2 to 1.[41] Even so, rural-urban inequality was below pre-reform levels. The overall effect during the early post-Mao period was a small gain in the economic status of peasants relative to urban workers, yet a still-wide gulf in socioeconomic conditions.

Of perhaps more immediate relevance to the political attitudes and behavior of farmers was the rise of new socioeconomic inequalities *among* rural residents. As described earlier, these inequalities arose from the duality of continued state controls over agriculture and the uneven spread of market opportunities. Under the collective agricultural system of the Mao era, income differentials in the countryside had been practically nonexistent. With everyone "eating from the same big pot" (*chi daguo fan*), official sources estimate that the rural Gini coefficient in the pre-reform period was a low 0.21.[42] In the first phase of the post-Mao era, rural inequality increased dramatically, reaching a Gini score of 0.31 in 1990.[43] To a large degree, this resulted from the unequal geographic distribution of successful TVEs, which made rural incomes much higher in coastal provinces than in central and western areas.[44] Between 1984 and 1988, for example, net daily income rose nearly 46 percent for nonagricultural industries, while that for grain production rose by about 15 percent.[45] Consequently, while economic circumstances improved dramatically in villages with nonagricultural income, for those relying only on agriculture, subsistence conditions prevailed.[46]

In localities where nonagricultural opportunities were more abundant, inequality *within* villages also rose, as individuals able to establish successful private enterprises or obtain employment in prosperous TVEs became much wealthier than those who could not or did not pursue income opportunities outside of farming. In less-developed localities lacking lucrative nonagricultural revenue sources, within-village economic inequality remained low.[47] Even so, in both prosperous and poor villages, households with political connections generally were more prosperous than those lacking such ties. As Andrew Walder and Litao Zhao found in a nationally representative survey undertaken in the mid-1990s, rural "households with no political ties [had] the lowest earning power, those with kinship ties [to political officials] [had] tangible income advantages, and cadres households [had] even larger advantages. The more direct the connection of a household to rural political office, the larger its earning power."[48]

Meanwhile, peasants' economic dependence on the regime declined dramatically as compared with the Mao period. Whereas the commune system forced rural residents to be almost entirely reliant on the party-state, the household responsibility system gave peasants much greater economic independence. Importantly, unlike rank and file SOE workers, who lamented their new economic independence from the party-state and felt abandoned by the regime as a result of economic reform, farmers welcomed the severance of their prior material ties with the party-state, for they felt that their Mao-era economic dependence had trapped them in poverty.

At the same time, some of the socialist policies that were perpetuated in the first phase of the post-Mao era prevented peasants from becoming wholly independent of the state for their livelihood. For peasants lacking nonagricultural income sources, basic sustenance was tied to the party-state's provision of land. Yet dependence on the state for land also limited peasants' ability to progress economically. Although leases were fairly long, local authorities were empowered to reallocate land, and they often did so much more frequently than was stipulated in national policy.[49] As a result, peasants were loath to invest in long-term improvements to their plots. In addition, the central government required that farmers meet gain quotas in exchange for land rights, thus limiting their ability to grow more profitable crops or to leave the village to earn income through wage work. Throughout much of the early reform period, the *hukou* system tied peasants to their place of official residence.

Peasants in the early reform period were presented with a number of political options that detracted from their perceived need to challenge the overall governmental system. In cases in which local political structures collapsed, peasants could ignore the political system entirely or rely on clan and temple associations to provide the public goods that formal political institutions failed to supply. In places where local authorities were both predatory and powerful, villagers could threaten to or actually engage in collective action. Along with submitting petitions to higher-level authorities, villagers could attempt to attract central leaders' attention by taking to the streets in protest. Tax limits promulgated by the central state, as well as party pronouncements regarding the need for rural stability, gave peasants some leverage in this regard. In addition, beginning in the late 1980s, farmers increasingly were able to elect new village leaders or even run for office themselves. Thus, although peasants had some real reasons to desire fundamental political change, the existing system provided options that enabled them to voice their grievances without challenging overall CCP rule.

In addition, in the early reform era when urban groups (such as college students, intellectuals, and state-owned enterprise workers) took to the streets to call for more systemic political reforms, they made virtually no effort to mobilize farmers to join them. When urban residents spoke of democracy in the late 1970s and 1980s, they showed little interest in the political enfranchisement of the rural masses.[50] Thus, for most peasants, participation in protests directed at the central regime never appeared as a practical or appealing option.

Political Attitudes and Behavior

Peasant perceptions of socioeconomic mobility, relative socioeconomic status, economic ties to the party-state, and political options shaped their political views and behavior. To the extent that farmers attributed their improved material conditions to party-state policies, their support for the regime was strengthened. As mentioned above, most farmers were highly critical of the forced egalitarianism of the Mao era, feeling that it did not reward hard work and that it had impaired the economic advancement of both individual households and the community as a whole. Against this backdrop, most welcomed the state's new landholding system as well as the state's encouragement of TVEs, seeing them as ways to enhance household and village prosperity. Although many outside observers expected that farmers would be unhappy with their insecure land rights, in fact, the household responsibility system's combination of socialist assets and market mechanisms appeared quite popular. In numerous surveys undertaken in the early 1990s, a majority of peasants expressed opposition to the extension of land tenure or outright land privatization and showed a preference for the existing system's guaranteed access to sufficient land through periodic reallocations to adjust for changes in household size. Further, peasants almost universally supported the egalitarian distribution of land and resources that was required by national guidelines.[51] As Eduard Vermeer reports, "rich or poor, most villagers felt that land, as common property, should remain accessible to all villagers."[52]

Simultaneously, many peasants felt that their ability to rise economically was limited by socialist legacies and state controls. They were critical of the residential registration system that disadvantaged them relative to urban *hukou* holders and of grain production requirements that constricted their ability to engage in more profitable pursuits. In addition, large numbers of peasants believed that local cadres were illegitimately benefiting from economic reform. In a 1990 survey of fifty-seven villages in four provinces, 65 percent of respondents expressed the belief that most officials in their locality were corrupt.[53] Another study undertaken toward the end of the early reform period found that no matter what the source of a local official's economic success, "villagers tend[ed] to suppose it [was] [the cadre's] privileged power position which [was] the determining factor."[54]

At the same time, peasants displayed the socialist mentality that the accumulation of wealth was illegitimate if it harmed community interests. In one poor village, for example, "the head of the construction team had aroused the peasants' anger. He was said to have used his connections (*guanxi*) with local cadres, and to possess no special qualifications other than his extensive social connections. In addition, he had hired no peasant [from the village] in his team." Local villagers "would scarcely talk to him, expressing in private conversations the hope that he would eventually meet with failure." Not only had this man prospered as a result of his political ties, but he had "caused the families in that village to be denied a profit which they felt entitled to in the name of community solidarity."[55]

Still, the level of farmer discontent varied by locality. In coastal areas with greater opportunities to accumulate wealth through entrepreneurship, many households without ties to the local political establishment became quite prosperous—sometimes even wealthier than local cadres. In these areas, politically unconnected peasants evidenced relatively little bitterness toward those with political ties.[56] Further, inasmuch as local authorities in more prosperous villages were able to provide government benefits and services without relying on heavy household taxes, even residents without political ties benefited from the political status quo. As a result, these areas witnessed very little peasant unrest in the early reform period. In addition, in more-developed areas where free and fair Village Committee elections were held, wealthy villagers without ties to existing political leaders began to run for office—and win.[57]

In contrast, politically unconnected residents of poorer central and western villages with fewer entrepreneurial possibilities often exhibited serious dissatisfaction with local authorities. As Isabelle Thireau reports, "the feeling that exploitation of connections as a means of allocating resources [was] illegitimate increase[d] in relationship to the scarcity of the desired assets or services."[58] Unlike in wealthier areas, in poor localities a clear socioeconomic division arose between the wealthy and politically connected on the one hand and the poor and unconnected on the other. When leaders in these villages attempted to impose burdensome taxes and fees on common farmers or charge prices above state-mandated rates for agricultural inputs (such as fertilizer), peasants' anger often led them to engage in contentious collective action.

In fact, virtually all of the rural unrest that appeared in the first phase of the post-Mao period occurred in relatively undeveloped areas with few nonagricultural opportunities and featured conflict between members of the same locality—typically politically unconnected and relatively poor villagers protesting against what in their view were the illegitimate gains of local political leaders and individuals with ties to them.[59] Although reliable data on the frequency of farmer protests in the early reform period is scarce, by the late 1980s central authorities clearly feared that rural order was deteriorating in the less-developed villages of central and western China. In most cases, peasants appear to have organized petition efforts. When such actions failed, some took to the streets or even committed acts of revenge against local leaders—sacking their fields, destroying equipment, raiding local government-controlled supplies, or even beating them.[60] According to official sources, peasants evidenced a "rebellious mentality" and "fierce dissatisfaction," leading to "vicious incidents" and "fierce reactions."[61]

In the vast majority of poor villages, however, even disgruntled peasants were quiescent. When local authorities were weak and unable to collect taxes and fees, most villagers ignored the government. As Kevin O'Brien relates, peasants in these circumstances displayed "little interest in affairs outside private life."[62] As of 1990, the Ministry of Civil Affairs estimated that this type of situation prevailed in roughly 20 percent of all villages—particularly those that were poor and remote and had few collective enterprises.[63] Even in localities where taxes and fees were collected coercively and village elections were fixed or ignored by local political authorities, residents generally did not act on their dissatisfaction. In large part, this was due to their perception of their lack of power to effect a change in their situation through individual or collective action. Yet at the same time, O'Brien found that although authoritarian local leadership typically was not the "first choice" of peasants, it was not always their least desirable option. As long as local officials could provide public security and attend to basic village needs, authoritarian governance often appeared to peasants as preferable to having no government at all.[64]

THE LATE REFORM ERA (EARLY 1990s THROUGH THE PRESENT)

In the late reform era, state-led development policies, market forces, and socialist practices have had a mixed impact on peasants—in some respects improving their quality of life and diminishing their political dissatisfaction, yet in other ways creating new types of hardship and political complaints. Since the early 1990s, China's farmers have been ever more directly impacted by market forces deriving from China's late entry into the global capitalist system. Following Deng Xiaoping's 1992 "Southern Tour," the capital cities of all inland provinces and autonomous regions were opened to international trade and investment, and scores of free trade zones, economic and technological development zones, and high-tech industrial development zones were established in medium and large cities.[65] In 2000 the central regime's "Go West" policy further opened China's interior areas to foreign investment and industrial development. As free-trade and foreign investment zones have spread in the late reform period, the expanding job market has given peasants new opportunities to find wage work and earn income through nonagricultural pursuits. Simultaneously, changes in state-led development policies have eased internal migration restrictions, thus increasing peasants' ability to seek nonfarm work.

Yet diminished party-state control and increased market influence over the economic fate of rural *hukou* holders have not been entirely beneficial to China's farmers; along with greater opportunities for economic advancement has come increased competition. Continued party-state direction of farmers' economic pursuits via local government directives to develop particular rural industries and enterprises has only exacerbated this trend. Although TVE output increased between the late 1980s and late 1990s, as TVEs proliferated, competition rose, with the result that profit did not grow commensurately. To deal with the dual problem of too many TVEs and too little profits, local officials privatized virtually all small and/or marginally profitable TVEs. The end of formal government ownership in these enterprises subjected employees to the vicissitudes of the market, allowing enterprise managers previously constrained by popular views of employment rights in collective enterprises to fire workers, to demand more stringent work conditions, and to reduce wages.[66] At the same time, competition among rural *hukou* holders rose as official constraints on internal migration diminished.

Around 2005, this trend began to abate, as unskilled labor shortages appeared in some coastal provinces. The result was a slight improvement in wages and working conditions in these areas. However, this positive development for peasants seeking wage work proved to be short-lived. In part, this was due to the mobility of capital. Although some factories responded to the dearth of cheap unskilled labor in coastal areas by moving inland within China, many others simply packed up and left the PRC.[67] Unskilled labor shortages disappeared with the economic crisis in the United States (the major importer of Chinese exports) that began in late 2008. As of this writing, the combined result has been a contraction of job opportunities for unskilled workers, such as peasants in search of wage work.

Similarly, sideline production schemes among peasants have been both encouraged and hampered by the combination of state direction and market forces. In countless cases, township or village officials have decided that profits may be made through a particular product, such as bricks, mushrooms, gloves, plastic, cable, or fertilizer. Subsequently, local authorities have ordered households and villages to sink money into this new enterprise. The consistent result has been increased demand for inputs and increased supply of outputs, such that the price of inputs has risen and the value of the final product has declined. Often the peasants have been left worse off than they were when they started.[68]

In addition, China's increasing immersion in the global economy has subjected peasants to severe fluctuations in agricultural prices. Although government policies such as tariffs on agricultural imports and domestic agricultural subsidies have kept competition with foreign suppliers somewhat at bay, the diminution of state purchases of grain at fixed prices has meant that an increasing portion of the crops produced by China's peasants has been affected by domestic and international market forces. When domestic harvests were good (as was the case in 1991, 1992, and 1997), crop prices fell dramatically.[69] Further, when world crop prices plummeted in the late 1990s, crop prices in China dropped by more than one-third.[70] Since China's ascension into the World Trade Organization in 2001, farmers have become only more vulnerable to global price fluctuations, as China's agricultural tariffs have dropped by about 20 percent and export subsidies have been discontinued.[71] In 2007–8, rising crop prices made farming more profitable. Even so, international market forces have constrained the potential gains of China's farmers. Because the household responsibility system allots peasants only small and scattered plots of land, China's peasants have had limited ability to compete with the large-scale and mechanized farm complexes that predominate in major agricultural exporters such as the United States.

In localities with fewer opportunities for successful nonagricultural pursuits, these problems were compounded in the 1990s by further increases in local government financial extractions from the peasantry.[72] Yet, in the first few years of the 2000s the trend toward ever-increasing rural exactions was not only halted; it was reversed. Beginning in 2000, central authorities initiated pilot projects to gradually phase out rural taxes and fees in some provinces. In 2002, party leaders announced national reforms requiring that all formal taxes and informal charges be phased out by 2006.[73] National authorities made concrete efforts to ensure that this new policy would be realized. Provinces were given centrally prescribed benchmarks, which were then handed down to township and village leaders.[74] With promotion clearly tied to the fulfillment of these benchmarks, local leaders readily complied. In addition, some provincial governments sent each household a letter explaining the new tax and fee reforms, and asking them to sign and return it.[75] With peasants made aware of the new central policies, it was difficult for local leaders to ignore or circumvent them. As a result, the pace of implementation was surprisingly rapid. By 2004 virtually all rural taxes and fees had been abolished.[76]

Although peasants have enjoyed a reduction in government exactions as a result of this reform, the broader impact of this change has varied by location. In wealthier coastal areas where market opportunities have been more abundant and local authorities have been less reliant on agricultural taxes, local enterprises have provided adequate revenue to make up for the decline in tax funds. As discussed earlier, in many such localities, the peasant tax burden was negligible even before the early 2000s tax reforms. In these cases, local governments have continued to pay cadre salaries and provide public services and benefits.

In more remote and economically undeveloped localities, conditions have deteriorated. This is because the structural flaw that led to increasing farmer burdens in the first place—insufficient funds for cadre salaries and public services at the township and village levels—has only worsened. Although the central government increased budget transfers to compensate for local revenue shortfalls, very little of this money has trickled down as it has passed through the provincial and county governmental levels. In a 2003–4 study of twenty townships, for example, only three received transfer funds, and they got only enough to pay a small supplement to some cadre salaries.[77] As a result, large numbers of township and village governments have been in debt since the first decade of the twenty-first century. To pay cadre salaries and provide centrally mandated services such as education, most have borrowed money. When the local government's credit rating has been so poor that loans have not been forthcoming, some individual cadres have taken out personal loans to pay for collective expenses. Still, funds have been inadequate in most central and western localities. In the 2003–4 study, only seven of the twenty surveyed townships were able to pay cadre salaries in full and on time. Many owed two or three months' back pay to their staff, and some were behind by as much as two years. The situation at the village level typically has been worse.[78]

Because scarce township and village funds have gone almost entirely to salaries in poor rural areas, public services have withered.[79] In 2004, central authorities issued a new rural policy document that attempted to address the problem. Most importantly, the document instituted a five-fold increase in rural spending.[80] As of this writing, this policy appears to have done little to ameliorate the depressed conditions of poor villagers. However, it has at least given peasants the impression that the national regime is concerned about their plight.

Meanwhile, the new millennium has witnessed an increase in the requisitioning of peasant land for nonagricultural development. Although by the late 1990s this practice already had become common, since the first decade of the twenty-first century, it has been pandemic in rural areas that are close to urban zones.[81] In the first half of 2004 alone, government sources reported nearly forty-seven thousand cases of "illegal land activities" nationwide.[82] The impact of land requisitions on the peasantry has been uneven. In some locations, land revenues have been used to provide public services or give villagers regular stipends that provide them with a higher and more stable income than they had earned from farming.[83] Yet in many cases, peasants have received little compensation.[84] For example, a 1999 study of a township in Yunnan province found that county and township governments took 60 to 70 percent of all income from land sales, village governments received 25 to 30 percent, and farmers were given only 5 to 10 percent. In one particular sale, the land had sold for 150,000 yuan per mu of land, but villagers received only 28,000 yuan/mu.[85] In 2006, central officials attempted to address this problem by directing provincial governors and local leaders to reduce government requisitions of land that has been allocated to rural residents.[86] As of this writing, the directive appears to have had little impact. Yet, as with the 2004 rural policy document mentioned earlier, it has indicated to peasants that party elites are on their side.

Perceptions of Socioeconomic Mobility, Relative Socioeconomic Status, Material Dependence on the Party-State, and Political Options

The mixture of beneficial and harmful developments that have arisen from the configuration of state-led development policies, market forces, and socialist legacies in the late reform period has had a similarly mixed impact on peasant perceptions of socioeconomic mobility, relative socioeconomic status, material dependence on the part-state, and political options. On the whole, the late post-Mao period has brought continued upward mobility to farmers. Using 2003 as a baseline, between 1989 and 2005, the yearly real per capita income of rural residents rose by 300 percent—from approximately 1,000 to 3,000 yuan (roughly US$125 to US$375).[87] Similarly, China's rural residents have enjoyed many more consumer goods as the late reform era has progressed. Between 1985 and 1998, per capita consumption of meat, eggs, and fish increased by roughly 50 to 100 percent. During the same period, the number of washing machines per 100 rural households climbed from 1.9 to 22.81, the number of refrigerators from .06 to 9.25, color TV sets from .8 to 32.59, and motorcycles from .1 to 13.52.[88] In a nationwide survey undertaken by Chunping Han and Martin King Whyte in 2004, among major socioeconomic sectors, farmers exhibited some of the highest levels of optimism.[89]

These general trends mask great variation in the lived experiences of China's peasants since the early 1990s. In more-developed rural areas where residents have been less reliant on agriculture for their income, virtually all have expressed the belief that they have moved upward materially. In a 2000 survey conducted in the prosperous southern region of Jiangsu province, for example, close to 90 percent of villagers reported that their standard of living had "noticeably improved."[90] As one peasant said in the late 1990s, "We get food from our farm, and profits from our factory. Everything that townspeople have, we have too. Houses, modern furniture, TVs, fridges, we've got them all. We've got a phone, too, so we can get through to anywhere in the country. How could I not be satisfied?"[91]

In marked contrast, peasants who have continued to depend on agriculture "have experienced absolute, not just relative, declines in their standard of living" in the late reform period.[92] Although the tax reforms of the first decade of the new millennium have lightened the tax burdens of poor peasants, most farmers have remained at a subsistence level. As late as 2000 in one poor village, residents lived in caves that were roughly 3 meters wide and 7 meters long. Until the late 1990s, they had no electricity, and as of 2000, they had no electrical appliances aside from a light. In 2000 their kitchen was outdoors, consisting of a cooker made of mud bricks and two burners. A typical resident consumed only 2 to 4 catties (2.6 to 5.2 pounds) of cooking oil and 1 to 2 catties (1.3 to 2.6 pounds) of meat per year. On most days, breakfast was noodle soup, lunch consisted of wheat flour gruel (sometimes with a few homegrown vegetables), and dinner was a soup made of millet or corn and some steamed buns.[93] For agriculturally reliant peasants whose land has been expropriated with little compensation in the late reform period, even this kind of bare survival has not been assured. In addition, to the extent that the second phase of the post-Mao era has witnessed a withering of government-funded services such as education, infrastructure, and utilities in poor villages, residents' living standards have suffered.

Relative to other groups, peasants' socioeconomic status has declined in the late reform period. From 1997–2003, for example, annual average per capita rural income reportedly rose 25 percent, but urban incomes increased by 65 percent.[94] From a ratio of 2.1 to 1 in 1990, the urban-rural income gap grew to 3.3 to 1 in 2007.[95] If the social welfare benefits of urban residents are included, the economic disjuncture between urban and rural residents has been even larger.[96] In another illustration of this disparity, as of 1999, 25 percent of the rural population consumed less than US$1 per day, compared to .5 percent of urban dwellers.[97]

Among rural residents, material disparities shifted somewhat in the late reform period. In the 1990s the income gap between those predominantly engaged in agriculture and those relying primarily on other sources of income grew larger. Beginning around 2000, tax reforms ameliorated this imbalance somewhat, as the poorest peasants that had paid the highest proportion of taxes relative to their income received the most economic relief. In addition, the rise in agricultural commodity prices in 2007–8 was a boon to China's farmers. Further, although coastal villages remain far more prosperous than those in China's interior, the spread of specially designated development zones and loosening of migration restrictions since the early 1990s have decreased the degree of interprovincial rural inequality.[98]

Within villages, however, economic inequality has increased over the course of the late reform period.[99] As in the early post-Mao era, the most politically well-connected households in a locality have been the most prosperous. Able to occupy upper-tier jobs close to home, they have earned healthy incomes without having to migrate in search of work. Meanwhile, the poorest and least politically connected families have remained engaged only in farming. Most of those with a middling level of connections and resources have sent some family members out in search of off-farm work, leaving the less able-bodied at home to tend to the farm.[100] As in the early reform period, material inequalities that correlate with the unequal distribution of political power have been a major source of peasant discontent. As Melanie Manion finds in multi-village surveys conducted in 1990 and 1996, "against an historical background of Maoist egalitarianism, many [peasants] associate growing inequality with the low moral scruples of those with wealth and power."[101]

Reflecting the economic inequalities and local budget shortfalls that have appeared in rural areas in the reform era, village elections increasingly have been dominated by the relatively wealthy. As Richard Levy notes, because many localities have been unable to pay cadre salaries, only those with independent income have been able to afford to serve. In addition, village governments and residents have relied on the resources of prosperous villagers.[102] In one famous case from the first decade of the new millennium, the winning candidate actually paid each villager 1,800 yuan (roughly US$225)—roughly two-thirds of the average rural resident's annual income![103]

Meanwhile, the late reform era has witnessed further increases in peasants' economic independence from the party-state. To begin, the power of rural officials to control the issuance of residence permits has declined.[104] Similarly, the tax reforms that began in 2000 have made farmers more autonomous vis-à-vis local authorities. Yet peasants have continued to be economically tied to the state for their land. They also have had to abide by the party-state's grain quota and price stipulations. Among those whose land has been requisitioned in the late post-Mao period, this tie has been severed. For peasants who subsequently have received regular payments from the local government, a new and more appealing form of economic dependence has taken its place, so systemic political reform holds little material appeal. In quite contrasting circumstances are farmers who have had neither land nor government support and have become completely independent of the party-state for their livelihood. Political discontent has run high in this group.

Along with their dependence on the state, peasants' political options in the post-Mao period have also undercut their interest in opposing the overall political system. As in the early reform period, farmers have been able to submit petitions or request government hearings. In addition, relative to the first phase of the post-Mao era, village elections have become more meaningful. In 1998 the party promulgated a new Organic Law regarding village governance. Among other things, the law stipulated that VCs should allow Village Assemblies to discuss and decide on matters such as village expenditures and revenues, applications, plot allocations, family planning actions, and collective contracts. The law also instructed VCs to publicize local government allocations and decisions. In addition, the new law gave all adult villagers the right to run for election, to directly nominate candidates, and to recall VC members before their term of office is complete.[105] According to various reports, the quality of village elections has improved. Although in 1990 the Ministry of Civil Affairs estimated that only about 15 percent of Village Committees nationwide were operating in accordance with central policies, in 2003 a Carter Center report found that this was true in 40 percent of China's villages.[106] Similarly, in a comparison of elections in rural Shaanxi province in 2000 and 2004, John James Kennedy found "clear improvements in the quality of village elections regarding the nomination of candidates and the competitiveness of elections." In addition, Kennedy reports that "once [village] elections are fully implemented, it is difficult to revert to semi-open elections or no elections."[107] Also in the first decade of the twenty-first century, Richard Levy found that village government transparency had increased, particularly in wealthier areas. In the late 1990s, for example, a county official in a moderately economically developed area estimated that "20 to 30 percent of villages did their transparency work well, 60 percent satisfactorily, and 10 to 20 percent poorly." According to Levy, the situation in this county had improved by the first decade of the new millennium.[108] To the degree that these institutionalized political mechanisms have increased the system's responsiveness to the demands and interests of peasants, challenging the CCP-led political system has not been an appealing option.

Political Attitudes and Behavior

Peasant perceptions of economic mobility, relative socioeconomic status, dependence on the state, and political options in the late reform era have in some areas bred extensive political dissatisfaction with local elites. At the same time, peasants have evinced a generally favorable view of the central regime. Even so, compared to other socioeconomic sectors, peasant support for continued CCP rule has been tenuous and declining.

As noted earlier, peasants have been quite restless in the late post-Mao period. In 1993, central authorities reported well over six thousand cases of "turmoil" in the countryside. In nearly one thousand of these instances, five hundred or more protestors were involved. In all, more than eight thousand deaths occurred, and 200 million yuan worth of property was destroyed. In 1995 and 1996, similar waves of peasant uprisings occurred.[109] In 1997, nearly 900,000 peasants in nine provinces participated in collective petition efforts and public demonstrations that in many cases involved violent confrontations with the authorities. In 1999 roughly five million farmers participated in such political activities, and in 2003, nearly two million did the same.[110] Since 2005, government statistics on the frequency of popular unrest have not been forthcoming, but both official media reports and independent observations suggest that peasant uprisings have remained frequent and widespread.

In addition to street protests, millions have participated in collective petition efforts. Although data since 2006 are not available, the total number of petitions skyrocketed from 2000–2005.[111] In 2003, the government petition office received more than ten million petitions. In 2005, this number rose to thirteen million. Official and scholarly reports estimate that approximately 60 to 80 percent of these petitions were initiated by peasants, and related to land disputes.[112]

The content and geographic distribution of peasant grievances shifted over the course of the 1990s and first decade of the 2000s. Between the early 1990s and the first decade of the new millennium, the major peasant concern was excessive taxes; as Thomas Bernstein and Xiaobo Lu report, discontent with tax and fee burdens during this period was "widespread and chronic."[113] Because local government exactions were much steeper in central and western provinces than in coastal zones, peasants in the former reported much higher levels of dissatisfaction and displayed a much greater proclivity to engage in contentious collective action.[114] Since the tax reforms that were initiated in 2000, protests and petition efforts revolving around excessive taxation virtually have disappeared, and China's western and central villages have been relatively quiet. Meanwhile, peasant discontent and unrest seem to have increased in China's coastal provinces, where most cases of land requisitions have occurred. In 2004, 87 percent of known cases of rural disturbances reportedly arose from land disputes.[115]

Despite these shifts in grievances and geography, peasants' basic political attitudes have been remarkably consistent between the mid-1990s and the time of this writing. In Ethan Michelson's 2002 survey of five provinces and the municipality of Chongqing, farmers reported general satisfaction with the ability of local leaders to resolve most basic villager problems.[116] Yet when it has come to tax disputes and land requisitions, peasants often have expressed grave discontent with local authorities. In these cases, farmers have insisted that their outrage is not simply due to the material hardship that local government actions have caused. Rather, their dissatisfaction has derived from their view that tax and land revenues have gone almost entirely into the pockets of local political leaders and their cronies. Meanwhile, peasants have displayed faith in the central government. In surveys conducted by Lianjiang Li between 1999 and 2001, a substantial majority of villagers expressed belief that the national government was well intentioned, but that when it came to tax disputes, local authorities thwarted the capacity of the center to implement its benevolent policies.[117] As a farmer engaged in tax protests in the late 1990s stated,

> Damn those sons of bitches [township and village cadres]! The Center lets us ordinary people have good lives; all central policies are very good. But these policies are all changed when they reach lower levels. It's entirely their fault. They do nothing good, spending their whole day wining and dining. The only thing they don't forget is to collect money.[118]

Myriad studies and interviews have uncovered an identical frame of mind among rural protestors. Indeed, research on rural tax and land conflicts universally has concluded that what has encouraged peasants to undertake collective action in the first place has been their belief that local authorities have not been implementing central policies designed to protect peasants' interests.[119] Kevin O'Brien and Lianjiang Li's 2003–4 survey found that 78 percent of respondents agreed or strongly agreed that "the Center is willing to listen to peasants who tell the truth and welcomes our complaints," and 87 percent agreed or strongly agreed that "the Center supports peasants in defending their lawful rights and interests."[120]

Still, compared to other socioeconomic groups, peasant support for the CCP-led political system has appeared weak. First, farmers have shown relatively little interest in joining the CCP or participating in its affiliated organizations. As of 2006, only 3.07 percent of those living in the countryside were party members, as opposed to 8.9 percent of urban residents.[121] Further, farmers have appeared more likely than other socioeconomic sectors to believe that "the well-being of the country should depend on the masses instead of state leaders."[122] When they feel wronged, peasants have reported less reluctance than urban residents to argue with the political authorities. In addition, farmers have shown more support for free-market capitalism and a greater belief in core democratic values such as free and fair elections and freedom of speech and expression.[123]

The future trajectory of peasants' political attitudes and behavior may depend on the extent to which the central regime succeeds in promoting mechanisms within the existing political system that satisfactorily address peasant grievances. Important in this regard is the degree to which village elections are meaningful. As Melanie Manion writes, high-quality local elections seem to promote both public trust in government and government trustworthiness.[124] Although Kevin O'Brien and Rongbin Han note that procedural improvements have been more impressive than have been changes in the actual exercise of power, free and fair village elections do seem to have become more prevalent over time.[125] To the extent that this trend continues, one might expect that peasant support for the existing political system will only rise in the future. Of course, if meaningful local elections become the norm in China, the political system will in reality be more democratic than is currently the case.

Similarly, the perceived responsiveness of the petition and hearing systems is important. Christopher Heurlin and Susan Whiting's 2005 survey of seventeen provinces found that in 68 percent of petition cases (virtually all of which concerned land compensation), the government either refused to increase the peasants' compensation (36 percent) or took no action at all (32 percent).[126] Lianjiang Li's 2003–5 survey of villagers in two provinces uncovered even more disturbing results: More than 60 percent of petitioners had been subjected to one or more forms of local repression, including being subjected to fines (28.2 percent); having their homes demolished or destroyed (21.8 percent); having their homes ransacked, properties confiscated, and valuables taken away (31.4 percent); being beaten or having their family members beaten (46.8 percent); and being detained, arrested, and sent to labor camps (41.1 percent). Still, in Li's survey roughly 40 percent reported satisfaction with the result of their petitioning effort.[127] In Heurlin and Whiting's research, among the 32 percent of cases where petitions resulted in increased compensation, 12 percent of respondents were satisfied with the amount.[128]

Not surprisingly, Li found that peasants who have had good experiences with petitioning have expressed increased trust in the central government, while those with bad experiences have displayed diminished faith in and lowered support for the ruling regime.[129] Yet interestingly, regardless of a person's assessment of the outcome, those who had petitioned central authorities in Bejing reported reduced trust in the national regime. As a whole, these petitioners were roughly 31 percent less likely than other peasants to agree that "the Center" truly cared about farmers, nearly 41 percent less likely to agree that "the Center" welcomed farmers to petition, and approximately 47 percent less likely to agree that petitioning Beijing was very useful.[130] Thus, even though beneficent national laws and pronouncements have encouraged peasants to take action within existing political structures, when their efforts have come to naught, they have become disillusioned with the political system as a whole. As one petitioner relates, "when we returned [home], seven of us were detained for a few weeks. It's useless to seek justice. Opposing graft and corruption means time in prison. There is no place to look for justice."[131]

For some, the response has been despair. Among Li's respondents, more than 13 percent of unsuccessful petitioners said that they would give up. But for most others, the reaction has been rage and determination.[132] In Li's survey, roughly 82 percent of failed petitioners said that they would continue petitioning until their goals were achieved; approximately 74 percent asserted that they would publicize policies and mobilize the masses to defend their lawful rights; slightly more than 45 percent said that they would "do something that cadres would be afraid of"; and nearly 56 percent said that they would establish an organization to defend farmers' lawful rights.[133] Although not common, some even expressed the desire to bring down the regime. In the words of one peasant whose repeated collective petition efforts had failed, "If we do not get the expected response in a given period of time, then we will go all out to mobilize the masses to struggle for peasant's right to life and democratic rights by starting a democratic revolutionary movement."[134]

It must be emphasized that the vast majority of peasants in the late reform era have not petitioned the government or engaged in protests. In the first decade of the twenty-first century, only about 1.4 percent of China's rural residents undertook petition efforts, and only .25 percent participated in public "disturbances."[135] Yet to the extent that these actions continue to rise and the government's response is not seen as satisfactory, peasant discontent may be expected to become more widespread and deep. Given that most unsuccessful petitioners have not given up but, rather, have continued their activism—often in a more confrontational way—peasant-based challenges to the ruling regime are likely to increase.

CONCLUSION

As of the time of this writing, party elites are presented with a quandary. To the extent that continued economic growth requires that agricultural land be developed, farmers must be displaced. Yet the party-state cannot afford to provide their sustenance, and the market offers insufficient opportunities for unskilled labor. As of 2009, national leaders have been able to provide peasants with just enough support and political opening to dissipate their more unabated fury. Yet recent trends in farmer attitudes and actions suggest that this state of affairs may not persist.

7 CONCLUSION

AS THE PRECEDING CHAPTERS have shown, China's combination of state-led development policies, market forces associated with late industrialization, and socialist legacies has given most Chinese citizens good reason to accept the authoritarian political status quo. First, this confluence of factors has improved the economic conditions of most socioeconomic sectors. Of equal importance, unlike in countries such as England around the time of the Industrial Revolution, most upwardly mobile citizens have believed that their material improvement has been facilitated by the ruling regime. In turn, these individuals have had no pressing motivation to agitate for systemic political transformation.

Second, key sectors have been economically dependent on the CCP. As detailed in Chapters 2 and 4, this clearly has been the case for private enterprise owners and state sector workers. The material reliance of these groups on the government has derived from the fact that, as in other state-led developers, in China the state has retained control of key economic resources. Because the economic prosperity and security of dependent groups have rested largely on their special connection with the party-state, they have had material reasons to tolerate continued CCP rule. At the same time, they have had disincentives to support liberal democratic political changes that might imperil their privileged position. For rank-and-file state sector workers, these considerations have been heightened by the job insecurity and competition that have emerged alongside China's late opening to the global capitalist system. Should the CCP fall from power, or should less-advantaged workers (such as rural migrants) become politically empowered, state sector workers might lose the few advantages that they have held in the labor market. In addition, because state sector workers have tended to espouse socialist-era beliefs that such privileges are legitimate and morally just, these workers' material motivation to support the political status quo has been intertwined with their ideal sense of what is right.

As shown in Chapters 5 and 6, farmers and rank-and-file private sector workers have not enjoyed a similarly privileged political position, and as a result, they have had less reason to support the existing political system. Even so, to the degree that the party-state has provided these groups with a basic safety net in the form of land rights, they have not had a pressing material reason to push for regime change. Further, as with common state sector workers, inasmuch as farmers and regular private sector workers have continued to believe that the government has a moral duty to ensure the basic livelihood of the people, the regime's provision of this safety net has enhanced the legitimacy of the CCP in farmers' and private sector workers' eyes.

Third, the confluence of state-led development policies and market forces associated with late opening to the global capitalist system has engendered a highly skewed socioeconomic structure in the shape of an onion dome. The egalitarianism of China's pre-reform past has made this economic imbalance especially glaring. As noted in Chapter 1, in the span of a few decades, China has moved from the ranks of the most economically equal countries in the world to a position among the most unequal. As economic privatization and marketization have progressed over the course of the post-Mao period, the distribution of wealth has become only more unbalanced.

For groups enjoying a position at or near the top of the onion dome—namely, private enterprise owners and professionals—liberal democratic reform has not been attractive. As detailed in Chapters 2 and 3, wealthy and even self-perceived "middle class" individuals have had little sense of common interests or values with the poor and, indeed, in some cases have openly expressed disdain for them. This, in turn, has undercut the potential material and ideal desires of wealthy and "middle class" individuals to promote the political empowerment of the masses or to embrace the principle of majority rule. For private enterprise owners, this tendency has been heightened by the possibility that working-class enfranchisement would undermine the ability of business owners to pay low wages and work their employees relentlessly. Given the still socialist expectations and values of most rank-and-file workers (reviewed in Chapters 4 and 5), such concerns have been well founded.

For groups in the vast lower tier of China's onion dome (namely, rank-and-file state and private sector workers, and farmers), one might expect that majority rule would hold an appeal. However, the factors outlined above (and detailed in Chapters 4, 5, and 6) have engendered incentives to tolerate the political status quo. Farmers and private sector workers generally have experienced upward socioeconomic mobility and have tended to feel that their material advance has been facilitated by the central party-state. In addition, the groups and individuals in China's lower economic tier have lacked a sense of common cause and interests. State sector workers have continued to enjoy an elevated political position and have continued to receive benefits from the party-state that have been unavailable to other poor individuals. These divisions have been heightened by party-state policies that have distinguished between rural and urban *hukou* holders, privileging the latter over the former. As discussed in Chapters 4 and 5, the overall result has been that unskilled laborers with urban and rural residential registrations have tended to view each other as competitors, often with mutual disdain. Consequently, they have had little inclination to press for their common political enfranchisement. Finally, the basic needs of China's poor have been protected by government-provided safety nets—something that those in the lower tier of China's socioeconomic structure have tended to believe is both right and just. Thus, the potential interest of the poor in pressing for systemic political change has been undermined.

Fourth, as the post-Mao period has progressed, central authorities have been able to take credit for widening opportunities for popular input and oversight within the existing political system. As detailed in Chapters 2 and 6, village elections, initiated in the late 1980s, have given farmers the opportunity and power to elect and remove local leaders, and successful businesspeople have been able to become local officials. Meanwhile, the rights to petition and to seek legal adjudication have given citizens greater means to voice their grievances. Inasmuch as these mechanisms have been perceived by citizens as a successful central effort to reduce local corruption and abuse, citizens have had decreased reason to desire systemic political change.

These realities have been reflected in the political attitudes and behavior of the Chinese public in the post-Mao era. At an aggregate level, remarkable support for the CCP-led political system has been found in countless national public opinion polls. Further, even citizens that have engaged in collective action to remedy their troubles have exhibited faith in the central regime and scant desire for a more liberal democratic national political structure.

THE POLITICAL EFFECTS OF ECONOMIC LIBERALIZATION
IN POST-SOCIALIST STATES

A look at other countries with histories of statist economic controls, late opening to the global capitalist system, and socialist labor and welfare provisions illuminates how these factors more generally may shape popular political cal views of democracy and authoritarianism in the aftermath of neoliberal economic reform. The cases of Vietnam and Russia are particularly relevant and instructive. Like China, these countries have legacies of "homegrown" (rather than externally imposed) socialism, including extensive state economic controls and state-provided social welfare benefits and protections. Each also opened its economy to the global capitalist system relatively late. In all three states, socioeconomic groups that benefited from socialist economic policies prior to economic liberalization have maintained a commitment to government-backed labor protections and benefits and have expressed skepticism about free-market capitalism.

Beyond these similarities, neoliberal economic reform in China and Vietnam has been accompanied by relatively strong support for the political status quo—despite the fact that the government has remained authoritarian. In Russia in the 1990s, in contrast, the transition to free-market capitalism was coupled with deep political dissatisfaction, even though the governmental system became markedly more democratic. Interestingly, popular political satisfaction in Russia has risen in the first decade of the 2000s—at the same time that the ruling regime has become more authoritarian. Although the explanation for these variations surely is complex, a comparison of these cases reveals some clear patterns in terms of economic mobility, socioeconomic polarization, material dependence on the state, and political options.

Vietnam

Vietnam is most similar to China in terms of its developmental trajectory. In the past few decades, both China and Vietnam have liberalized their previously socialist economies, and in both cases the authoritarian ruling party has attempted to provide basic socioeconomic protections. Meanwhile, national-level political change has been minimal. As in China, in Vietnam these contextual developments have coincided with upward socioeconomic mobility, growing socioeconomic inequality, key groups' economic dependence on the state, and greater political opportunities to work within the existing governmental system. At the same time, similar to the Chinese, Vietnam's citizens have displayed a continued commitment to socialist economic values, remarkably high levels of support for the still-authoritarian national government, and little interest in pursuing systemic regime change.

Although Vietnam's socialist economic period was much shorter and less encompassing than that in China, its reform-era experience has been quite similar.[1] As in China, Vietnam's liberal economic reforms began in agriculture, with the establishment in the late 1970s and early 1980s of a contract system allowing peasants to lease government-owned land for fifteen-year terms.[2] In addition, after meeting state-mandated crop requirements, rural residents were given the freedom to determine land use and to sell their products on the open market. In 1986, Vietnam's leaders embarked on a policy of *doi moi* (renovation) designed to gradually but more generally liberalize the economy. As in China, this entailed opening the economy to foreign investment, allowing the establishment of private businesses, and privatizing many state-owned enterprises (SOEs). In all of these respects, but especially with regard to SOE reform, both China and Vietnam moved slowly. Through the early 1990s, SOE workers experienced little change in their employment conditions. Subsequently, the number of SOEs was roughly halved, and a significant number of SOE workers were retrenched.[3]

To an even greater extent than in China, Vietnam's reform-era political leadership has retained key state controls over the economy. Unlike China, in Vietnam most foreign investment has been channeled into SOEs through joint-owned enterprises. As a result, the state sector's contribution to Vietnam's GDP has risen—from 33 percent in 1990 to 40 percent in 2005.[4] Further, in contrast to China, the state sector in Vietnam has been more vibrant than the private sector.[5] Thus, whereas state enterprises in China have had to demand more of their employees in order to compete with prosperous private businesses, in Vietnam, state-owned enterprises have been able to "set the bar" for employment practices.

In addition, Vietnam's Communist Party leaders have evidenced a stronger commitment to socialist values and policies than has been the case in reform-era China.[6] Vietnam's party-state has backed labor protections and raised minimum wages in both the state and private sectors and has supported workers who have protested or gone on strike. Unlike in China, where the leaders of collective labor actions typically have received harsh punishment at the hands of both local and central authorities, Vietnamese officials have not only declined to repress protest leaders but have actively supported aggrieved workers. In one notable example in late 2005, Vietnamese Communist Party (VCP) elites announced that the minimum wage in foreign-invested enterprises would rise by roughly 40 percent. When many firms announced their desire to defer the wage increases for a few months, tens of thousands of workers went on wildcat strikes at scores of foreign-invested enterprises.[7] Although the strikes technically were illegal (because they had not been sanctioned by Vietnam's official labor union), central leaders did not stop them. Instead, government authorities supported the workers' demands and forced the companies to increase wages. This chain of events was not an aberration; similar occurrences transpired throughout the late 1990s and first decade of the twenty-first century.[8] As a 2002 report by the *Economist* magazine's pro-business Economist Intelligence Unit lamented, "labour rights sentiments in Vietnam [have been] backed by a conciliation system and a judiciary sympathetic to labor demands."[9] Similarly, the manager of a Taiwanese factory complained in the first decade of the millennium that "in Vietnam [the government's] protection of labour rights is too stringent."[10]

These contextual developments have coincided with upward socioeconomic mobility for the vast majority of the population.[11] Although Vietnam's reform-era economic performance has not matched China's, it still has been impressive. Between 1986 and 1990, Vietnam's economy grew by an average of nearly 4 percent annually, and from 1991 to 2007 it rose by an average of roughly 8 percent each year.[12] Inflation has been high, but poverty was roughly halved over the course of the 1990s.[13] In addition, compared to China, few Vietnamese have experienced a material decline. Only about 1.5 percent of the Vietnam's total population has suffered SOE layoffs.[14] Further, for unskilled workers in both the state and private sectors, wages have risen and working conditions have been fairly good. Unlike in China, wages generally have been paid in full and on time, and the typical work week has been 48 hours within six days, with an "absolute maximum" of 12 hours of overtime.[15] In addition, Vietnam's unskilled private sector workers generally have not been subject to the harsh workplace discipline that has been characteristic in China.[16]

In terms of material inequality, like China, Vietnam's distribution of wealth has become more polarized as a result of economic liberalization. Even so, the change in Vietnam has not been as dramatic as it has been in China. On the eve of Vietnam's economic reforms, its Gini coefficient stood at 0.24—a figure somewhat higher than that of Mao-era China. By the mid-1990s Vietnam's level of inequality had risen to about 0.35, and since then, it has remained roughly the same.[17] Thus, although its level of material polarization is much higher than it was before economic reform, as of 2008 it was significantly lower than that in China and the United States. As in China, those at the top of Vietnam's socioeconomic hierarchy have prospered largely through their connections with the party-state. Thus, they have had little incentive to challenge it. Further, as a wealthy minority sitting atop an economic pyramid wherein a majority of the population is relatively poor, those at the top have had little reason to embrace democracy. Meanwhile, the dissatisfaction of those at the bottom of the socioeconomic structure has been undermined by socialist policies that attend to their basic needs and by improved living conditions.

The economic dependence of the Vietnamese on the party-state is quite similar to that of the Chinese. Despite a general increase in material independence for most groups in the reform era, two key Vietnamese sectors have depended on the regime for their livelihood: state-owned enterprise workers and business elites. State sector workers have continued to receive socioeconomic benefits that are unavailable to non-state workers. In addition, wages for rank-and-file state sector workers have tended to be substantially higher than those of rank-and file-private sector workers.[18] As in China, the security and benefits of government employment have remained attractive to unskilled workers in reform-era Vietnam.[19] Thus, rather than seeking to distance themselves from the party-state, common citizens have displayed the desire to be more closely connected with it.

Unlike in China, the most prosperous businesspeople in Vietnam manage state-owned enterprises. However, like China, Vietnam's business elite has close ties to the party-state. To an even greater extent than in China, Vietnam's ruling regime has continued to control key economic resources. As political scientist Martin Gainsborough reports, "to succeed in business, [Vietnamese] companies are still very reliant on the state for licenses, contracts, access to capital and land, and very often, protection." Not surprisingly, Gainsborough adds, "many of [Vietnam's] new entrepreneurs have emerged from within the existing system, are currently serving or former officials, or are the children of the political elite."[20] Similarly, a researcher at the Hanoi Institute of Sociology states that "most of the rich work for the government. With power and access, you can change your life. Without them, you can't get rich."[21] As in China, these circumstances have given Vietnam's successful businesspeople strong reasons to support the political status quo.

In terms of political options, Vietnamese citizens in the reform period generally have been able to express and address their grievances within the existing system. Since 2001, individuals who are not members of the ruling Vietnamese Communist Party (VCP) have been able to nominate themselves as candidates for direct National Assembly elections. Research suggests that VCP and non-VCP candidates have received equal coverage in the official media and have received balanced treatment in government-sponsored public meetings with their electoral constituencies prior to an election.[22] In the two most recent National Assembly elections (in 2002 and 2007), roughly 8 percent of successful National Assembly candidates were not affiliated with the VCP, although only a tiny handful of them were self-nominated.[23] At the same time, compared to the Chinese, Vietnam's citizens have had more freedom to voice collective concerns and undertake collective actions without fear of punishment. To the extent that the regime has been open and responsive to the demands of the public, the citizenry has had little incentive to press for systemic change.

This configuration of factors is reflected in the political attitudes and behavior of the Vietnamese public. As in China, business elites in Vietnam express satisfaction with the country's political leadership. In a late 1990s survey, political scientist Thomas Heberer asked this group if they believed that their interests were "adequately taken into account in the business policies of the local government"; about 80 percent responded "yes" or "to some extent," and only 20 percent said "no."[24] Because most businesspeople either have close ties to government representatives or are themselves political officials, this finding is not surprising.

As in China, workers and peasants in Vietnam have engaged in collective protest actions in the reform era—especially since the early 1990s. Unfortunately, research on the demands and political views of these disgruntled individuals is scarce. Yet it appears that, as in China, rural protests have arisen when peasants have believed that land has been unfairly allocated or expropriated by corrupt local leaders. In Vietnam, rural unrest also has been connected with ethnic conflict.[25] However, Gainsborough argues that there is nothing to indicate that Vietnam's peasants have "an organization with a common institutional base" or a "coherent critique of party rule."[26] In urban areas, worker protests have focused on higher wages and improved working conditions. As noted above, these disgruntled individuals have had good reason to view the central state as their protector and savior, rather than their antagonist.

National public opinion surveys in reform-era Vietnam have uncovered a high level of support for the political status quo—in fact, more so than has been the case in China. When asked in the World Values Survey of 2001 to assess "how the political system is going" on a scale of 1 to 10 (with 10 representing "very good"), more than 81 percent of respondents answered with ratings between 8 and 10. When asked about Vietnam's political institutions, nearly 98 percent reported "a great deal" or "quite a lot" of confidence in the national government, about 97 percent expressed a similar degree of confidence in the National Assembly, roughly 92 percent had faith in political parties, and more than 79 percent reported confidence in the civil service. The corresponding figures in China were 97 percent (national government), 95 percent (National People's Congress), 93 percent (parties), and 66 percent (civil service) (see illustration on page 173). Similarly, more than 91 percent of Vietnamese expressed the belief that the "country is run for all the people." In China, roughly 84 percent of respondents espoused this view.

Overall, like China, there is little to suggest that capitalist economic development in Vietnam has engendered increased strain between society and the authoritarian governing regime. To the contrary, public support for the political status quo in reform-era China and Vietnam has been as high, or higher, than in any country in the world—including the most democratic and prosperous. Further, the relatively high level of popular political satisfaction in Vietnam in comparison with China correlates with the fact that in Vietnam's reform era, economic dependence on the party-state has been relatively high, and the party-state's commitment to socialist values and policies has been relatively strong. These factors seem important in explaining why public support for the existing political system is higher in Vietnam than in China—despite the fact that economic growth has been much more impressive in China than it has in Vietnam.

Russia

As in China and Vietnam, Russian citizens have displayed a strong commitment to socialist economic values in the country's "post-socialist" reform era.[27] Unlike in China and Vietnam, the Russian populace has expressed great disillusionment with the political regime that ushered in neoliberal economic reform. The basic reason is that, for most Russian citizens, economic liberalization coincided with downward socioeconomic mobility, rising material inequality, and severed economic ties to the state.

In the late 1980s, Communist Party General Secretary Mikhail Gorbachev attempted to dismantle Russia's planned economy and implement reforms like those promoted in China. Although foreign trade was opened, changes in agriculture and the state sector were minimal. It was not until Russian Federation President Boris Yeltsin's "shock therapy" of 1992 that neoliberal economic reforms became effective. The changes were far more extensive and rapid than was the case in either China or Vietnam: Price controls were lifted, substantial state sector privatization began, and the Russian ruble generally was allowed to float. Simultaneously, Russia's political system largely was democratized.[28]

Although most Russians rejoiced at the end of authoritarian communist rule, their enthusiasm for the new and more democratic system quickly waned. In the 1990s, along with economic and political liberalization, Russia experienced a severe economic decline. From 1992 to 1999, Russia's GDP shrank, contracting by 12 percent in 1994 alone.[29] Simultaneously, inflation skyrocketed. Between 1992 and 1993, real wages dropped, fluctuating between 50 and 75 percent of 1990 levels. Meanwhile, unemployment became widespread. In 1992, nearly 2 percent of Russia's workers were dismissed from their jobs.[30] Although some were reemployed in the private sector, most were unable to find new work. Further, many who remained employed in the state sector were given only part-time work or were forced to take extended leave with reduced or delayed pay.[31] Consequently, whereas less than 2 percent of the population fell below the poverty line on the eve of Russia's economic reforms, by the mid-1990s 40 percent of the citizenry was impoverished and at least another 10 percent had incomes only marginally above the poverty line.[32]

Public support for Russia's new democratic government also was negatively influenced by growing levels of socioeconomic inequality. Although most of the population experienced downward socioeconomic mobility in the 1990s, a small group of politically connected individuals became fantastically wealthy. This development is reflected in Russia's Gini coefficient, which rose from an average of about 0.27 in the pre-reform period to roughly 0.40 in 2000.[33]

In terms of material reliance on the government, aside from public pensions, Yeltsin's "shock therapy" severed the Russian working public's material ties to the state. To an even greater degree than in China and Vietnam, in Russia the loss of these state-provided benefits and guarantees was both sudden and widespread. Although in pre-reform China and Vietnam only a small minority of citizens enjoyed secure and benefit-rich employment in SOEs, in

Russia this was true of roughly 95 percent of the public. With economic reform, virtually the entire populace was left on its own to eke out a livelihood. Because the experience of communism had instilled in the Russian public a feeling of entitlement to government-assured socioeconomic security, this abrupt disappearance of government-assured sustenance coincided with disillusionment with the democratic ruling regime that presided over Russia's early reform period and nostalgia for the communist past.

As discussed in Chapter 1, public opinion polls conducted in the 1990s uncovered low levels of confidence in Russia's "democratic" postcommunist political institutions, positive views of communism, and increasing openness to authoritarian rule. Buttressing the findings of Richard Rose, William Mishler, and Neil Munro, the 1999 World Values Survey found that more than 90 percent of respondents reported "not very much" or "no" confidence in the parliament (the Duma), and 62.2 percent and 63.8 percent expressed similarly dismal views of the civil service and justice system, respectively (see illustration on page 173). As noted earlier, World Values Surveys undertaken around the same time in relatively "authoritarian" China and Vietnam show roughly the same percentage of citizens expressing "a great deal" or "quite a lot" of confidence in national government institutions.[34] Similarly, in political scientist Bruce Gilley's late 1990s/early 2000s study of levels of state legitimacy in seventy-two countries, "democratic" Russia ranked last with a score of 2.4 out of 10, whereas "authoritarian" China ranked thirteenth with a score of 6.2.[35] Indicating nostalgia for Russia's socialist past, in both the 1995 and the 1999 Russian World Values Surveys, a significant plurality (roughly 26 to 28 percent) of respondents stated that they would vote for the Communist Party as their first choice in elections. No other party came close in terms of expressed support.[36] Further, whereas in 1991, 51 percent of Russians reported that they would prefer a democratic form of government over "a leader with a strong hand," in 2002, only 21 percent gave this response.

In the first decade of the 2000s, Russia has experienced growing authoritarianism in the political system, a reassertion of state economic controls, and economic recovery. Between 2000 and 2006, the nonprofit, pro-democracy organization Freedom House dropped Russia's rating on political rights by two points, indicating that Russia's political system had moved from being "partly free" to "not free."[37] Simultaneously, Russia's GDP resumed positive growth. As of this writing, these economic gains have enabled per capita incomes to surpass their pre-reform levels for the first time since 1991.[38] These

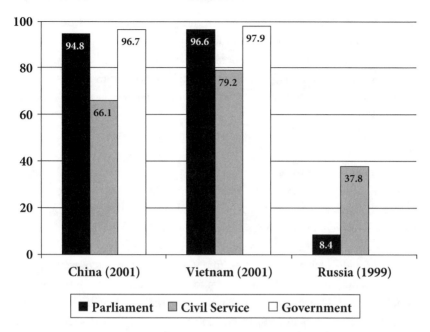

Percentage of citizens reporting "a great deal" or "quite a lot" of confidence in the "Parliament," the "Civil Service," and "Government." Source: World Values Survey, http://www.worldvalues survey.org/.

economic improvements have coincided with the government's renationalization of many state assets and renewed payment of pensions and state salaries.

At the same time, the public has displayed extremely high levels of support for Russia's more authoritarian political leadership. Although Vladimir Putin (Russia's president from 2000–2008) is seen as the architect of Russia's authoritarian regression, in a variety of national Russian public opinion surveys in the middle part of the first decade of the 2000s, 75 to 80 percent of respondents expressed confidence in his governance.[39] Similarly, in 2006, 61 percent of Russians stated that they preferred "a leader with a strong hand."[40]

Overall, in Russia, China, and Vietnam one finds that popular views of the present are colored by the citizenry's experience of communism and reform. Although Russian, Chinese, and Vietnamese citizens have recognized the limitations of the prior planned economy, most have continued to support government-provided benefits and guarantees. At the same time, whereas the upward economic mobility experienced by most Chinese and Vietnamese citizens has bred support for the Communist Party–led political system that has facilitated the public's relative material prosperity, the downward economic mobility suffered by a substantial portion of Russia's citizenry in the 1990s bred skepticism for the democratic institutions that ushered in Russia's economic downturn and openness toward the authoritarian leadership that has re-asserted state controls over the economy and overseen Russia's relative economic improvement.

Patterns

This comparative survey uncovers some apparent patterns in the relationship between economic liberalization and popular political attitudes in countries with a socialist economic past. First, individuals and groups that benefited from socialist economic policies typically retain socialist values in the aftermath of economic liberalization. Given this, governments that have continued to provide socioeconomic benefits and protections (such as in China, Vietnam, and post-Yeltsin Russia) seem to be rewarded with higher levels of popular trust and legitimacy. When added to the fact that these countries have entered the global capitalist system relatively late, statist social welfare policies have been particularly important in helping to shield rank-and-file workers and farmers from the harmful effects of extreme labor competition and capital mobility.

Second, public attitudes toward the post-reform governing regime are shaped by the perceived economic results of neoliberal change. Where economic liberalization has coincided with economic growth and upward socioeconomic mobility (as in China and Vietnam), the populace has displayed satisfaction with the political status quo. When the opposite has occurred (as in 1990s Russia), political dissatisfaction has been rife. Importantly, these patterns seem to hold regardless of whether or not the post-reform political system is authoritarian or democratic. When economic liberalization coincides with political liberalization but also economic decline (as in 1990s Russia), even democratic regimes may have low legitimacy. When economic liberalization is coupled with authoritarian rule and economic improvement (as in China, Vietnam, and post-2000 Russia), faith in an authoritarian regime can be high. Popular support is magnified when the government also provides socioeconomic protections and guarantees (as in China, and even more so in Vietnam). More broadly, the cases of China and Vietnam suggest that in countries with socialist economic legacies, capitalist economic growth may not necessarily lead to public pressures for democratic political change.

THE POLITICAL EFFECTS OF CAPITALIST ECONOMIC GROWTH IN AUTHORITARIAN STATE-LED LATE INDUSTRIALIZERS

China's experience also buttresses Eva Bellin's argument that the combination of state-led development and late industrialization may thwart the expected relationship between capitalist economic growth and public pressures for democracy. When the state controls key economic resources, individuals and groups that depend on the state for their material livelihood have an interest in perpetuating the political status quo—even when it is illiberal and undemocratic. In China in the reform era, this has been particularly true of private entrepreneurs and state sector workers. As Bellin notes, it also has been the case in many other state-led late developers with authoritarian political regimes. Close connections with the ruling regime engendered little enthusiasm for democracy among business owners in Tunisia from the 1960s through the 1990s; Syria from the 1970s through the present; Brazil from the mid-1960s through the mid-1980s; Singapore from the 1960s through the present; Indonesia from the 1950s through the 1990s; and South Korea between the 1960s and the early 1980s. Material dependence on the state coincided with support for authoritarian rule by organized labor in Tunisia from the 1960s through the 1990s; Mexico from the 1940s through the late 1990s; Venezuela from the late 1940s to the late 1980s; and Peru between the mid-1940s and late 1980s.[41] Historically, socioeconomic sectors have pressed for democratic political change only when they have been economically independent of the state. Significant examples include private capital holders in England in the late 1700s and early 1800s; private capital holders in South Korea beginning in the mid-1980s; organized workers in Chile in the late 1980s; organized workers in Zambia in the 1980s; organized workers and professionals in South Korea between the 1960s and 1980s; and private capital holders and professionals in Taiwan from the 1950s through the 1990s.

The political consequences of material dependence on the state are magnified in countries entering the global capitalist system relatively late. As time has passed, countries embarking on industrialization have been subject to increased competition and capital mobility. The result is that economic growth has tended to exacerbate economic inequality. In late industrializers where there is a wide gap between the rich and the poor and only a small "middle class," upper-level socioeconomic sectors have had reason to fear majority rule. In post-socialist states where rank-and-file workers retain a commitment to socialist economic values, this has been particularly true. Although growing economic polarization might be expected to propel lower-level socioeconomic sectors to press for democratic political change, this potential has been undermined when the authoritarian state has provided benefits and protections that mitigate the potential harmful effects of market forces. In addition, when authoritarian regimes have provided socioeconomic protections and benefits to some lower-level socioeconomic strata (such as state sector workers in China), these relatively advantaged groups have shown little sense of common cause with other low-income sectors and scant interest in regime change.

LIKELY SOURCES OF ATTITUDINAL CHANGE IN CHINA

Although the confluence of state-led development, late industrialization, and socialist legacies helps to explain popular support for CCP rule in reform-era China, it is important to recognize that the present constellation of factors is not set in stone. In the coming years, the Chinese public may indeed turn against the existing political system. The factor that is most certain to change is the public's memory of China's socialist economy prior to neoliberal reform. As of this writing, individuals who are under thirty years of age have had no direct experience of the Maoist economic system. They constitute slightly more than 43 percent of the total population but less than 20 percent of the adult population.[42] By 2050, they will make up virtually the entire population. As this demographic shift transpires, the effect of China's socialist legacies on the political attitudes and behavior of the public will fade and eventually disappear. When the quasi-capitalist system of the reform era becomes the only lived experience of China's citizenry, the populace will no longer judge the performance of the current economic system against that of China's Maoist past. The public also will be less likely to expect the socioeconomic security and benefits that the ruling regime offered in the pre-reform period.

The precise impact of this generational change on the political attitudes and behavior of the Chinese populace is difficult to predict. Surveys conducted by Jie Chen and Wenfang Tang in the late 1990s found that as the age of the respondent declined, support for the ruling regime was lower and openness to liberalization and democratization was higher.[43] Researchers also have found a significantly higher level of nationalism among young people. As seen in Chinese students' emotional opposition to criticism of China's Tibet policy in conjunction with the 2008 Beijing Olympics, this nationalism often has coincided with a distrust of the West and a belief that powerful countries (particularly the United States) press China to liberalize its political system only in order to weaken China's international reputation and strength.

Apart from the demographic changes that are sure to diminish popular memories of China's Maoist past, three possible developments might reduce the public's current acceptance of China's existing political system. First, an economic slowdown (such as that which began in late 2008) may diminish popular support for continued CCP rule. In 2007, China's economic statistics could not have been more phenomenal: real annual GDP growth was a staggering 11.4 percent, industrial production rose by 18 percent, urban real per capita income grew by 12.2 percent, and rural real per capita income climbed by 9.5 percent.[44] Among migrant workers, the unskilled labor shortages that appeared in southeastern China in the middle part of the first decade of the 2000s led to wage increases of 4.9 percent in 2005, 9.8 percent in 2006, and an estimated 20 percent in 2007.[45] Yet in the second half of 2008, ominous signs of downturn appeared. By the end of 2008, real GDP growth had fallen to 6.8 percent, and industrial production growth had dropped to 5.7 percent.[46] With the United States—the major importer of Chinese goods—falling deeper into recession in early 2009, experts predicted 6 percent GDP growth in China in 2009, with the possibility of growth as low as 4 percent.[47] Yet by late 2009, China's economy had picked up steam, and was estimated by the Asian Development Bank to close the year with an impressive 8.2 percent growth rate— just above the 8 percent rate that is portrayed by Chinese officials as the minimum level required to prevent an increase in unemployment.[48]

If an economic downturn were to cause Chinese citizens to experience a decline in their material conditions, their tolerance of CCP rule might dissipate. Yet, the likelihood of such a development also depends on the actions taken by central leaders in the face of economic downturn. In 2008, CCP elites moved swiftly to prevent significant declines. Almost immediately after China's economy began to slide in late 2008, the regime passed a US$585 billion economic stimulus package that included fiscal spending and tax reductions and cut interest rates by a hefty 1.08 points. Though the gains reaped as a result of this package may prove to be short-lived, as of late 2009, the stimulus had been successful in helping to resuscitate China's economy. If China remains one of the few countries in the world to experience positive economic growth amidst a global economic recession, central CCP leaders may be expected to enjoy bolstered popular support.

A second variable that might make the public more likely to support systemic regime change would be an increase in the citizenry's economic independence from the state. Although most state sector workers and private entrepreneurs remain materially tied to the CCP as of this writing, their dependence has been diminishing over time. With the passage of the 2008 Labor Law, the protections and benefits once provided only to state sector workers formally have been extended to those in the private sector. Further, the *hukou* system that traditionally has privileged urban residents over ruralites continues to be weakened. As state sector workers become less politically privileged and more economically independent of the state, they will have less reason to support CCP rule. At the same time, the divisions among China's lower-level socioeconomic sectors that have inhibited a sense of common interest in mass political empowerment will recede. Similarly, the trend among China's successful private entrepreneurs has been toward greater distance from the ruling regime. Although most private entrepreneurs in the post-Mao period have prospered as a result of their political connections, in more recent years successful businesspeople have pursued tech-intensive and creative enterprises that do not substantially rely on governmental ties. As long as these more independent entrepreneurs experience upward economic mobility that is not thwarted by the state, they may tolerate the political status quo. Even so, they have little reason to actively support it. Finally, farmers and rank-and-file private sector workers with rural residence registration increasingly have experienced the severance of their last major economic tie to the state: their land. Should this trend continue, the basic safety net that has protected farmers and rural migrant workers from the vicissitudes of the free market will be gone. With it, their acceptance of CCP governance may disappear.

A third variable is China's level of domestic economic inequality. Should future economic development lead to a decline in material inequality in China such that the socioeconomic structure comes to resemble a diamond more than an onion dome, those at the top of the socioeconomic structure will be closer to the majority of the population in material terms and thus may have less reason to fear democratic change.[49] Similarly, should most who currently sit at the wide base of the onion dome become part of a large middle class, they will have less cause to cling to the existing authoritarian state for economic protection. Since the first decade of the twenty-first century, CCP elites have pursued policies designed to address China's growing inequality. As of late 2009, the effects have been minimal. Should China's leaders become more successful at reducing the polarization of wealth in the future, they may unwittingly undermine the forces that have led many to accept authoritarian rule.

Even if one or more of these factors shifts to the extent that large portions of the Chinese public ceases to accept continued CCP rule, a dramatic transition to liberal democracy should not be assumed. If the people themselves have any say in the matter, what is more likely to emerge is a form of social democracy that prioritizes economic and social security. And, as has been the case in post-socialist Russia, the Chinese public may be willing to support—or at least accept—a new authoritarian regime that attends to the public's ideal desires and material needs.

CLOSING THOUGHTS

In terms of the broader relationship between capitalist economic development and popular pressures for democracy, this book suggests that countries with a socialist economic past are subject to distinct attitudinal features that may confound prevalent assumptions that economic liberalization and growth lead to strain between an authoritarian regime and the society that it governs. When coupled with state-led development policies and market forces associated with late immersion in the global capitalist system that render key groups both vulnerable and dependent on the state, authoritarian political rule in post-socialist states may be much more resilient than many have imagined.

At the same time, these findings underscore the idea that the reform process is a sequenced one and that succeeding phases of reform may support, at different moments, different political relationships. In addition, it should be remembered that a regime's success in co-opting the population in one phase does not preclude quite different outcomes in a later phase. Thus, although at present, socialist legacies, state-led development policies, and market forces associated with late industrialization have enabled the CCP to enjoy substantial popular acceptance, these seemingly "fixed, fast-frozen relations" may prove to be both transitory and fragile.[50]

NOTES

Chapter 1

1. I use quotation marks here to denote that I am using the term "class" loosely, in reference to groups at different levels of material prosperity. As used here, the term is not meant to imply class consciousness or solidarity, common relations to the means of production, or a common occupation.

2. Since the Maoist era, all Chinese citizens have held an official household registration card (*hukou*) that designates one's residential status as urban or rural.

3. Regarding the protests of 1989, see Walder and Gong, "Workers in the Tiananmen Protests." For the Democracy Wall movement of 1978–80, see Wei Jingsheng's famous call for "The Fifth Modernization." In this piece, Wei calls for a form of social democracy wherein "the laboring masses" hold political power, and the people have the right to "choose their own representatives to work according to their will and in their interests." Expressing commitment to socialist economic values, Wei states that "people . . . have worked as hard as they could and actually produced much wealth. But where has all the wealth gone? [Without democracy,] it can never get into the hands of the laboring people" (Wei Jingsheng, "Fifth Modernization"). The university-based protests of 1986–87 emphasized political and intellectual freedom, with less emphasis on social democratic economic rights and protections. [For an analysis of the views of the most prominent leader of these protests, see Williams, "Fang Lizhi's Expanding Universe."]

4. This vulnerability became particularly apparent in the global economic crisis that was precipitated by the U.S. financial meltdown in the fall of 2008. See Chapters 5 and 7 for discussion of the effects of this crisis on China's unskilled laborers.

5. The 0.496 figure is reported in the *2007 CASS Blue Book*. The 0.561 figure comes from a Chinese People's University [*Renmin Daxue*] study. Both are cited in Fewsmith, "Assessing Social Stability," 9.

6. CIA World Fact Book, "Brazil: Economy," https://www.cia.gov/library/publica tions/the-world-factbook/geos/br.html, and "United States: Economy," https://www .cia.gov/library/publications/the-world-factbook/geos/us.html (accessed October 4, 2009).

7. Fewsmith, "Assessing Social Stability," 9.

8. *Zhongguo tongji nianjian* [China Statistical Yearbook] (2007). See also Li S., "Shuji xianshi woguo zhongchan jieceng zhan jiuye renkou 11%," cited in An Chen, "Why Does Capitalism Fail," 154. In terms of the actual number or percentage of "middle class" citizens in China, researchers have not reached a consensus. If one looks at consumption, roughly 35 percent of Chinese citizens have electronic goods such as a television, refrigerator, washing machine, air conditioner, or microwave. If the require-ment is a "white collar" profession, then just under 16 percent of the citizenry may be considered "middle class." If one includes "individual industrial or commercial work-ers" (some of whom may be viewed as "white collar" workers), this percentage rises to 27 percent. When these various criteria are combined, the proportion of "middle class" individuals shrinks dramatically, to about 6 percent of the population (aged sixteen to seventy). See Fewsmith, "Political Implications," 3–4.

9. *Zhongguo tongji nianjian* [China Statistical Yearbook] (2007). The exchange rate in June 2007 was roughly 7.6:1, so RMB$16,004 was equivalent to approximately US$2,106.

10. Wang Junxiu, *2007 CASS Blue Book*, as cited in Fewsmith, "Assessing Social Stability," 6.

11. Peilin Li, Guangjin Chen, and Wei Li, "Report on the Situation of Social Har-mony and Stability of China in 2006," 21. Two other surveys, conducted in 2001 and 2004, show a higher percentage of citizens who identify themselves as "middle class" than was found in the 2006 study by Peilin Li, Guangjin Chen, and Wei Li. However, it is impossible to compare the results of these two surveys, or with Peilin Li, Guangjin Chen, and Wei Li's 2002 and 2006 surveys, as their parameters (in terms of age, oc-cupational status, and place of residence) varied dramatically. For details on the 2001 and 2004 surveys, see Fewsmith, "Political Implications," 3–4.

12. Data on the extent and impact of these government-provided benefits can be found in Appleton et al., "Labour Retrenchment," 32–34. Further anecdotal evidence can be found in Guiheux, "Promotion of a New Calculating Chinese Subject."

13. As is discussed in Chapter 6, the abolition of rural taxes also has had a nega-tive impact, resulting in a decline in public services in the countryside.

14. Skocpol, *States and Social Revolutions*.

15. See O'Donnell and Schmitter, *Transitions from Authoritarian Rule*.

16. For a recent review of the concept of "political opportunity structures," see Meyer, "Protest and Political Opportunities."

17. Wright, "China Democracy Party."

18. Marquand, "Zhao Remembered"; Pan, "Thousands Mourn"; and Kahn, "China's Fear of Ghosts."

19. Marquand, "After Dark, Remembering Zhao."

20. Kahn, "Cautiously, China Honors Leader"; Jiangtao Shi, "Select Few Flout News Blackout"; Huang, "Official Praise"; and Irene Wang, "Public Praise." The same is true of the June 2005 funeral for Zhao's top aide. See Rui and Cheung, "State Media Silent."

21. Irene Wang, "Incidents of Social Unrest." Since 2006, the Chinese government has not publicized statistics on unrest.

22. In 2006, the number of mass incidents reportedly declined by 16.5 percent—the first such decrease in thirteen years.

23. As reported by Ching Kwan Lee, in 2003, 3 million individuals participated in 58,000 "mass disturbances." Among the participants, the largest group (1.66 million, or 46.9 percent) were laid-off, retired, and active workers (Ching Kwan Lee, *Against the Law*, 5). Among the more than 37,000 workers who participated in protests in Fujian from 2000–2002, 49 percent were laid-off workers (i.e., still maintained a connection with their firm), 33 percent had been fired, and 4 percent were retired (Chung, Lai, and Xia, "Mounting Challenges," 7 n19). See also Tanner, "China Rethinks Unrest," 136.

24. Ching Kwan Lee, *Against the Law*, 112.

25. Ibid., 200, citing Thireau and Hua, "Moral Universe."

26. Chung, Lai, and Xia estimate that in 2000 roughly half of the participants in "mass disturbances" were rural residents (Chung, Lai, and Xia, "Mounting Challenges," 7 n17).

27. O'Brien and Li, *Rightful Resistance*. See also Bernstein and Lu, *Taxation Without Representation*, 139–40.

28. O'Brien and Li, *Rightful Resistance*, 122.

29. Ibid.

30. To be sure, one may raise questions regarding the reliability of these survey responses. Most obviously, it is possible that respondents' answers reflect a fear of punishment should a "wrong" response be provided. However, studies find virtually no correlation between a respondent's stated fear of political persecution and his or her reported level of regime support (Jie Chen, *Popular Political Support*, 35–36; and Tianjian Shi, "Cultural Values and Political Trust," 405–7). Alternatively, respondents' stated support for the existing political system may be thought to reflect indoctrination via the officially controlled media. Yet, research shows that exposure to the domestic media in China actually has a negative effect on reported confidence in the government (Xueyi Chen and Tianjian Shi, "Media Effects on Political Confidence.")

31. Jie Chen, *Popular Political Support*, 29. Indeed, this is true despite the fact that most respondents gave the ruling regime only mediocre—and sometimes poor—marks on its handling of specific issues, such as corruption and inflation (Jie Chen, *Popular Political Support*, 28–29 and 48–52).

32. Tang, *Public Opinion*, 71.

33. Lianjiang Li, "Political Trust in Rural China."

34. Lianjiang Li, "Political Trust and Petitioning," 8.

35. East Asian Barometer 2002; and World Values Survey 2001.

36. World Values Survey 2001. In the United States, 37.8 percent of 2,000 WVS respondents expressed confidence in the government, and 38.1 percent expressed confidence in Congress.

37. World Public Opinion.org and the Program on International Policy Attitudes, "World Public Opinion on Governance and Democracy."

38. East Asian Barometer 2002; and World Values Survey 2001.

39. This law was amended in 1998.

40. Jie Chen, "Sociopolitical Attitudes of the Masses and Leaders," 447.

41. Josephine Ma, "Create a Uniform System."

42. O'Brien and Li, "Accommodating 'Democracy.'" See also Oi, "Realms of Freedom"; Tianjian Shi, "Village Committee Elections in China"; Xu Wang, "Mutual Empowerment," 1431–42; Howell, "Prospects for Village Self-Governance"; Kelliher, "Chinese Debate"; and O'Brien, "Implementing Political Reform."

43. O'Brien and Li, *Rightful Resistance*, 100.

44. Lianjiang Li and Kevin O'Brien, "Struggle over Village Elections," 140.

45. O'Brien and Li, *Rightful Resistance*, 108.

46. In urban areas, a 1990 Organic Law called for the election of Residents' Committees by residents of urban neighborhoods. In 2000, these bodies were told to transform into Community Residents' Committees, with Committee leaders directly nominated and elected by local residents. As of late 2003, only an estimated 10 percent of Community Residents' Committees had been elected via free and fair competitive elections (Jie Chen and Chunlong Lu, "Social Capital in Urban China," 423–24). I am not aware of any studies of the public response to these Committees.

47. Tang, *Public Opinion*, 104, referencing the 2000 World Values Survey.

48. World Values Survey 2007.

49. Tang, *Public Opinion*, 104, referencing the 1990–96 World Values Surveys and the 1995–95 Freedom House ratings.

50. Jie Chen and Chunlong Lu, "Social Capital," 431. See also Tang, *Public Opinion*, 114.

51. See, for example, Putnam, *Bowling Alone*; and Brehm and Rahn, "Individual-level Evidence."

52. Jie Chen and Chunlong Lu, "Social Capital," 431, citing Tang, *Public Opinion*, ch. 5.

53. Tang, *Public Opinion*, 114.

54. Jie Chen, *Popular Political Support*, 32.

55. Tang, *Public Opinion*, 72.

56. Ibid., 70.

57. Dowd, Carlson, and Shen, "Prospects for Democratization," 371.

58. World Values Survey 2007.

59. Tang, *Public Opinion*, 60–61.

60. World Values Survey 2000, Questions E036 and E067. At the same time, it should be noted that on questions asking respondents to value "egalitarianism" v. "competition" and "people should take more responsibility" v. "the government should take more responsibility," the responses were almost evenly mixed.

61. Han and Whyte, "Social Contours," 13.

62. Tang, *Public Opinion*, 75. As is elaborated in Chapter 4, it is important to emphasize that this adherence to socialist economic values does not mean that workers and other citizens wish to return to the state-planned economy of the past.

63. Jie Chen, *Popular Political Support*, 79.

64. Tang, *Public Opinion*, 78

65. Jie Chen, *Popular Political Support*, 93. Using a different measure, Tang finds that those of lower socioeconomic status appear to be more politically "obedient" than those of higher socioeconomic status (Tang, *Public Opinion*, 71).

66. Jie Chen, *Popular Political Support*, 93. Tang finds that "high earners" were more satisfied with the overall reforms of the post-Mao period. Interestingly, though, Tang's data also show that high income respondents are less politically "obedient" than those of lesser economic means (Tang, *Public Opinion*, 67, 72).

67. Jie Chen, *Popular Political Support*, 82. At the same time, Tang finds that men appear to be more negative than women regarding the "overall effect of reform" (Tang, *Public Opinion*, 67).

68. Jie Chen, *Popular Political Support*, 86–89. Chen notes that the lower support of college students may be more strongly explained by their age.

69. Dong and Shi, "Reconstruction of Local Power," 224.

70. Ibid.

71. Kellee Tsai, "Capitalists Without a Class."

72. See North and Weingast, "Constitutions and Commitment."

73. Kellee Tsai, "Capitalists Without a Class," 1150.

74. Dickson, *Red Capitalists in China.*

75. Kellee Tsai, *Back-Alley Banking*; Alpermann, "'Wrapped Up in Cotton Wool,'" 34; and Jianjun Zhang, "Marketization, Class Structure, and Democracy," 426–29.

76. Alpermann, "'Wrapped Up in Cotton Wool,'" 34; Jianjun Zhang, "Marketization, Class Structure, and Democracy," 426–29.

77. Alpermann, "'Wrapped Up in Cotton Wool,'" 60; and Jianjun Zhang, "Marketization, Class Structure, and Democracy," 426–29.

78. Jie Chen, *Popular Political Support*, 56–57.

79. Ibid., 92–93. Chen explains the rising support of the lower "classes" by pointing to the government's increased flow of resources to alleviate urban poverty in the mid-1990s. While similarly time-spanning surveys since the start of the new millennium do not exist, the support of more well-to-do Chinese citizens may well have increased since the time of Chen's surveys, as a result of the official inclusion of "advanced productive forces" (such as private entrepreneurs and skilled workers) in the party via the adoption of Jiang Zemin's theory of the "Three Represents" in 2002.

80. Lipset, "Some Social Requisites of Democracy."

81. For a recent, methodologically rigorous example, see Boix and Stokes, "Endogenous Democratization."

82. Burkhart and Lewis-Beck, "Comparative Democracy," 907.

83. Przeworski and Limongi, "Modernization," 158.

84. Boix and Stokes, "Endogenous Democratization," 544.

85. Bellin, "Contingent Democrats," 177.

86. Moore, *Social Origins of Dictatorship and Democracy*.

87. Boix and Stokes, "Endogenous Democratization," 539–40.

88. Rueschemeyer, Stephens, and Stephens, *Capitalist Development and Democracy*, 59.

89. Bellin, "Contingent Democrats," 186, 194.

90. Ibid.

91. See, for example, Rowen, "When Will the Chinese People Be Free?" 41; and Freidman, *Lexus and the Olive Tree*.

92. Kristof, "Tiananmen Victory," cited in Mann, *China Fantasy*, 49.

93. Rowen, "When Will the Chinese People Be Free?" 38.

94. Ibid., 39, citing Barro, "Determinants of Democracy."

95. Ibid., 39, citing Barro, "Rule of Law."

96. Clinton, *Between Hope and History*, 36.

97. Bush, "A Distinctly American Internationalism," cited in Mann, *China Fantasy*, 2.

98. Bush, cited in Mann, *China Fantasy*, 110.

99. "Blair Presses for China Democracy."

100. Mann, *China Fantasy*, 14.

101. Ibid., 110.

102. Nathan, "Authoritarian Resilience."

103. Minxin Pei, "How Will China Democratize?"

104. Kroeber, "Durable Communist Party."

105. Dickson, *Democratization in China and Taiwan.*

106. Kellee Tsai, *Capitalism Without Democracy.*

107. Bueno de Mesquita and Downs, "Development and Democracy"; Dickson, *Red Capitalists in China.*

108. Bueno de Mesquita and Downs, "Development and Democracy," 78, 84.

109. Ibid., 78.

110. Perry, "Studying Chinese Politics," 10.

111. Ibid., 9.

112. Ibid., 13.

113. Ibid.

114. Ibid.

115. Dickson, *Red Capitalists in China.*

116. Nathan, "Authoritarian Resilience"; and Yang, *Remaking the Chinese Leviathan.*

117. Saich, Review of Dali Yang, 539.

118. Yang, "State Capacity on the Rebound"; Ibid., 47.

119. Nathan, "Authoritarian Resilience."

120. Ibid., 16.

121. Ibid., 13.

122. Ibid., 13–15.

123. Ibid., 7.

124. Gilley, "Limits of Authoritarian Resilience," 23. See also Gilley, *China's Democratic Future.*

125. Liddle, "Indonesia," 70, cited in Gilley, "Limits of Authoritarian Resilience," 25.

126. Minxin Pei, *China's Trapped Transition,* 42.

127. Gerschenkron, *Economic Backwardness.*

128. Bellin, *Stalled Democracy,* 154.

129. Ibid., 153.

130. Bellin, "Contingent Democrats," 182.

131. Bellin, *Stalled Democracy,* 153.

132. Ibid., 144.

133. Bellin, "Contingent Democrats," 187.

134. Ibid., 186–87. See also Bellin, *Stalled Democracy,* 160–62. For an earlier formulation of this argument with regard to China, see Solinger, "Urban Entrepreneurs."

135. Jones, "Democratization, Civil Society," 159–60.

136. Bellin, "Contingent Democrats," 189–95.

137. Ibid., 183.

138. Ibid.

139. Ibid.

140. Ibid.

141. For a discussion of this development, see Pierson, *Hard Choices*.

142. Rose, Mishler, and Munro, *Russia Transformed*, 12.

143. Ibid., 169.

144. Ibid., 153.

145. Ibid.

146. Ibid., 132.

147. Ibid., 131.

148. Ibid., 132.

149. Howard, *Weakness of Civil Society*, 10, 29, 122.

150. Rose, Mishler, and Munro, *Russia Transformed*, 127.

151. Ibid., 129.

152. Ibid., 127.

153. Howard, *Weakness of Civil Society*, 140.

154. Kullberg and Zimmerman, "Liberal Elites, Socialist Masses," 324.

155. Ibid., 354.

156. Ibid., 324.

157. Fuller, "Socialism and the Transition in Eastern and Central Europe," 599.

158. Ibid.

159. Rose, Mishler, and Munro, *Russia Transformed*, 67.

160. Ibid., 137. Nineteen percent endorsed "pro-market" principles, and 40 percent eschewed all political labels.

161. For a discussion of the relationship between material and ideal interests, see Weber, *Sociology of World Religions*.

Chapter 2

1. In both official and colloquial language, private businesses with fewer than eight employees are referred to as "shops" (*shangdian*) or "stalls" (*tanzi*), and their owners are described as "individual entrepreneurs" (*getihu*). The owners of businesses with eight or more employees are referred to officially as "private entrepreneurs" (*siying qiyezhu*). See Wank, "Private Business," 59; and Kellee Tsai, "Capitalists Without a Class."

2. As of 1999, "individual entrepreneurs" made up 4.2 percent of China's population, and "private entrepreneurs" made up .6 percent of the population (Lu Xueyi, *Dangdai Zhongguo*, cited in Yongnian Zheng, "Party, Class, and Democracy," 232–34).

3. For a discussion of whether or not China's private entrepreneurs should be viewed as a "class," see Kellee Tsai, "Capitalists Without a Class."

4. L. Wei, "Wider Market Access," cited in Kellee Tsai, "Capitalists Without a Class," 1132.

5. According to Huang Mengfu (vice-chair of the National Committee of the Chinese People's Political Consultative Conference and chair of the All-China Federation of Industry and Commerce), domestic private business accounted for 49.7 percent of GDP in 2005 (Xiao Ma, "Private Firms Crucial"). According to the central government's economic blueprint for 2007, domestic private business generates one-third of China's GDP ("Across PRD," *China Daily* [Hong Kong edition], September 19, 2007; and Zhuang, "New Social Strata").

6. Xiao Ma, "Private Firms Crucial."

7. Haoting Liu, "Private Firms Propel Innovation."

8. State-owned enterprises are controlled by the central government, but collective enterprises are controlled by local governments. Zhang Houyi, Ming Zhili, and Liang Zhuanyun, *Zhongguo siying qiye fazhan baogao*, vol. 5.

9. Ibid.

10. Kroeber and Yao, "SOEs in Pictures," 39; and "Non-public Economy Blooming in China."

11. Qiang Li, as cited in Yongnian Zheng, "Party, Class and Democracy," 240. See also Hong, "Mapping the Evolution," 33.

12. For a seminal analysis of the private sector during the Maoist and early post-Mao eras, see Solinger, *Chinese Business Under Socialism*.

13. An Chen, "Why Does Capitalism Fail," 150.

14. Solinger, *Chinese Business Under Socialism*, 201.

15. Young, "Policy, Practice," 58; and Guiheux, "Political 'Participation.'"

16. "Constitution of the People's Republic of China," *People's Daily*, http://english.peopledaily.com.cn/constitution/constitution.html (accessed October 4, 2009).

17. Wank, *Commodifying Communism*, 191–92.

18. Young, "Policy, Practice," 59–60. See also Solinger, *Chinese Business Under Socialism*.

19. Solinger, *Chinese Business Under Socialism*, 203.

20. Hong, "Mapping the Evolution," 27–28.

21. Ibid., 28–29.

22. Dickson, "Dilemmas of Party Adaptation," 146.

23. Dickson, *Red Capitalists*, 38.

24. Ibid., 22, 96; Kellee Tsai, *Capitalism Without Democracy*, 3 n8. See also Wank, "Private Business," 55–71; and Pearson, *China's New Business Elite*.

25. Guiheux, "Political 'Participation.'"

190 NOTES TO CHAPTER 2

26. Dickson, "Dilemmas of Party Adaptation," 147. See also Wank, "Private Business."

27. Unger and Chan, "Inheritors of the Boom," 51.

28. Kellee Tsai, "Adaptive Informal Institutions," 130.

29. Dickson, "Dilemmas of Party Adaptation," 147.

30. Unger and Chan, "Inheritors of the Boom," 51.

31. "CPC Amends Constitution to Foster Private Sector."

32. Many "shareholding" enterprises are restructured state-owned enterprises.

33. Sisci, "Fiscal Democracy," 34; and Eva Cheng, "Public Sector."

34. Cai, *State and Laid-off Workers*; and Wank, "Private Business," 54, 62.

35. Hong, "Mapping the Evolution," 29.

36. Ibid., 29–30. For elaboration on the effects of "forced shareholding" on former public sector workers, see issues of the China Labour Bulletin (http://www.china-labour.org.hk/).

37. Hong, "Mapping the Evolution," 30.

38. In 2005, some areas of China—especially the southeast—experienced a tightening of the labor supply, and even some labor shortages. This situation persisted until the fall of 2008, when China's economic slowdown (precipitated by economic recession in the United States) led to a renewed surfeit of unskilled labor available to private entrepreneurs.

39. Hong, "Mapping the Evolution," 23–42.

40. See Han and Whyte, "Social Contours of Distributive Injustice."

41. Reed, review of Kellee Tsai, *Back-Alley Banking*, 552.

42. Shih, "Factions Matter," 3; and Kellee Tsai, *Capitalism Without Democracy*, 84.

43. See, for example, Dickson, *Red Capitalists*, 106.

44. Hong, "Mapping the Evolution," 31.

45. Kellee Tsai, *Capitalism Without Democracy*, 201.

46. Ibid.

47. Ibid., 202–9.

48. Dickson, "Integrating Wealth and Power," 834.

49. Dickson, *Red Capitalists* and "Integrating Wealth and Power."

50. See, for example, An Chen, "Why Does Capitalism Fail"; Dickson, *Red Capitalists*; and Hong, "Mapping the Evolution."

51. Kellee Tsai, *Capitalism Without Democracy*, 77.

52. Zhang Houyi and Liu Wenpu, *Zhongguo de siying jingji yu siying qiye zhu*, 408; and Zhang Houyi, Ming Zhili, and Liang Zhuanyun, *Zhongguo siying qiye fazhan baogao*, vol. 4, 31.

53. "Siying jingji sanfen tianxia," cited in Hong, "Mapping the Evolution," 33.

54. Kellee Tsai, "Capitalists Without a Class," 1140; and Alpermann and Gang, "Social Origins," 6.

55. "Number of CPC Members Increases by 6.4 Million over 2002."

56. Li Qiang, as cited in Yongnian Zheng, "Party, Class," 240. See also Hong, "Mapping the Evolution," 33.

57. Dickson, *Red Capitalists*, 107, and "Integrating Wealth and Power," 838. Similar findings are reported in surveys conducted by Alpermann and Gang in 2002 and 2006 (Alpermann and Gang, "Social Origins"). See also Zhang Houyi, Ming Zhili, and Liang Zhuanyun, *Zhongguo siying qiye fazhan baogao*, vol. 4, 31.

58. Dickson, "Integrating Wealth and Power," 838.

59. Ibid.

60. Goodman, "Localism and Entrepreneurship," 159–60.

61. Ibid., citing "Siying yiyezhu shi jianshezhe haishi xinxing zichang jieji?"

62. Ibid.

63. Dickson, *Red Capitalists*, 74.

64. Ibid., 25.

65. Ibid., 74.

66. Alpermann, " 'Wrapped Up in Cotton Wool,' " 46.

67. Dickson, *Red Caplitalists*, 57.

68. Jianjun Zhang, "Marketization, Class Structure, and Democracy," 427–29.

69. Dickson, "Integrating Wealth and Power," 845. It should be noted that this percentage declined slightly between 1999 and 2005 in Dickson's surveys.

70. Dickson, *Red Capitalists*, 123.

71. Ibid., 125.

72. He Li, "Middle Class," 90.

73. Dickson, *Red Capitalists*, 122, and "Integrating Wealth and Power," 844.

74. "Siying jingji sanfen tianxia," cited in Hong, "Mapping the Evolution," 34.

75. Peng Cong and Liu Lantao, "Zhongguo fuhao zai renda."

76. Lang Y. and Guo Xiajuan, "Renda daibiao zhidu yu xianfu qunti de zhengzhi suqiu" [The People's Congress System and the Political Articulation of the New Rich Groups], presented at the Symposium on Social Change and Political Studies in China (Guangzhou, China, 2005), cited in Yang, "Economic Transformation," 157.

77. Kellee Tsai, *Back-Alley Banking*.

78. Dickson, *Red Capitalists*.

79. Alpermann, " 'Wrapped Up in Cotton Wool,' " 37–38.

80. Ibid., 34.

81. See North and Weingast, "Constitutions and Commitment."

82. Jianjun Zhang, "Marketization, Class Structure, and Democracy," 436.

83. Ibid., 433.

84. Ibid., 435.

85. Ibid.

86. Ibid., 433.

87. Ibid., 435.

88. Ibid., 427.

89. Alpermann, "'Wrapped Up in Cotton Wool'," 54.

90. Jianjun Zhang, "Marketization, Class Structure, and Democracy," 440.

91. Jianjun Zhang, *Marketization and Democracy in China*, 234.

92. Ibid., 233.

93. Przeworski, "Some Problems in the Study."

Chapter 3

1. As noted in Chapter 1, in 2005 the average per capita income in China was roughly 14,000 yuan. In that year the average professional made between 60,000 and 500,000 yuan.

2. Moore, *Social Origins*. Moore considers other factors to be of critical importance as well; in particular, he emphasizes the commercialization of agriculture such that the landed gentry ceases to be a dominant social force and the peasantry becomes uprooted.

3. Goodman, "New Middle Class," 243–44.

4. Li Chunling, "Dangian gaoshouru chunti de shehui goucheng ji tezheng."

5. Goodman, "New Middle Class," 244.

6. Wang, Davis, and Bian, "Uneven Distribution," 326.

7. Thorgersen, "Through the Sheep's Intestines," 33. It should be noted that, despite its more academic focus, the new version of the exam still includes an ideological component.

8. "Education Finance," 27.

9. From 1979 to 1989, the number of university students rose from 1 to 2 million, while the total population increased from roughly 980 million to 1.12 billion. See Guo, "Party Recruitment," 373.

10. Thorgersen, "Through the Sheep's Intestines," 52.

11. Guo, "Party Recruitment," 386.

12. The actual financial "return" from a college education during this period has been calculated at 4 percent ("Education Finance," 26).

13. Goldman, *Sowing the Seeds.*

14. From 1975 to 1977, college students were accepted based on recommendations from their local work unit or party organizations, such as the Communist Youth League. See Guo, "Party Recruitment," 374.

15. Ibid., 373.

16. Ibid., 376–78.

17. Ibid., 376.

18. Kwong, "1986 Student Demonstrations."

19. Ibid., 977.

20. Ibid.

21. Rosen, "China in 1987," 36.

22. Kwong, "1986 Student Demonstrations," 983.

23. Ibid., 981–82.

24. Note that few of the casualties on June 4, 1989 involved students. Virtually all of the dead and wounded were city residents who went into the streets to try to block the military from advancing to the city center. When the soldiers reached Tiananmen Square, they did not harm the roughly five thousand students who remained at the Square.

25. "Recognize the Essence of Turmoil and the Necessity of Martial Law," 12; and Chen Xitong, *Report on Checking the Turmoil and Quelling the Counter-Revolutionary Rebellion.*

26. Rosen, "State of Youth," 164.

27. "Education Finance," 25–26.

28. Rosen, "State of Youth," 166.

29. Huang Zhijian, "Qingnian xiaofei wu da qushi." For per capita income, see http://asiaecon.org/aei/index.php/inside_asia/country/china#econ_ind (accessed March 1, 2008).

30. Rosen, "Victory of Materialism," 35.

31. Junyan Liu, "Chinese College Students," 146.

32. "Education Finance," 27.

33. Guo, "Party Recruitment," 374.

34. Ibid., 386–87.

35. "Education Finance," 26.

36. Buckley, "How a Revolution Becomes a Dinner Party," 215.

37. For a more extended discussion of this debate, see Rosen, "State of Youth," 170–72.

38. Rosen, "Victory of Materialism," 47–48.

39. Guo, "Party Recruitment," 387. See also Rosen, "State of Youth," 169.

40. Pan Duola, "Ye tan 'ru dang dongji.'"

41. Rosen, "State of Youth," 168.

42. Bobai Li and Andrew Walder, "Career Advancement," cited in Rosen, "State of Youth," 168.

43. Rosen, "State of Youth," 169.

44. Ibid., 169 and n56.

45. Ibid., 168 and n52.

46. Ibid., n52.

47. Ibid., 169 and n56. See Li Zhidong, "Dangdai daxuesheng zhengzhiguan, daodeguan, jiazhiguan diaocha yanjiu," 52.

48. Rosen, "State of Youth," 168.

49. "Number of CPC Members Increases by 6.4 Million over 2002."

50. Rosen, "State of Youth," 170.

51. Wright, "China Democracy Party."

52. Guo, "Party Recruitment," 388.

53. Rosen, "State of Youth," 170.

54. Ibid.

55. Guo, "Party Recruitment," 389.

56. Deng Xiaoping, "Speech at the Opening Ceremony," 113.

57. Goldman, *From Comrade to Citizen*, 12.

58. Hamrin and Cheek, *China's Establishment Intellectuals*.

59. Fewsmith, *China Since Tiananmen*, 11–12.

60. For more detailed accounts of the movement, see Nathan, *Chinese Democracy*; and Goldman, *From Comrade to Citizen*, chap. 1.

61. Goldman, *From Comrade to Citizen*, 35–36.

62. Ibid., 35.

63. Minzhu Han, *Cries for Democracy*, 108.

64. Goldman, *From Comrade to Citizen*, 49–50.

65. Ibid., 59.

66. Ibid., 60.

67. Ibid., 61.

68. Ibid., 62–65.

69. Fewsmith, *China Since Tiananmen*, 16.

70. Ibid., 17.

71. Ibid., 12.

72. Yongnian Zheng, "Party, Class," 250.

73. Fewsmith, *China Since Tiananmen*, 15.

74. Ibid., 14–15.

75. Ibid., 15.

76. Ibid., 12.

77. *Xinhua*, June 20, 1991, in FBIS, June 21, 1991, cited in Dickson, *Red Capitalists*, 35.

78. Yongnian Zheng, "Party, Class," 250.

79. Ibid.

80. Ibid.

81. Goldman, *From Comrade to Citizen*, 7–8.

82. Wright, "China Democracy Party." Note that the CDP continues its work publicly outside of the PRC.

83. China Democracy Party Beijing-Tianjin Branch Establishment Announcement (#2) (November 9, 1998). In China Democracy Party (CDP) Data Collection [*Zhongguo Minzhudang Ziliao Huipian*], 5.

84. Ibid.

85. Hebei CDP Branch Notice, March 26, 1999, CDP Data Collection, 136.

86. Hebei CDP Branch, "Statement on the Coming of the Anniversary of June 4," May 2000, CDP Data Collection, 144.

87. CDP Beijing-Tianjin Branch Establishment Announcement (#2) (November 9, 1998). In CDP Data Collection, 5.

88. Jie Tang and Anthony Ward, *Changing Face*, 145.

89. Personal communication with Christopher McNally, October 2007.

90. Between 1950 and 1957, there were about 2,500 lawyers in China, all of whom were employed by the party-state. Between 1957 and 1977, lawyers were castigated as "rightists," and the profession was abolished. See Zheng et al., *Zhonghua renmin gongheguo lushifa quanshu*, 40; and Tao Mao et al., *Lushi shiyong daquan*, 23.

91. Michelson, "Lawyers," 362, 365; and Yuwen Li, "Lawyers in China," 23.

92. Sida Liu and Terence Halliday, "Dancing Handcuffed," citing Article 3 of the 1980 Interim Regulation on Lawyers.

93. For a list of specific qualifications, see Michelson, "Lawyers," 366.

94. Ibid., 365.

95. Ibid., 366–67.

96. Ibid., 370–71.

97. Ibid., 362.

98. "Lushimen de hushing."

99. Michelson, "Lawyers," 365.

100. Ibid., 372–73.

101. Michelson, "Practice of Law," 11.

102. Ibid., 12.

103. Ibid., 11.

104. Michelson, "Lawyers," 367. The bar exam had been administered since 1986 but was required only after the 1996 enactment of the Law on Lawyers. Note that many individuals who act as lawyers are not officially certified to do so.

105. Michelson, "Lawyers," 367.

106. Ibid., 370, 399.

107. Ibid., 368. In 1986, China had about 25,000 lawyers.

108. Proctor and Qiu, "Lack of Professionals."

109. Sanderson, "Rights Group."

110. Michelson, "Lawyers," 401.

111. Ibid., 401.

112. Ibid., 381.

113. I am grateful to Merle Goldman for these points.

114. Human Rights Watch, "'Walking on Thin Ice.'"

115. Ibid. See also Hualing Fu and Richard Cullin, "Weiquan [Rights Protection] Lawyering."

116. Luo, "Bolstering the Teaching," and "The Political and Legal Organs," cited in Human Rights Watch, "'Walking on Thin Ice.'"

117. Human Rights Watch, "'Walking on Thin Ice.'"

118. Personal communication with Christopher McNally, October 2007.

119. Jie Tang and Anthony Ward, *Changing Face*, 145.

120. Similarly, China's state-owned quantity surveying companies were ordered in the late 1990s to abolish their links with government bodies and become independent private professional services, either in the form of partnerships or limited liability corporations (Ibid., 147).

121. Proctor and Qiu, "Lack of Professionals."

122. For a discussion of these individuals and their actions, see Goldman, *From Comrade to Citizen.*

123. Cai, "China's Moderate Middle Class," 792.

124. Ibid., 798.

Chapter 4

1. In 1980–81, roughly 139 million individuals held urban residence cards. Among them, slightly more than 50 percent (69.5 million) were employed. Of these, 32.1 million worked in state-owned enterprises (Walder, *Communist Neo-traditionalism*, 41, 43).

2. Solinger, "New Crowd of the Dispossessed," 50; and Weston, "Iron Man Weeps," 69.

3. Solinger, "New Crowd of the Dispossessed," 50–52.

4. A notable exception was the summer of 2009, when there were at least three major strikes at SOEs in Jilin, Henan, and Hunan provinces. See "China's State-Owned Enterprises Back in the Spotlight"; "Hunan Coalminers Strike Over Privatization Plans"; and "Manager Killed During Protest Over Steel Plant Privatization."

5. As explained by Walder, urban collectives first formed in the 1950s to organize craftworkers and the unemployed. In the late 1950s, they became a major source of employment for urban women. In the late 1970s, urban collectives were opened to

unemployed youths returning from their forced move to the countryside during the Cultural Revolution (Walder, *Communist Neo-traditionalism*, 43).

6. Ibid., 41.

7. Ibid., 58–59, 66–67.

8. Ibid., 41.

9. Ibid., 16, 42, 60, 62–66.

10. Ibid., 40.

11. Ibid., 16.

12. Ibid., 69.

13. Ibid., 67.

14. Ibid., 46–48.

15. Ibid., 43, 46.

16. Ibid., 48–54.

17. Ibid., 60.

18. Whyte, "Changing Role of Workers," 187; and Solinger, "Path Dependency Reexamined."

19. Walder, *Communist Neo-traditionalism*, 225.

20. Ibid., 225.

21. Ibid., 226.

22. Ibid., 226, 238.

23. Ibid., 227.

24. Ibid.

25. Ibid., 225.

26. In 1988, the United States had a Gini score of 0.395 (Scipes, "International Income Inequality").

27. Tang and Parish, "Chinese Labor Relations," 371–72. The 1986 survey, conducted by the All-China Federation of Trade Unions (ACFTU), included 640,000 workers in 519 enterprises. The 1991–92 survey was conducted by Tang and Parish and included 8,000 employees in 100 industrial enterprises.

28. Ibid., 372.

29. Ibid.

30. Dickson, *Red Capitalists*, 32.

31. Tang and Parish, "Chinese Labor Relations," 371. The survey was conducted by the ACFTU (see note 27).

32. As reported by Dickson, the 1982 survey was conducted by the Central Secretariat Research Office of the CCP. The 1990 survey was conducted by the Chinese Mechanical and Electrical Industry Staff and Workers Ideological and Political Work Society. Both are described in Gong Kaijin, "Qiye lingdao tizhi yu dang zuzhi zai qiyezhong de diwei," 25–28. See Dickson, *Red Capitalists*, 34n13.

33. On the general causes of the protests of 1989, see Francis, "Progress of Protest"; Unger, "Introduction"; Feigon Lee, *China Rising*; and Hartford, "Political Economy."

34. The immediate spark of the movement was the April 15, 1989, death of former CCP General Secretary Hu Yaobang, who had been dismissed from his post in 1987 due to his perceived support of student-led calls for greater political reform.

35. The WAFs were led by workers with limited formal education, though a few university students also worked with the organizations. Steel workers, builders, bus drivers, machinists, railway workers, and office staff made up the bulk of the membership ("Tiananmen—Ten Years On," 3).

36. Ibid.

37. Beijing Workers Autonomous Federation Preparatory Committee, "Provisional Memorandum," May 28, 1989.

38. "Tiananmen—Ten Years On," 3.

39. Walder and Gong, "Workers in the Tiananmen Protests," 12.

40. Beijing Workers Autonomous Federation Preparatory Committee, "Provisional Memorandum."

41. Walder and Gong, "Workers in the Tiananmen Protests," 12.

42. Garnaut, Song, and Yao, "Impact and Significance," 37–38.

43. Ibid., 38.

44. Ibid.

45. Ibid., 42. See also *China Labour Bulletin* 6–17 (September 1995) and 37 (July–August 1997).

46. See *China Labour Bulletin* 6–17 (September 1995) and 37 (July–August 1997).

47. Garnaut, Song, and Yao, "Impact and Significance," 42–43, 48.

48. Ibid., 48–49, 56.

49. Ibid., 51.

50. Ibid., 53.

51. Frazier, "China's Pension Reform," 101n11. It should be noted that this rise also is related to increased life expectancy.

52. Hurst and O'Brien, "China's Contentious Pensioners," 349n22. The legal retirement age is fifty-five for women and sixty for men.

53. Garnaut, Song, and Yao, "Impact and Significance," 54; Li and Sato, "Introduction," 2–3.

54. Appleton et al., "Labour Retrenchment," 30, 36–37.

55. Qiao, "2003 nian: Xin yilun jiegou tiaozheng xia de laodong guanxi," 285.

56. Shi Li and Hiroshi Sato, "Introduction," 2; Solinger, "Path Dependency Reexamined."

57. Shi Li and Hiroshi Sato, "Introduction," 3; Solinger, "Path Dependency Reexamined."

58. Appleton et al., "Labor Retrenchment," 32.

59. Ibid., 33.

60. Ching Kwan Lee, *Against the Law*, 46; Trinh, "China's Pension System." See also Lardy, *China's Unfinished Economic Revolution*, 45; and Whyte and Parish, *Urban Life in Contemporary China*, 73. William Hurst and Kevin O'Brien note that inflation has eroded the value of these benefits (Hurst and O'Brien, "China's Contentious Pensioners," 348).

61. Efimov, "The Retirement Blues," 39; "China Won't Change Retirement Age."

62. Ching Kwan Lee, *Against the Law*, 48. See also Hurst and O'Brien, "China's Contentious Pensioners."

63. Cai, *State and Laid-off Workers*, 59, 106.

64. Frazier, "China's Pension Reform," 106–9.

65. Li Peilin, "Zhongguo jingji shehui fazhan de wenti he qushi," 76.

66. Trinh, "China's Pension System," 7; and "240 million Chinese Covered by Social Pension System," *Xinhua*, December 5, 2007. As of 2004, there were 265 million urban workers, 123 million of whom had pension coverage. In 2006 the number of covered urban workers was 187.6 million.

67. "China to Raise Pension Fund as of Jan."

68. Cai, *State and Laid-off Workers*, 23–24, 86.

69. Solinger, "Labour Market Reform," 314n38; and Solinger, *Contesting Citizenship*, 115.

70. Cai, *State and Laid-off Workers*, 86.

71. Garnaut, Song, and Yao, "Impact and Significance," 56.

72. *South China Morning Post*, January 11, 2003, cited in Guiheux, "Promotion," 151.

73. "Don't Sweat Joblessness: Be Your Own Boss," *China Daily* (Hong Kong edition), July 19, 2004, cited in Guiheux, "Promotion," 151.

74. Guiheux, "Promotion," 168.

75. Ibid., 157.

76. Ibid. See also Ching Kwan Lee, *Against the Law*.

77. Ibid., 167–68.

78. Gallagher, *Contagious Capitalism*, 1, 31.

79. Ibid., 105–10.

80. Ibid., 46–48, 144.

81. Ibid., 62.

82. Ching Kwan Lee, *Against the Law*, 23.

83. Ibid., 125.

84. Ibid., 56.

85. Ibid., 126.

86. Jian Li and Xiaohan Niu, "New Middle Class," paragraph 26.

87. *China Daily*, January 4, 2002, cited in Tomba, "Residential Space," 939.

88. *Nanfang Zhoumou*, May 29, 2003.

89. Jian Li and Xiaohan Niu, "New Middle Class," paragraph 51.

90. Tomba, "Creating an Urban Middle Class," 19.

91. Jian Li and Xiaohan Niu, "New Middle Class"; Tomba, "Creating an Urban Middle Class."

92. Ching Kwan Lee, *Against the Law*, 125.

93. Ibid., 128. Lee finds that this is especially true when funds are pooled in households that include more than two adults—a very common occurrence.

94. Solinger, "Labour Market Reform," 311.

95. Solinger, "Path Dependency Reexamined," 50.

96. Shi Li and Hiroshi Sato, "Introduction," 3

97. Cai, *State and Laid-off Workers*, 30.

98. Ibid., 28.

99. Ibid., 28–29.

100. Ching Kwan Lee, *Against the Law*, 130–31; and Solinger, "New Crowd of the Dispossessed."

101. Mok and He, "Beyond Organized Dependence," 73.

102. Chen Wuming, "Fubai manyan de tedian jiqi yanzhong weihai."

103. Whyte, "Changing Role of Workers," 192.

104. Mok and He, "Beyond Organized Dependence," 73.

105. Solinger, "Labor Market Reform," 309.

106. Ibid., 309–10; and Solinger, "Path Dependency Reexamined," 52.

107. Liang, "Zhongguo dangzheng ganbu ji ganqun guanxi de diaocha fenxi," 35.

108. Mok and He, "Beyond Organized Dependence," 75.

109. Ibid., 79.

110. Ching Kwan Lee, *Against the Law*, 202.

111. Ibid., 195.

112. Ibid., 217.

113. Ibid.,199.

114. Ibid., 198.

115. Ibid., 84. Indeed, many laid-off and unemployed SOE workers live and eat at their parents' homes, living off parents' pensions (Ibid., 93).

116. Reinforcing this view has been a widespread public perception that the moral and legal claims of retirees are more legitimate than those of laid-off or unemployed SOE workers (see Hurst and O'Brien, "China's Contentious Pensioners," 350; and Ching Kwan Lee, *Against the Law*, 79, 84).

117. Ching Kwan Lee, *Against the Law*, 77–78.

118. Dickson, *Red Capitalists*, 35.

119. Gallagher, *Contagious Capitalism*, 134.

120. Ibid., 148.

121. "Facing Up to Unemployment, What Should Chinese Workers Do?" *Shenyang Daily*, March 12, 1997, cited in Gallagher, *Contagious Capitalism*, 150.

122. Blecher, "Hegemony and Workers' Politics"; and Cai, *State and Laid-off Workers*, 89.

123. Mok and He, "Beyond Organized Dependence," 72.

124. Dickson, *Red Capitalists*, 165.

125. *Liaoning Daily*, August 13, 1999, cited in Cai, *State and Laid-off Workers*, 33.

126. Ching Kwan Lee, *Against the Law*, 64.

127. "Hu Pledges Political Reform, Stronger Party."

128. "Hu Jintao Vows to 'Reverse Growing Income Disparity.'"

129. Ching Kwan Lee, *Against the Law*, 70.

130. Ibid.

131. Cai, *State and Laid-off Workers*, 32.

132. Thireau and Hua, "Moral Universe," 85–87.

133. Thireau and Hua, "Moral Universe"; Ching Kwan Lee, *Against the Law*; and Gallagher, *Contagious Capitalism*.

134. Cai, *State and Laid-off Workers*, 63, 72, and 102.

135. Ching Kwan Lee, *Against the Law*, 106.

136. Ibid., 121; and Kellee Tsai, "Capitalists Without a Class."

137. Ching Kwan Lee, *Against the Law*, 140.

138. See, for example, Ching Kwan Lee, *Against the Law*, 140; and Blecher, "Hegemony and Workers' Politics," 288.

139. See Ching Kwan Lee, *Against the Law*; Michael Zhang, "Social Marginalization"; Thireau and Hua, "Moral Universe"; Hurst and O'Brien, "China's Contentious Pensioners"; Feng Chen, "Privatization and Its Discontents"; Feng Chen, "Industrial Restructuring"; Cai, *State and Laid-off Workers*; and Solinger, "New Crowd of the Dispossessed." A notable exception is Blecher's 1995–99 study of workers in the city of Tianjin (Blecher, "Hegemony and Workers' Politics").

140. Ching Kwan Lee, *Against the Law*, 140.

141. Ibid., 141–42.

142. Ibid., 141.

143. Ibid., 143, 148.

144. Ibid., 143.

145. Ibid.

146. Ibid.

147. Ibid., 141.

148. Ibid., 142.

149. Ibid., 26.

150. Feng Chen, "Privatization and Its Discontents," 47–48.

151. Ibid., 48.

152. Feng Chen, "Industrial Restructuring," 247.

153. Ching Kwan Lee, *Against the Law*, 99.

154. Cai, *State and Laid-off Workers*, 89.

155. Whyte, "Chinese Popular Views," 7.

156. Lu Xueyi, *Dangdai zhongguo shehui ge jieceng fenxi*, 115 n14.

157. For statistics, see *Xinhua*, June 29, 1995, in FBIS, June 30, 1995, pp. 12–13, cited in Dickson, *Red Capitalists*, 35.

158. In 2004, official statistics show that 7.676 million SOE workers were party members. Nationwide, there were 49.22 million SOE workers and 69.603 million CCP members. See "Latest Inner-Party Statistics of 2004 Show the Vitality of Party Ranks."

159. "Members of Communist Party of China Grow to 70.8 Million."

160. Tanner, "China Rethinks Unrest," 136. According to Ministry of Public Security statistics, between 1993 and 2005 the number of "mass incidents" in China each year grew from 10,000 to 87,000, while the number of yearly participants rose from 730,000 in 1993 to 3.8 million in 2004. In 2006 the number of mass incidents reportedly declined by 16.5 percent—the first such decrease in thirteen years. Ministry of Public Security statistics from 2004 show that the major cause of mass protests was labor-management disputes, followed by land disputes, forced evictions, and issues specifically arising from the privatization of SOEs ("Food and Fuel Price Hikes Spark Protests in China"; "Incidents of Social Unrest Hit 87,000").

161. Weston, "Iron Man Weeps," 69.

162. Solinger, "Path Dependency Reexamined," 53.

163. Ibid., 53.

164. Ching Kwan Lee, *Against the Law*, 21.

165. Weston, "Iron Man Weeps," 75.

166. Ibid.

167. Ching Kwan Lee, *Against the Law*, 28.

168. Ibid., 24.

169. Ibid., 91.

170. Ibid., 28.

171. Weston, "Iron Man Weeps," 75.

172. Solinger, "Path Dependency Reexamined."

173. Ibid.

174. Cai, *State and Laid-off Workers*, 33; and Cai, "Managed Participation," 429–30.

175. Thireau and Hua, "Moral Universe," 87.

176. Ibid., 91.

177. Ibid., 99.

178. Ibid., 93.

179. Ibid., 99–100.

180. Frazier, "China's Pension Reform," 111.

181. Hurst and O'Brien, "China's Contentious Pensioners," 346–47; and Ching Kwan Lee, *Against the Law*, 77.

182. Ching Kwan Lee, *Against the Law*, 82.

183. Ibid., 81.

184. Hurst and O'Brien, "China's Contentious Pensioners," 351.

185. Ibid., 351.

186. Ibid., 358.

187. Ibid., 121. See also Perry, "Studying Chinese Politics."

188. See, for example, Solinger, "Clashes Between Reform and Opening."

189. Hurst, "Forgotten Player," 4–10. In addition, Frazier emphasizes that the level and extent of pension payments to SOE retirees widely varies by locality, due in part to the relative economic status of the local government and enterprises, and in part to the attitudes of local officials and firm managers (Frazier, "China's Pension Reform").

190. Though note the outbreak of major protests in the summer of 2009 (see note 4).

191. See, for example, Harrison, *Before the Socialists*.

192. See, for example, Bendix, *Nation Building and Citizenship*, 61–74.

193. Katznelson, "Working Class Formation," 38. See also Bridges, "Working Classes in the United States," 157–96.

194. Bellin, *Stalled Democracy*, 127–56.

195. Ibid., 167–68.

Chapter 5

1. Xiao Ma, "Private Firms Crucial"; Zhuang, "New Social Strata"; Haoting Liu, "Private Firms Propel."

2. Ching Kwan Lee, *Against the Law*, 6; Guang, "Guerilla Workfare," 482; and Boyd, "Migrant Labour Mechanisms," 29.

3. Solinger, *Contesting Citizenship*, 44–49.

4. As noted in Chapter 1 (note 2), since the Maoist era, all Chinese citizens have held an official household registration card (*hukou*) that designates one's residential status as urban or rural.

5. In late 1984, peasants were allowed to apply for "urban registration for those with self-supplied grain" (*zili kouliang changzhen hukou*). In the summer of 1985,

authorities created a special "card for residents living with others" (*jizhu zheng*) for longer-term peasants with urban jobs (Solinger, *Contesting Citizenship*, 49–50).

6. Ibid., 50–51.

7. Ibid., 50.

8. From 1984 through the early 1990s, the housing department enforced a regulation against renting state-owned housing to "outsiders" (Ibid., 65).

9. Ibid., 87.

10. Ibid., 135–36.

11. These numbers refer to "migrants away from their place of household registration for more than six months" (Feng Wang, "Boundaries of Inequality," 3). See also Kam Wing Chan, "Recent Migration," 131.

12. *State Administration for Industry and Commerce Statistical Collection, 2003* (Beijing: State Administration for Industry and Commerce, 2004).

13. Wank, "Private Business," 59.

14. This range reflects great variation by city (Solinger, *Contesting Citizenship*, 47, 243–44).

15. *State Administration for Industry and Commerce Statistical Collection* (2003).

16. *Zhongguo tongji nianjian* (2006). Another report finds that, if one includes within the "private sector" partially privatized state enterprises and excludes collective enterprises, in 2005 roughly 50 percent of capital and employment were in domestically owned enterprises and 16 percent in foreign-owned firms (Chengshui Li, cited in Eva Cheng, "Public Sector Less than 40% of Economy." Li was the head of China's National Bureau of Statistics from 1981–84).

17. *State Administration for Industry and Commerce Statistical Collection* (2003).

18. For example, a 2003 study by Chinese researcher Kaiming Liu found that migrant workers made up 57 percent of the manufacturing sector, more than 80 percent of the construction sector, and 50 percent of the service sector. See Froissart, "Escaping from under the Party's Thumb," 213n1.

19. Ching Kwan Lee, *Against the Law*, 39.

20. Two separate 2006 government surveys undertaken by the Research Office of the State Council and the National Bureau of Statistics found that roughly 54 percent of migrant workers had signed job contracts, 30.6 percent had not, and 15.7 percent did not know what a labor contract was ("Woguo nongmin gong de shengcun xianzhuan"; and Social Trends Analysis and Forecasting Topic Group, Chinese Academy of Social Sciences, "Zhongguo jinru quanmian jianshe hexie shehui xin jieduan"). In Ching Kwan Lee's study, as of the middle part of the first decade of the 2000s one-third had signed contracts (Ching Kwan Lee, *Against the Law*, 164–65).

21. Ching Kwan Lee, *Against the Law*, 161, 163.

22. China Labour Bulletin, "Speaking Out," 3.

23. Ibid., 26.

24. Ching Kwan Lee, *Against the Law*, 57.

25. *China Labour Bulletin* #11 (February 1995), 9, 11.

26. Ngai, "Becoming Dagongmei (Working Girls)," 6; Anita Chan, *China's Workers Under Assault*.

27. "Laboring over Workers' Rights."

28. Social Trends Analysis and Forecasting Topic Group, "Zhongguo jinru quanmian jianshe hexie shehui xin jieduan."

29. Ching Kwan Lee, *Against the Law*, 79, 94. See also Solinger, *Contesting Citizenship*; Anita Chan, *China's Workers Under Assault*; and Anita Chan, "Emerging Patterns."

30. For a vivid depiction of working conditions in domestically funded private enterprises, see the film *China Blue* (Bullfrog Films, 2005). Other examples may be found in *China Labour Bulletin* #1, #12, #13, #14, #17, #23, #24, #49, #51, and *China Labour Bulletin Action Express* #24; and Ching Kwan Lee, *Against the Law*, 166–74.

31. Official statistics from 2002 report that 70 percent of construction workers were rural migrants (Guang, "Guerilla Workfare," 482).

32. Solinger, *Contesting Citizenship*, 48.

33. Ibid., 211.

34. Guang, "Guerilla Workfare," 498.

35. Ibid.

36. Solinger, *Contesting Citizenship*, 79.

37. Ibid., 129.

38. For the text of the law, see http://www.jus.uio.no/lm/china.labor.law.1994/doc.html.

39. Anita Chan, "Recent Trends," 27.

40. "A Better Day for Beggars."

41. Hon, "Beijing Signs Pact." It should be noted that these reforms were very slow in coming (I am grateful to Dorothy Solinger for this point).

42. China Labour Bulletin, "Speaking Out," 32.

43. Josephine Ma, "'Make Sure Migrant Workers Get Paid,'" 6.

44. China Labour Bulletin, "Speaking Out," 7.

45. For the text of the law, see http://www.law-lib.com/law/law_view.asp?id=204461 (Chinese) or http://lawprofessors.typepad.com/china_law_prof_blog/files/070629_labor_contract_law_en.pdf (English).

46. Solinger, "New Crowd of the Dispossessed," 58.

47. Chunguang Wang, "Changing Situation of Migrant Labor," 189.

48. Ching Kwan Lee, *Against the Law*, 221.

49. Ibid., 206.

50. Ibid., 230.

51. For example, a mid-1980s study found that workers employed "outside" of the state plan in Guangdong earned roughly half the salary of regular SOE employees (Ji Y., "Dangqian wosheng jihuawai yonggong qingkuang poxi," 20). A 1996 study reaches similar conclusions (Yaohui Zhao, "Foreign Direct Investment").

52. Ngai, "Becoming Dagongmei," 2.

53. Ibid., 4.

54. Ibid., 7.

55. Solinger, *Contesting Citizenship*, 283.

56. Guang, "Guerilla Workfare," 498.

57. Guang and Zheng, "Migration," 41, 44.

58. William Parish, X. Zhe, and F. Li, "Nonfarm Work"; Guang and Zheng, "Migration," 25.

59. Solinger, "China's Floating Population," 233.

60. Ibid., 234.

61. Ibid., 235.

62. Ibid., 230.

63. Guang, "Guerilla Workfare," 492.

64. Solinger, *Contesting Citizenship*, 63.

65. Ibid., 84.

66. Ibid., chap. 6.

67. See Davies and Ramia, "Governance Reform."

68. *Shenzhen shi laowugong sixiang daode zhaungkuang diaocha* (A Survey Regarding the Ideological and Moral Situation of Migrant Workers in Shenzhen Municipality), June 1996, cited in Thireau and Hua, "Moral Universe," 84.

69. Ibid. Thireau and Hua note that the vast majority of unskilled private enterprise workers who lodged complaints with government offices went to Letters and Visits Offices. Meanwhile, workers who were educated and skilled or were affiliated with the state sector were more likely to approach arbitration committees. In large part, this difference resulted from manual private sector workers' lack of resources, as arbitration costs nearly four times their mean monthly wage, while submitting a complaint with a Letters and Visits Office is free (Thireau and Hua, "Moral Universe," 89–90).

70. See Anita Chan, "Recent Trends," 26.

71. Ching Kwan Lee, *Against the Law*, 177.

72. Solinger, *Contesting Citizenship*, 284.

73. China Labour Bulletin, "Speaking Out," 25.

74. Solinger, *Contesting Citizenship*, 284; China Labour Bulletin, "Speaking Out," 20.

75. When some machinery and other items belonging to the factory were damaged in the course of the protest, several dozen employees were arrested—including two sixteen-year-old workers who had been underaged when hired. With the help of a lawyer hired by the Hong Kong-based labor activist group China Labour Bulletin, as well as domestic media coverage that was sympathetic to the workers, Stella expressed its "sadness" at the detention of the workers, leading to their ultimate release. ("Stella Shoe Workers Protest," *China Labour Bulletin*, http://www.china-labour.org.hk. For other examples, see China Labour Bulletin, "Speaking Out," 20–24; and "Cry for Justice," 46–54.)

76. Thireau and Hua, "Moral Universe," 97.

77. Ching Kwan Lee, *Against the Law*, 174.

78. Thireau and Hua, "Moral Universe," 98.

79. Ibid., 99.

80. Ching Kwan Lee, *Against the Law*, 201.

81. See, for example, "Release and Sentence Reductions for Stella Shoe Factory Workers," "Xianyang Textile Workers Detained for Leading Historic Seven-week Strike are Released," and "Female Workers at Wal-Mart Supplier in Shenzhen Demand Union," *China Labour Bulletin*, http://www.china-labour.org.hk/ (accessed September 1, 2005); and China Labour Bulletin, "Speaking Out," 27.

82. Dickson, *Red Capitalists*, 44.

83. Ibid.

84. Anita Chan, "Emerging Patterns."

85. China Central Television (CCTV) 1, December 4, 2003, cited in Froissart, "Escaping from under the Party's Thumb," 202.

86. Froissart, "Escaping from under the Party's Thumb," 202.

87. Ching Kwan Lee, *Against the Law*, 230.

88. "Three Million Chinese Farmers a Year Expected to Lose Land."

Chapter 6

1. "NBS: China's Rural Population Shrinks to 56% of Total."

2. "Urbanization Is Reducing China's Rural Population." In 1990, 74 percent of China's citizens were rural residents; in 2001, 64 percent lived in rural areas ("NBS: China's Rural Population Shrinks to 56% of Total").

3. *Zhongguo tongji nianjian 2000*, 369; and *Zhongguo xiangzhen qiye nianjian 2001*, 95.

4. Planning Department of the Ministry of Agriculture, *Nongye jingji ziliao, 1949–83*, 82–83.

5. For a more detailed discussion of this period, see Oi, *State and Peasant in Contemporary China*.

6. This occurred in Anhui province in late 1978 and reportedly also in a village in Guizhou province as early as the late 1960s.

7. The official lease term was lengthened to thirty years in 1998.

8. Brandt et al., "Land Rights in Rural China," 73–75; and Cheng and Tsang, "Agricultural Land Reform in a Mixed System."

9. Murphy, "Introduction," in Cao, *Huanghe biande Zhongguo*, 7.

10. Cui, "Ruhe renshi jinri Zhongguo."

11. *Zhongguo tongji nianjian 1989.*

12. Oi, "Two Decades of Rural Reform," 619; and Brandt et al., "Land Rights," 68.

13. *Zhongguo tongji nianjian 1989.*

14. *Zhongguo xiangzhen qiye nianjian* 1991, 137–39.

15. Kung, "Evolution of Property Rights," 105; see also 114–15.

16. Oi, *Rural China Takes Off*, 78.

17. China Internet Information Center, "Opening to the Outside World."

18. Oi, *Rural China Takes Off*, 61.

19. As of 2003, China had 19,600 towns and 18,400 townships (*Zhongguo tongji nianjian 2004*, 21).

20. There are two types of villages: administrative villages (*xingzhengcun*) and natural villages (*zirancun*). Some administrative villages encompass multiple natural villages, some large natural villages are divided into two administrative villages, and some administrative and natural villages are the same. See Lianjiang Li, "Direct Township Elections," 100; and Ho, "Contesting Rural Spaces," 94–95.

21. Lianjiang Li, "Direct Township Elections," 101.

22. In the mid-1980s, fiscal reforms known as "eating in separate kitchens" made townships self-financing. Under this system, a township was given quotas for tax revenues that were shared with higher governmental levels. The township was to collect and turn over all revenue designated as central taxes and keep revenues designated as local taxes. With the latter, the township was required to balance its own budget (Oi and Zhao, "Fiscal Crisis in China's Townships," 76).

23. Bernstein and Lu, "Taxation Without Representation," 743.

24. Oi and Zhao, "Fiscal Crisis," 81; and Cao, *Huanghe biande Zhongguo*, 133. The central job allocation system for township posts continued through 2001.

25. Oi and Zhao, "Fiscal Crisis," 89; and Cao, *Huanghe biande Zhongguo*.

26. Oi, *Rural China Takes Off*, 79–80.

27. Wong, *Financing Local Development*, 199; and Oi and Zhao, "Fiscal Crisis," 83.

28. O'Brien, "Implementing Political Reform in China's Villages"; An Chen, "Failure of Organizational Control," 162–69; Levy, "Village Elections and Anticorruption," 22; and Lily Tsai, "Cadres, Temple and Lineage Associations."

29. Bernstein and Lu, "Taxation Without Representation," 743.

30. Ibid., 746–47.

31. Li Qin, "Dui woguo nonmin fudan zhuangkuang de fenxi"; Kennedy, "Implementation of Village Elections," 48.

32. Khan and Riskin, "Income and Inequality," 249.

33. Lianjiang Li and Kevin O'Brien, "Struggle over Village Elections."

34. In situations where the village population is too large or scattered to meet regularly as a group, some provinces allowed for the establishment of Village Representative Assemblies consisting of representatives of each household (O'Brien, "Implementing Political Reform," 42–43; and Lawrence, "Democracy, Chinese Style," 61).

35. O'Brien, "Implementing Political Reform," 39.

36. Ibid., 41.

37. This estimate comes from the Ministry of Civil Affairs. See O'Brien, "Implementing Political Reform," 51.

38. "Shehui shouru fenpei bugong wenti yantaohui zongshu" (Summing up of the Conference 'Unfair Distribution of Income in Society'), *Shehuixue yanjiu* (Social Studies Research) 1 (1992): 80–82; Ge Yanfeng and Yue Songdong, "Dui woguo xianjieduan shouru fenpei wentidi jidian zairenazhi" (Another Consideration of some Points of the Distribution Problem in our Country's Present Stage), *Shehuixue yanjiu* 1 (1992): 83–84, cited in Eduard Vermeer, "Egalitarianism and the Land Question in China," *China Information* 18 (2004): 113n18. See also Ching Kwan Lee, *Against the Law*, 206, 221–22. The only nostalgia that rural residents have shown for the past is for the anti-corruption campaigns of the Mao era. See O'Brien and Li, "Campaign Nostalgia."

39. These are rough figures; as Lardy notes, reliable statistics on inflation during this time span are scarce. To make these calculations, I have slightly increased the World Bank calculation of 6.6 percent yearly rural price increases to 7 percent. Over the course of six years (1978–83), this amounts to a 39 percent rural inflation rate. During the same period, nominal per capita farm income rose 130 percent, and nominal per capita rural income rose 230 percent (Lardy, "Consumption and Living Standards," 851, 861).

40. Benjamin, Brandt, and Giles, "Evolution of Income Inequality," 776–78, 784. This finding is based on data from the National Bureau of Statistics and the Ministry of Agriculture's Research Center for Rural Economy.

41. *Zhongguo tongji nianjian*, various years.

42. Tang Ping, "Woguo nongcun jumin shouru shuiping ji chayi yanjiu" [Research into the Levels and Disparities in Income Among China's Village Residents], *Jingji yanjiu cankao* [Economic Research Reference Materials] 158 (October 14, 1994), 27, cited in Chan, Kervliet, and Unger, eds., *Transforming Asian Socialism*, 123.

43. Zhang Ping, "Zhongguo nongcun jumin quyujian shouru bupingdeng yu fei-nongjiuye," 60. For a discussion of official statistics on household income and inequality, see Bramall, "Quality of China's Household Income Surveys."

44. In 1990, the ratio of agricultural income in eastern, central, and western provinces was roughly 1.5 to 1.2 to 1. In the same year, the ratio of nonagricultural workers' wage income was approximately 1.7 to 1.2 to 1 ("Why the Chinese Income Gap Is Widening").

45. Oi, *Rural China Takes Off*, 77.

46. Kerkvliet and Selden, "Agrarian Transformation in China and Vietnam," in Chan et al., eds., *Transforming Asian Socialism*, 113.

47. Walder and Zhao, *Political Office*.

48. Ibid., 12.

49. Although leases were supposed to run fifteen years, Brandt et al. find that between 1983 (when the household responsibility system formally began) and 1996, the average village underwent 1.7 land reallocations. The average allocation typically involved slightly more than 50 percent of village land and roughly 75 percent of village households (Brandt et al., "Land Rights," 75–77).

50. For a discussion of this phenomenon in the spring of 1989, see Perry, "Casting a Chinese 'Democracy' Movement."

51. See, for example, Kung, "Equal Entitlement"; Kung and Liu, "Farmers' Preferences"; and Xiaoyuan Dong, "Two-Tier Land System" (referenced in Brandt et al., "Land Rights," 68).

52. Vermeer, "Egalitarianism," 127. See also Cao, *Huanghe biande Zhongguo*, 86.

53. Manion, "Democracy, Community, and Trust," 307.

54. Thireau, "From Equality to Equity," 53.

55. Ibid., 47.

56. Chan, Madsen, and Unger, *Chen Village Under Mao and Deng*; Chih-jou Jay Chen, "Local Institutions"; Ya-ling Liu, "Reform from Below"; Parris, "Local Initiative"; and Unger and Chan, "Inheritors of the Boom."

57. For a discussion of this phenomenon in Wenzhou, see Jianjun Zhang, *Marketization and Democracy*.

58. Thireau, "From Equality to Equity," 52. See also O'Brien, "Implementing Political Reform," 53.

59. Thireau, "From Equality to Equity," 43.

60. Ibid., 56. Given the deterioration of local state structures in poor villages in the latter half of the 1980s, when peasants acted violently against local authorities, public security forces often were insufficient to stop or punish the perpetrators (Bernstein and Lu, "Taxation Without Representation," 757; and O'Brien, "Implementing Political Reform," 53).

61. Bernstein and Lu, "Taxation Without Representation," 753.

62. O'Brien, "Implementing Political Reform," 52.

63. Ibid., 51–53.

64. Ibid., 56–57.

65. China Internet Information Center, "Opening to the Outside World."

66. Kung, "Evolution."

67. "China May Face Labor Shortage in 2010."

68. For numerous specific examples of this process, see Cao, *Huanghe biande Zhongguo.*

69. Oi, "Two Decades of Rural Reform," 619.

70. Benjamin, Brandt, and Giles, "Evolution of Income Inequality," 770–71.

71. "The U.S.–China WTO Accession Deal," *FAS online* (U.S. Department of Agriculture).

72. Bernstein and Lu, "Taxation Without Representation."

73. Ran and Qin, "How Has Rural Tax Reform Affected Farmers," 20–21.

74. Linda Chelan Li, "Working for the Peasants?" 102.

75. Oi and Zhao, "Fiscal Crisis," 82.

76. Ran and Qin, "How Has Rural Tax Reform"; and Oi and Zhao, "Fiscal Crisis." According to a 2005 survey undertaken by the Center for Chinese Agricultural Policy, total rural exactions declined by more than 50 percent between 2000 and 2004 (Ran and Qin, "How Has Rural Tax Reform," 23). A 2004 report by the National Bureau of Statistics states that the peasant tax burden declined by more than 27 percent between 2003 and 2004 (Oi and Zhao, "Fiscal Crisis," 82).

77. Oi and Zhao, "Fiscal Crisis," 80.

78. Ibid., 83–86, 90.

79. Oi and Zhao note that this expenditure priority results from the fact that unpaid cadres are more likely to rebel than are ordinary peasants deprived of government services. And, in order to protect their chances of job retention and promotion, township cadres must prevent local instability or protests that might come to the attention of political higher-ups (Oi and Zhao, "Fiscal Crisis," 89, 94–95).

80. Yeh, "Rural Policy"; and Forney, "Trouble in the 'New Socialist Countryside.'"

81. A 2003–4 study by the Institute of Rural Development at the Chinese Academy of Social Sciences found that between 1990 and 2002, more than sixty million farmers lost their land. The study's authors assert that this number has increased in more recent years. See Ling Zhao, "Significant Shift." Technically, land is under the collective ownership of the village, and as such is subject to Village Committee (VC) control. Yet VCs do not have the power to expropriate land for compensatory use. Rather, this power is held by the county government. In most cases, it appears that

land expropriation is initiated by the township, which then appeals to the county for approval and also attempts to convince the relevant VC to relinquish the land (Xiaolin Guo, "Land Expropriation," 424–26).

82. Ling Zhao, "Significant Shift."

83. Oi and Zhao, "Fiscal Crisis," 93.

84. Since 1999, compensation fees for the loss of crops on expropriated land have been six to ten times the value of the average annual output of the land over the prior three years (Xiaolin Guo, "Land Expropriation," 427).

85. Ibid., 427–28. One mu is roughly equal to one-sixth of an acre.

86. Yeh, "Rural Policy"; and Forney, "Trouble in the 'New Socialist Country-side.'"

87. Park, "Rural-Urban Inequality," 42.

88. Zhang and Yang, "Evaluation of People's Living Level."

89. Han and Whyte, "Social Contours of Distributive Injustice."

90. Yang Zhong, "Democratic Values Among Chinese Peasantry," 197.

91. Cao, *Huanghe biande Zhongguo*, 82.

92. Benjamin, Brandt, and Giles, "Evolution of Income Inequality," 770–71.

93. Cao, *Huanghe biande Zhongguo*, 226, 232–33.

94. Yeh, "Rural Policy," 26, citing Chen Xiwen, deputy director of China's Central Financial Work Leading Group.

95. *Zhongguo tongji nianjian*, various years.

96. Renwei Zhao, "Increasing Income Inequality."

97. Prosterman and Schwarzwalder, "From Death to Life," 20.

98. Benjamin, Brandt, and Giles, "Evolution of Income Inequality," 791–97.

99. Ibid., 799.

100. Guang and Zheng, "Migration," 44.

101. Manion, "Democracy," 314.

102. Guang and Zheng, "Migration," 30.

103. It should be noted that this candidate later lost his position. Although there was some debate as to whether or not he had engaged in bribery (since he paid all villagers, and not only his supporters), the city Discipline Department ruled that the election was invalid (Levy, "Village Elections," 35).

104. An Chen, "Failure of Organizational Control"; and Miller, "Hukou Reform."

105. Organic Law of the Villagers Committees of the People's Republic of China. Recall proceedings may be initiated by a petition signed by one-fifth of all villagers. The matter then goes to a vote, and a simple majority prevails. Note that the law also states that VCs should include "an appropriate number of women" (Article 9).

106. Josephine Ma, "Create a Uniform System," 5. Similarly, a study of rural Jiangsu province in 2000 found that 40 percent of village elections were free, fair, and com-

petitive (Jie Chen, "Sociopolitical Attitudes," 453). A 2004 survey of village elections in Shaanxi province reports that 80 percent of villages had conducted competitive elections, but the quality of the nomination process varied widely (Kennedy, "Implementation of Village Elections," 60). A 1999 Ministry of Civil Affairs report finds that 66 percent of village elections met national standards (*Xinhua*, July 11, 1999, SWB-FE 3585, July 13, 1999, and *South China Morning Post*, July 13, 1999, cited in Bernstein and Lu, "Taxation Without Representation," 762).

107. Kennedy, "Implementation," 55, 72.

108. Levy, "Village Elections," 38–39.

109. Bernstein and Lu, "Taxation Without Representation," 753–54; and *Cheng Ming* [Contention] (Hong Kong), in Bernstein, "Unrest in Rural China," 3–4.

110. *Cheng Ming*, in Bernstein, "Unrest in Rural China," 3–4.

111. "China's Land Grabs Raise Specter of Popular Unrest"; Kathy Chen, "Chinese Protests Grow More Frequent, Violent"; and Jianguo Li, "Protect the Right."

112. Ling Zhao, "Significant Shift."

113. Bernstein and Lu, "Taxation Without Representation," 756.

114. In a 2002 survey of rural households in six provinces, Michelson found that 85 to 90 percent of villagers in the central provinces of Hunan and Henan reported at least one grievance, as opposed to only 22 to 26 percent of villagers in coastal Shandong and Jiangsu provinces (Michelson, "Climbing the Dispute Pagoda," 475). On the geographic distribution of collective disputes in the 1990s and the first decade of the twenty-first century, see Bernstein and Lu, "Taxation Without Representation," and Ling Zhao, "Significant Shift."

115. Peasants' major complaints are that land is illegally or forcefully confiscated, or that compensation is too low (Ling Zhao, "Significant Shift").

116. Michelson, "Justice from Above or Below?"

117. Lianjiang Li, "Political Trust."

118. Zhu Anshun, "Ruci jian fang wei na ban?" 384, cited in O'Brien and Li, *Rightful Resistance*, 43.

119. For examples, see Bernstein and Lu, "Taxation Without Representation"; O'Brien and Li, *Rightful Resistance*; Xiaolin Guo, "Land Expropriation"; Ling Zhao, "Significant Shift"; and Yu and Xiao, "Ershinian lai dalu nongcun de zhengzhi wending zhangkuang."

120. O'Brien and Li, *Rightful Resistance*, 45.

121. In 2006, of a total of 73 million CCP members, an estimated 50.37 million (69 percent) were urban residents and 22.6 million (31 percent) were rural residents. The total urban population in 2006 was roughly 563 million, and the total rural population was roughly 727 million.

122. Yang Zhong, "Democratic Values Among Chinese Peasantry," 203.

123. Ibid., 194, 200, 203, 207; and Bernstein and Lu, "Taxation Without Representation," 759.

124. Manion, "Democracy, Community, and Trust," 319.

125. O'Brien and Han, "Path to Democracy?"

126. Heurlin and Whiting, "Villagers Against the State"; and Lianjiang Li, "Political Trust and Petitioning."

127. Lianjiang Li, "Political Trust and Petitioning."

128. Heurlin and Whiting, "Villagers Against the State," 20.

129. In Lianjiang Li's survey, successful petitioners became 45.7 percent more likely to agree that the central government truly cared about farmers and 63.7 percent more likely to agree that petitioning Beijing was very useful. Conversely, "local repression had a negative correlation with trust in the center" (Lianjiang Li, "Political Trust and Petitioning," 218).

130. Lianjiang Li, "Political Trust and Petitioning."

131. Lianjiang Li, "Political Trust in Rural China," 247.

132. See also O'Brien and Li, *Rightful Resistance*, chap. 4.

133. Lianjiang Li, "Political Trust and Petitioning."

134. Lianjiang Li, "Political Trust in Rural China," 247. For similar quotes, see Jianrong Yu, "Conflict in the Countryside," 149; and Cao, *Huanghe biande Zhongguo*, 253.

135. If one assumes that 80 percent of the roughly 13 million petitions submitted in 2005 related to land disputes (and therefore were initiated by peasants), then roughly 10.4 million of China's 737 million peasants submitted a petition. In 2003 roughly 2 million of China's roughly 800 million participated in public protests.

Chapter 7

1. By 1949 in China, virtually all citizens were subject to CCP governance, but in Vietnam, communist rule in the North was impeded by war through 1975, and communist governance was not established in the South until the same year. Following the war, agricultural collectives were the norm in North Vietnam but never were fully established in the South. Further, whereas approximately 20 percent of the populace in pre-reform China worked in the state sector and received attendant socialist socioeconomic benefits such as housing, medical care, and pensions, this was the case for only about 5 percent of the Vietnamese population. See Kerkvliet, Chan, and Unger, "Comparing Vietnam and China."

2. This term later was extended to twenty years.

3. Of the approximately 2.3 million Vietnamese who worked in SOEs in 1990, roughly half had been laid off by 1992. At the same time, the total number of SOEs diminished from approximately 12,000 to fewer than 6,000. See St. John, "End of

the Beginning," 178–79; and Dinh, "Political Economy of Vietnam's Transformation Process," 362. In 1990, Vietnam's population totaled 66 million; in 1992, it was 69 million.

4. U.S. Department of Commerce Report, cited in Kradjis, "Vietnam: 30 Years After Victory."

5. Dinh, "Political Economy," 363.

6. For a comparison, see Chan and Wang, "Impact of the State on Workers' Conditions."

7. Kradjis, "Big Strikes."

8. Ibid. See also Tan, "Alternatives to the 'Race to the Bottom' in Vietnam."

9. Economist Intelligence Unit, "Risk Wire."

10. Chan and Wang, "Impact of the State on Workers' Conditions," 633.

11. Amy Y. C. Liu, "Markets, Inequality, and Poverty in Vietnam," 232–33; Fforde, "From Plan to Market," 59; and Van Arkadie and Mallon, *Vietnam: A Transition Tiger?*, 28.

12. Asian Development Bank, *Asian Development Outlook 2007.*

13. Vietnam's inflation peaked in the late 1980s, with increases of 300 to 500 percent yearly. Since 2004, inflation rates have stabilized at about 7 percent annually. As of 1998, just over 26 percent of the citizenry was below the poverty line.

14. Of a total population of 69 million Vietnamese, 1.1 million SOE workers were laid off. This compares with roughly 5 to 8 percent in China. As Solinger documents, reliable figures on the total number of SOE layoffs in China in the mid-1990s are unavailable (Solinger, "Why We Cannot Count the 'Unemployed'"). Most estimates fall in the range of 50 to 100 million "retrenched" Chinese SOE workers in a population of 1.2 billion.

15. Chan and Wang, "Impact of the State on Workers' Conditions," 634.

16. Ibid., 632–33.

17. These Gini figures come from the World Bank.

18. For example, as of the middle of the first decade of the 2000s, the pay of state sector garment workers was about 30 percent higher than that in private and foreign firms (Kradjis, "Vietnam: 30 Years After Victory").

19. For example, an early 1990s survey of five universities and colleges in Hanoi found that 85 percent of respondents expressed a preference for jobs in the state sector (Heberer, *Private Entrepreneurs in China and Vietnam*, 6).

20. Gainsborough, "Political Change in Vietnam," 700.

21. *Far East Economic Review*, January 13, 1994, 71, cited in Heberer, *Private Entrepreneurs in China and Vietnam*, 5.

22. Gainsborough, "Party Control."

23. Ibid., 66. See also Heberer, *Private Entrepreneurs in China and Vietnam.*

24. Heberer, *Private Entrepreneurs in China and Vietnam*, 172. Interviewees in China responded even more positively: More than 37 percent said "yes," more than 57 percent chose "to some extent," and only about 6 percent said "no" (Ibid., 169).

25. This was the case in the Central Highlands protests of early 2001, the largest instance of rural protests in Vietnam's reform era.

26. Gainsborough, "Political Change," 699.

27. For a discussion of the concept of "post-socialism," see Chen and Sil, "Stretching Postcommunism."

28. Although powerful politicians and their financial backers manipulated Russia's political system during the 1990s, Freedom House categorizes Russia during this time as "partly free," giving it scores of 3 on "political rights" and 4 on "civil liberties." Countries with scores of 1 or 2 on these measures are considered by Freedom House to be "free."

29. Cook, "Negotiating Welfare in Postcommunist States," 42.

30. A total of 1.3 million workers were dismissed. Russia's total working population at the time was 73 million.

31. Cook, "Workers in the Russian Federation," 15–17.

32. Sil and Chen, "State Legitimacy," 356.

33. Doyle, "Distributional Consequences During the Early Stages of Russia's Transition"; and CIA World Factbook, "Russia: Economy."

34. World Values Survey.

35. Gilley, "Meaning and Measure of State Legitimacy."

36. World Values Survey.

37. "Freedom in the World."

38. Bernstam and Rabushka, "China vs. Russia."

39. Morin and Samaranayake, "Putin Popularity Score."

40. Ibid., citing Pew Global Attitudes surveys.

41. Bellin, "Contingent Democrats." See also Murillo, "From Populism to Neoliberalism."

42. As of 2007, 22.8 percent of the population fell between the ages of fifteen and twenty-nine.

43. Jie Chen, *Popular Political Support*; Tang, *Public Opinion*. For Chen's statistics on regime support, see Chapter 1.

44. *Zhongguo tongji nianjian, 2007*; "Urban, Rural Residents Income up over 15% in 2007"; and Economist Intelligence Unit Viewswire, "How Much Worse Will It Get?"

45. Garnaut, "Employment for the Masses in China."

46. Economist Intelligence Unit Viewswire, "How Much Worse Will It Get?"

47. These predictions were made by *The Economist*'s Economist Intelligence Unit and the international consulting firm, AT Kearney. The World Bank predicted a 2009

Chinese GDP growth rate of 7.5 percent. See Economist Intelligence Unit Viewswire, "How Much Worse Will It Get?"; and Bao and Xin, "China's Growth Rate May Fall to 6%: AT Kearney," *China Daily*, November 27, 2008.

48. Asian Development Bank, *Asian Development Outlook 2009*, 126.

49. See Boix, *Democracy and Redistribution*.

50. Marx, *Communist Manifesto*, 58.

BIBLIOGRAPHY

"Across PRD." *China Daily* (Hong Kong edition), September 19, 2007.

Alpermann, Bjorn. "'Wrapped Up in Cotton Wool': The Political Integration of Private Entrepreneurs in Rural China." *China Journal* 56 (2006): 33–61.

Alpermann, Bjorn, and Shuge Gang. "Social Origins and Political Participation of Private Entrepreneurs in Beijing." Unpublished paper, Wuerzburg University (Germany).

Appleton, Simon, John Knight, Linda Song, and Qingjie Xia. "Labour Retrenchment in China: Determinants and Consequences." In *Unemployment, Inequality and Poverty in Urban China*, edited by Shi Li and Hiroshi Sato, 19–42. New York: Routledge, 2006.

Asian Development Bank. *Asian Development Outlook 2007: Vietnam*. http://www.adb.org/Documents/Books/ADO/2007/VIE.pdf (accessed March 24, 2008).

———. *Asian Development Outlook 2009 Update: Broadening Openness for a Resilient Asia*. http://www.adb.org/Documents/Books/ADO/2009/Update/ (accessed October 11, 2009).

Bao, Wanxian, and Zhiming Xin. "China's Growth Rate May Fall to 6%: AT Kearney." *China Daily*, November 27, 2008.

Barro, Robert. "Determinants of Democracy." *Journal of Political Economy* 107 (December 1999): 158–83.

———. "Rule of Law, Democracy, and Economic Performance." *2000 Index of Economic Freedom*. Washington, DC: Heritage Foundation, 2000.

Beijing Workers Autonomous Federation Preparatory Committee. "Provisional Memorandum." May 28, 1989.

Bellin, Eva. "Contingent Democrats: Industrialists, Labor, and Democratization in Late-Developing Countries." *World Politics* 52, no. 2 (2000): 175–205.

———. *Stalled Democracy: Capital, Labor, and the Paradox of State-Sponsored Development*. Ithaca, NY: Cornell University Press, 2002.

Bendix, Reinhard. *Nation Building and Citizenship.* New York: John Wiley and Sons, 1964.

Benjamin, Dwayne, Loren Brandt, and John Giles. "The Evolution of Income Inequality in Rural China." *Economic Development and Cultural Change* 53, no. 4 (2005): 769–824.

Bernstam, Michael, and Alvin Rabushka. "China vs. Russia: Wealth Creation vs. Poverty Reduction." Hoover Institution, April 25, 2005. http://www.hoover.org/research/russianecon/essays/5084951.html (accessed March 21, 2008).

Bernstein, Thomas. "Unrest in Rural China: A 2003 Assessment." *Center for the Study of Democracy Paper* 13 (2004): 1–21.

Bernstein, Thomas, and Xiaobo Lu. *Taxation Without Representation in Contemporary Rural China.* Cambridge: Cambridge University Press, 2003.

———. "Taxation Without Representation: Peasants, the Central and the Local States in Reform China." *China Quarterly* 163 (September 2000): 742–63.

"A Better Day for Beggars." *Beijing Review* 46, no. 52 (December 25, 2003).

"Blair Presses for China Democracy," BBC News, September 6, 2005.

Blecher, Marc J. "Hegemony and Workers' Politics in China." *China Quarterly* 170 (2002): 283–303.

Boix, Carles. *Democracy and Redistribution.* Cambridge: Cambridge University Press, 2003.

Boix, Carles, and Susan Stokes. "Endogenous Democratization." *World Politics* 55, no. 4 (2003): 517–49.

Boyd, Mary. "Migrant Labour Mechanisms: The Down and Dirty." *China Economic Quarterly* Q3 (2005): 29.

Bramall, Chris. "The Quality of China's Household Income Surveys." *China Quarterly* 167 (September 2001): 689–705.

Brandt, Loren, Jijun Huang, Guo Li, and Scott Rozelle. "Land Rights in Rural China." *China Journal* 47 (January 2002): 67–97.

Brehm, John, and Wendy Rahn. "Individual-level Evidence for the Causes and Consequences of Social Capital." *American Journal of Political Science* 41 (July 1997): 999–1023.

Bridges, Amy. "The Working Classes in the United States Before the Civil War." In *Working Class Formation*, edited by Ira Katznelson and Aristide Zolberg, 157–96. Princeton, NJ: Princeton University Press, 1986.

Buckley, Christopher. "How a Revolution Becomes a Dinner Party: Stratification, Mobility, and the New Rich in Urban China." In *Culture and Privilege in Capitalist Asia,* edited by Michael Pinches, 209–30. New York: Routledge, 1999.

Bueno de Mesquita, Bruce, and George W. Downs. "Development and Democracy." *Foreign Affairs* 84, no. 5 (September/October 2005): 77–86.

Burkhart, Ross, and Michael Lewis-Beck. "Comparative Democracy: The Economic Development Thesis." *American Political Science Review* 88, no. 4 (December 1994): 903–10.

Bush, George W. "A Distinctly American Internationalism." Speech at Ronald Reagan Presidential Library, Simi Valley, CA, November 19, 1999.

Cai, Yongshun. "China's Moderate Middle Class: The Case of Homeowners' Resistance." *Asian Survey* 45, no. 5 (October 2005): 777–99.

———. "Managed Participation in China." *Political Science Quarterly* 119, no. 3 (2004): 425–52.

———. *State and Laid-off Workers in Reform China: The Silence and Collective Action of the Retrenched.* New York: Routledge, 2006.

Cao Jinqing. *Huanghe biande Zhongguo* [China Along the Yellow River]. Shanghai: Shanghai wenyi chubanshe, 2000.

Chan, Anita. *China's Workers Under Assault: The Exploitation of Labor in a Globalizing Economy.* Armonk, NY: M. E. Sharpe, 2001.

———. "The Emerging Patterns of Industrial Relations in China and the Rise of Two New Labour Movements." *China Information* 9, no. 4 (1995): 36–59.

———. "Recent Trends in Chinese Labour Issues: Signs of Change." *China Perspectives* 57 (January–February 2005): 23–31.

Chan, Anita, Benedict Kervliet, and Jonathan Unger, eds. *Transforming Asian Socialism: China and Vietnam Compared.* New York: Rowman and Littlefield, 1999.

Chan, Anita, Richard Madsen, and Jonathan Unger. *Chen Village Under Mao and Deng.* Berkeley: University of California Press, 1992.

Chan, Anita, and Hong-zen Wang. "The Impact of the State on Workers' Conditions—Comparing Taiwanese Factories in China and Taiwan." *Pacific Affairs* 77, no. 4 (Winter 2004–2005): 629–46.

Chan, Kam Wing. "Recent Migration in China: Patterns, Trends and Policies." *Asian Perspective* 24, no. 4 (2001): 127–55.

Chen, An. "The Failure of Organizational Control: Changing Party Power in the Chinese Countryside." *Politics and Society* 35, no. 1 (March 2007): 145–79.

———. "Why Does Capitalism Fail to Push China Toward Democracy?" In *Capitalism in the Dragon's Lair,* edited by Christopher McNally, 146–66. New York: Routledge, 2007.

Chen, Cheng, and Rudra Sil. "Stretching Postcommunism: Diversity, Context, and Comparative Historical Analysis." *Post-Soviet Affairs* 23, no. 4 (October–December 2007): 275–301.

Chen, Chih-jou Jay. "Local Institutions and the Transformation of Property Rights in Southern Fujian." In *Property Rights and Economic Reform in China,* edited by

Jean C. Oi and Andrew Walder, 49–70. Stanford, CA: Stanford University Press, 1999.

Chen, Feng. "Industrial Restructuring and Workers' Resistance in China." *Modern China* 29, no. 2 (April 2003): 237–62.

———. "Privatization and Its Discontents in Chinese Factories." *China Quarterly* 185 (2006): 42–60.

Chen, Jie. *Popular Political Support in Urban China.* Stanford, CA: Stanford University Press, 2004.

———. "Sociopolitical Attitudes of the Masses and Leaders in the Chinese Village." *Journal of Contemporary China* 14, no. 44 (August 2005): 445–64.

Chen, Jie, and Chunlong Lu. "Social Capital in Urban China: Attitudinal and Behavioral Effects on Grassroots Self-government." *Social Science Quarterly* 88, no. 2 (June 2007): 422–42.

Chen, Kathy. "Chinese Protests Grow More Frequent, Violent." *Wall Street Journal*, November 5, 2004.

Chen Wuming. "Fubai manyan de tedian jiqi yanzhong weihai" [The Features and Damages of Spreading Corruption]. *Zhenli de Zhuiqiu* [Seeking Truth] 122 (August 11, 2000): 22–31.

Chen, Xitong. *Report on Checking the Turmoil and Quelling the Counter-Revolutionary Rebellion.* Beijing: New Star Publishers, 1989.

Chen, Xueyi, and Tianjian Shi. "Media Effects on Political Confidence and Trust in the People's Republic of China in the Post-Tiananmen Period." *East Asia* 19, no. 3 (Fall 2001): 84–118.

Cheng, Eva. "Public Sector Less than 40% of Economy." *Green Left Weekly* 734, December 5, 2007. http://www.greenleft.org.au/2007/734/38026 (accessed January 25, 2008).

Cheng, Yuk-shing, and Tsang Shu-kai. "Agricultural Land Reform in a Mixed System." *China Information* 10, no. 3–4 (Winter 1995–Spring 1996): 1–29.

China Blue (documentary film). Bullfrog Films, 2005.

China Democracy Party Data Collection [*Zhongguo Minzhudang Ziliao Huipian*], in the author's possession.

China Internet Information Center (State Council Information Office). "Opening to the Outside World: Special Economic Zones and Open Coastal Cities." July 13, 2000. http://www.china.org.cn/e<->china/openingup/sez.htm (accessed May 25, 2008).

China Labour Bulletin. "Speaking Out: The Workers' Movement in China, 2005–2006." *China Labour Bulletin Research Reports* 5 (December 2007).

China Labour Bulletin (various issues). http://www.china-labour.org.hk.

China Labour Bulletin Action Express (various issues). http://www.china-labour.org.hk.

"China May Face Labor Shortage in 2010." *China Daily*, May 14, 2007.

"China to Raise Pension Fund as of Jan." *Xinhua*, December 15, 2007.

"China Won't Change Retirement Age." *People's Daily*, December 16, 2005.

"China's Land Grabs Raise Specter of Popular Unrest." *Washington Post*, October 5, 2004.

"China's State-Owned Enterprises Back in the Spotlight." *China Labour Bulletin*, September 14, 2009. http://www.china-labour.org.hk/en/node/100562 (accessed October 10, 2009).

Chung, Jae Ho, Hongyi Lai, and Ming Xia. "Mounting Challenges to Governance in China: Surveying Collective Protestors, Religious Sects and Criminal Organizations." *China Journal* 56 (July 2006): 1–31.

CIA World Factbook. "Brazil: Economy." https://www.cia.gov/library/publications/the-world-factbook/geos/br.html (accessed October 4, 2009).

———. "Russia: Economy." https://www.cia.gov/library/publications/the-world-factbook/geos/rs.html (accessed March 21, 2008).

———. "United States: Economy." https://www.cia.gov/library/publications/the-world-factbook/geos/us.html (accessed October 4, 2009).

Clinton, Bill. *Between Hope and History*. New York: Random House, 1996.

"Constitution of the People's Republic of China." *People's Daily*. http://english.peopledaily.com.cn/constitution/constitution.html (accessed October 4, 2009).

Cook, Linda. "Negotiating Welfare in Postcommunist States." *Comparative Politics* 40, no. 1 (October 2007): 41–62.

———. "Workers in the Russian Federation: Responses to the Post-communist Transition, 1989–1993." *Communist and Post-Communist Studies* 28, no. 1 (1995): 13–42.

"CPC Amends Constitution to Foster Private Sector." *Xinhua*, October 21, 2007.

"A Cry for Justice: The Voices of Chinese Workers." Albert Shanker Institute, 2008. http://www.shankerinstitute.org/ACryforJusticeFinal.pdf (accessed October 11, 2009).

Cui Zhiyuan. "Ruhe renshi jinri Zhongguo: 'xiaokang shehui' jiedu" [How to Comprehend Today's China: An Interpretation of the "Comparatively Well Off" Society]. *Dushu* [*Reading*] 3 (March 2004): 3–9.

Davies, Gloria, and Gaby Ramia. "Governance Reform Towards Serving Migrant Workers: The Local Implementation of Central Government Regulations." *China Quarterly* 193 (2008): 140–49.

Dickson, Bruce J. *Democratization in China and Taiwan: The Adaptability of Leninist Parties*. Oxford: Oxford University Press, 1998.

———. "Dilemmas of Party Adaptation: The CCP's Strategies for Survival." In *State and Society in 21st-century China*, edited by Peter Hays Gries and Stanley Rosen, 159–79. New York: Routledge, 2004.

———. "Integrating Wealth and Power in China: The Communist Party's Embrace of the Private Sector," *China Quarterly* 192 (December 2007): 827–54.

——. *Red Capitalists in China: The Party, Private Entrepreneurs, and Prospects for Political Change.* Cambridge: Cambridge University Press, 2003.

Dinh, Quan Xuan. "The Political Economy of Vietnam's Transformation Process." *Contemporary Southeast Asia* 22, no. 2 (August 2000): 360–88.

Dong, Xiaoyuan. "Two-Tier Land System and Sustained Economic Growth in Post-1978 Rural China." *World Development* 24, no. 5 (1996): 915–28.

Dong, Xuebing, and Jinchuan Shi. "The Reconstruction of Local Power: Wenling City's 'Democratic Talk in All Sincerity.'" In *The Search for Deliberative Democracy in China*, edited by Ethan J. Lieb and Baogang He, 217–28. New York: Palgrave, 2006.

Dowd, Daniel, Allen Carlson, and Mingming Shen. "The Prospects for Democratization in China: Evidence from the 1995 Beijing Area Study." *Journal of Contemporary China* 8, no. 22 (November 1999): 365–81.

Doyle, Chris. "The Distributional Consequences During the Early Stages of Russia's Transition." *Review of Income and Wealth* 42, no. 4 (1996): 493–505.

East Asian Barometer. 2002. http://www.jdsurvey.net/bdasepjds/easiabarometer/eab .jsp (accessed October 11, 2009).

Economist Intelligence Unit. "Risk Wire: Vietnam Risk." April 2, 2002, http://www .eiu.com (accessed February 19, 2009).

Economist Intelligence Unit Viewswire. "How Much Worse Will It Get?" *Economist,* February 3, 2009. http://www.economist.com/displaystory.cfm?story_id=13053205 (accessed February 19, 2009).

"Education Finance: Pay to Play." *China Economic Quarterly* Q4 (2005).

Efimov, Alexey. "The Retirement Blues." *China Economic Quarterly* Q3 (2007).

Fewsmith, Joseph. "Assessing Social Stability on the Eve of the 17th Party Congress." *China Leadership Monitor* 20 (Winter 2007): 1–24.

——. *China Since Tiananmen: The Politics of Transition.* Cambridge: Cambridge University Press, 2001.

——. "The Political Implications of China's Growing Middle Class." *China Leadership Monitor* 21 (Summer 2007): 1–8.

Fforde, Adam. "From Plan to Market: The Economic Transitions in Vietnam and China Compared." In *Transforming Asian Socialism: China and Vietnam Compared*, edited by Benedict Kerkvliet, Anita Chan, and Jonathan Unger, 43–72. New York: Rowman and Littlefield, 1999.

"Food and Fuel Price Hikes Spark Protests in China." *Straits Times* (Singapore), December 7, 2007.

Forney, Matt. "Trouble in the 'New Socialist Countryside.'" *China Economic Quarterly* Q1 (2006): 53–55.

Francis, Corrina-Barbara. "The Progress of Protest in China." *Asian Survey* 29, no. 9 (September 1989): 898–915.

Frazier, Mark. "China's Pension Reform and Its Discontents." *China Journal* 51 (January 2004): 97–114.

"Freedom in the World." Freedom House. http://www.freedomhouse.org/template .cfm?page=15 (accessed June 13, 2008).

Freidman, Thomas. *The Lexus and the Olive Tree.* New York: Anchor Books, 2000.

Froissart, Chloe. "Escaping from under the Party's Thumb: A Few Examples of Migrant Workers' Striving for Autonomy," *Social Research* 73, no. 1 (Spring 2006): 197–218.

Fu, Hualing, and Richard Cullin. "Weiquan [Rights Protection] Lawyering in an Authoritarian State." *China Journal* 59 (2008): 111–27.

Fuller, Linda. "Socialism and the Transition in Eastern and Central Europe: The Homogeneity Paradigm, Class, and Economic Inefficiency." *Annual Review of Sociology* 26 (2000): 585–609.

Gainsborough, Martin. "Party Control: Electoral Campaigning in Vietnam in the Run-up to the May 2002 National Assembly Elections." *Pacific Affairs* 78, no. 1 (Spring 2005): 57–75.

———. "Political Change in Vietnam: In Search of the Middle-Class Challenge to the State." *Asian Survey* 42, no. 5 (September–October 2002): 694–707.

Gallagher, Mary. *Contagious Capitalism: Globalization and the Politics of Labor in China.* Princeton, NJ: Princeton University Press, 2005.

Garnaut, John. "Employment for the Masses in China." *Sydney Morning Herald*, May 5, 2008.

Garnaut, Ross, Ligang Song, and Yang Yao. "The Impact and Significance of State-owned Enterprise Restructuring in China." *China Journal* 55 (January 2006): 35–65.

Gerschenkron, Alexander. *Economic Backwardness in Historical Perspective.* Cambridge, MA: Harvard University Press, 1962.

Gilley, Bruce. *China's Democratic Future.* New York: Columbia University Press, 2004.

———. "The Limits of Authoritarian Resilience." *Journal of Democracy* 14, no. 10 (2003): 18–26.

———. "The Meaning and Measure of State Legitimacy: Results for 72 Countries." *European Journal of Political Research* 45, no. 3 (May 2006): 499–525.

Goldman, Merle. *From Comrade to Citizen: The Struggle for Political Rights in China.* Cambridge, MA: Harvard University Press, 2005.

———. *Sowing the Seeds of Democracy in China: Political Reform in the Deng Xiaoping Era.* Cambridge, MA: Harvard University Press, 1994.

Goodman, David S. G. "Localism and Entrepreneurship: History, Identity and Solidarity as Factors of Production." In *China's Rational Entrepreneurs: The Development of the New Private Business Sector,* edited by Barbara Krug, 159–60. New York: Routledge, 2004.

―――. "The New Middle Class." In *The Paradox of China's Post-Mao Reforms*, edited by Merle Goldman and Roderick MacFarquhar, 241–61. Cambridge, MA: Harvard University Press, 1999.

Gong Kaijin. "Qiye lingdao tizhi yu dang zuzhi zai qiyezhong de diwei" [The Enterprise Leadership System and the Role Party Organizations within Enterprises]. *Qiye Wenming* [Enterprise Civilization] (Chongqing) (March 1995): 25–28.

Guang, Lei. "Guerilla Workfare: Migrant Renovators, State Power, and Informal Work in Urban China." *Politics and Society* 33, no. 3 (September 2005): 481–506.

Guang, Lei, and Lu Zheng. "Migration as the Second-Best Option: Local Power and Off-farm Employment." *China Quarterly* 181 (2005): 22–45.

Guiheux, Gilles. "The Political 'Participation' of Entrepreneurs: Challenge or Opportunity for the Chinese Communist Party?" *Social Research* 73 (Spring 2006): 219–44.

―――. "The Promotion of a New Calculating Chinese Subject: The Case of Laid-off Workers Turning into Entrepreneurs." *Journal of Contemporary China* 16 (February 2007): 149–71.

Guo, Gang. "Party Recruitment of College Students in China." *Journal of Contemporary China* 14, no. 43 (May 2005): 371–93.

Guo, Xiaolin. "Land Expropriation and Rural Conflicts in China." *China Quarterly* 166 (2001): 422–39.

Hamrin, Carol, and Timothy Cheek. *China's Establishment Intellectuals*. Armonk, NY: M. E. Sharpe, 1986.

Han, Chunping, and Martin King Whyte. "The Social Contours of Distributive Injustice Feelings in Contemporary China." In *Creating Wealth and Poverty in Post-Socialist China*, edited by Deborah Davis and Wang Feng, 193–212. Stanford, CA: Stanford University Press, 2009.

Han, Minzhu, ed. *Cries for Democracy: Writings and Speeches from the 1989 Chinese Democracy Movement*. Princeton, NJ: Princeton University Press, 1990.

Harrison, Royden. *Before the Socialists*. London: Routledge, 1965.

Hartford, Kathleen. "The Political Economy Behind the Beijing Spring." In *Perspectives on the Chinese People's Movement: Spring 1989*, edited by Tony Saich, 50–82. Armonk, NY: M. E. Sharpe, 1990.

Heberer, Thomas. *Private Entrepreneurs in China and Vietnam*. Leiden, Germany: Brill, N.H.E.J. N.V Koninklijke, Boekhandel en Drukkerji, 2003.

Heurlin, Christopher, and Susan Whiting. "Villagers Against the State: The Politics of Land Disputes." Paper presented at the annual meeting of the American Political Science Association, Chicago, August 30, 2007.

Ho, Peter. "Contesting Rural Spaces." In *Chinese Society*, 2nd ed., edited by Elizabeth Perry and Mark Selden, 93–112. New York: Routledge, 2003.

Hon, Chua Chin. "Beijing Signs Pact to Protect Migrant Workers." *Straits Times,* October 16, 2004.

Hong, Zhaohui. "Mapping the Evolution and Transformation of the New Capital Holders in China." *Journal of Chinese Political Science* 9, no. 1 (2004): 23–42.

Howard, Marc Morje. *The Weakness of Civil Society in Post-Communist Europe.* Cambridge: Cambridge University Press, 2003.

Howell, June. "Prospects for Village Self-Governance in China." *Journal of Peasant Studies* 25, no. 3 (1998): 86–111.

"Hu Jintao Vows to 'Reverse Growing Income Disparity.'" *Xinhua,* October 15, 2007.

"Hu Pledges Political Reform, Stronger Party." *South China Morning Post,* October 15, 2007.

Huang, Cary. "Official Praise for Deposed Party Chief." *South China Morning Post,* November 19, 2005.

Huang Zhijian. "Qingnian xiaofei wu da qushi" [Five Major Trends in Consumption Patterns of Youth]. *Liaowang xinwen zhoukan* [Outlook Weekly] 35, no. 27 (August 27, 2001): 38–40.

Human Rights Watch, "'Walking on Thin Ice'; Control, Intimidation and Harassment of Lawyers in China," April 2008. http://www.hrw.org/reports/2008/china0408/ (accessed March 30, 2009).

"Hunan Coalminers Strike Over Privatization Plans." *China Labour Bulletin,* September 1, 2009. http://www.china-labour.org.hk/en/node/100553 (accessed October 10, 2009).

Hurst, William. "The Forgotten Player: Local State Strategies and the Dynamics of Workers' Contention." Paper presented at a conference on Reassessing Unrest in China, Washington, DC, 2004.

Hurst, William, and Kevin O'Brien. "China's Contentious Pensioners." *China Quarterly* 170 (2002): 345–60.

"Incidents of Social Unrest Hit 87,000." *South China Morning Post,* January 20, 2006.

Ji Y. "Dangqian wosheng jihuawai yonggong qingkuang poxi" ["Analysis of the Current Conditions of Out-of-plan Workers"]. *Chuangyezhe* 11 (1986).

Jones, David Martin. "Democratization, Civil Society, and Illiberal Middle Class Culture in Pacific Asia." *Comparative Politics* 30, no. 2 (January 1998): 147–69.

Kahn, Joseph. "Cautiously, China Honors Leader Linked to Tiananmen Unrest." *New York Times,* November 19, 2005.

———. "China's Fear of Ghosts: Balancing Stability and Dissent." *New York Times,* January 30, 2005.

Katznelson, Ira. "Working Class Formation: Constructing Cases and Comparisons." In *Working Class Formation,* edited by Ira Katznelson and Aristide Zolberg, 3–44. Princeton, NJ: Princeton University Press, 1986.

Kelliher, Daniel. "The Chinese Debate over Village Self-Government." *China Journal* 37 (1997): 63–86.

Kennedy, John James. "The Implementation of Village Elections and Tax-for-Fee Reform in Rural Northwest China." In *Grassroots Political Reform in Contemporary China*, edited by Elizabeth Perry and Merle Goldman, 48–74. Cambridge, MA: Harvard University Press, 2007.

Kerkvliet, Benedict, Anita Chan, and Jonathan Unger. "Comparing Vietnam and China: An Introduction." In *Transforming Asian Socialism: China and Vietnam Compared*, edited by Benedict Kerkvliet, Anita Chan, and Jonathan Unger, eds., 1–14. New York: Rowman and Littlefield, 1999.

Kerkvliet, Benedict, and Mark Selden. "Agrarian Transformation in China and Vietnam." In *Transforming Asian Socialism: China and Vietnam Compared*, edited by Benedict Kerkvliet, Anita Chan, and Jonathan Unger, eds., 98–119. New York: Rowman and Littlefield, 1999.

Khan, Azizur Rahman, and Carl Riskin. "Income and Inequality in China: Composition, Distribution and Growth of Household Income, 1988 to 1995." *China Quarterly* 154 (June 1998): 221–53.

Kradjis, Michael. "The Big Strikes: Did the Government 'Cave In' to Workers or Did it Lead Them?" *Asian Analysis*, ASEAN Focus Group, The Australian National University, September 2006. http://www.aseanfocus.com/asiananalysis/article.cfm?articleID=984 (accessed June 11, 2008).

———. "Vietnam 30 Years After Victory: Towards Capitalism or Socialism?" GreenLeft.org, May 4, 2005. http://www.greenleft.org.au/2005/625/34772 (accessed June 24, 2008).

Kristof, Nicholas. "The Tiananmen Victory." *New York Times*, June 2, 2004.

Kroeber, Arthur. "The Durable Communist Party." *China Economic Quarterly* Q1 (2007): 14–18.

Kroeber, Arthur, and Rosealea Yao. "SOEs in Pictures: Large and in Charge." *China Economic Quarterly* 12, no. 2 (June 2008): 38–41.

Kullberg, Judith S., and William Zimmerman. "Liberal Elites, Socialist Masses, and Problems of Russian Democracy." *World Politics* 51, no. 3 (1999): 323–58.

Kung, James. "Equal Entitlement Versus Tenure Security Under a Regime of Collective Property Rights: Peasants' Preference for Institutions in Post-reform Chinese Agriculture." *Journal of Comparative Economics* 21 (1995): 82–111.

———. "The Evolution of Property Rights in Village Enterprises." In *Property Rights and Economic Reform in China*, edited by Jean Oi and Andrew Walder, 95–122. Stanford, CA: Stanford University Press, 1999.

Kung, James, and Shouying Liu. "Farmers' Preferences Regarding Ownership and Land Tenure in Post-Mao China." *China Journal* 38 (July 1997): 33–63.

Kwong, Julia. "The 1986 Student Demonstrations in China: A Democratic Movement?" *Asian Survey* 28, no. 9 (September 1988): 970–85.

"Laboring over Workers' Rights." *Bejing Review* 46, no. 52 (December 25, 2003).

Lardy, Nicholas. *China's Unfinished Economic Revolution.* Washington, DC: Brookings Institution Press, 1998.

———. "Consumption and Living Standards in China, 1978–83." *China Quarterly* 100 (December 1984): 849–65.

"Latest Inner-Party Statistics of 2004 Show the Vitality of Party Ranks." *People's Daily,* March 7, 2006.

Lawrence, Susan. "Democracy, Chinese Style: Village Representative Assemblies." *Australian Journal of Chinese Affairs* 32 (July 1994): 61–68.

Lee, Ching Kwan. *Against the Law: Labor Protests in China's Rustbelt and Sunbelt* Berkeley: University of California Press, 2007.

Lee, Feigon. *China Rising: The Meaning of Tiananmen.* Chicago: Ivan R. Dee, 1990.

Levy, Richard. "Village Elections and Anticorruption." In *Grassroots Political Reform in Contemporary China,* edited by Perry and Goldman, 20–47. Cambridge, MA: Harvard University Press, 2007.

Li, Bobai, and Andrew Walder. "Career Advancement as Party Patronage: Sponsored Mobility into the Chinese Administrative Elite, 1949–1996." *American Journal of Sociology* 106, no. 5 (March 2001): 1371–1408.

Li Chunling. "Dangian gaoshouru chunti de shehui goucheng ji tezheng" [The Social Composition and Special Characteristics of the Wealthy in Contemporary China]. *Zhongguo shehuixuewang* [Chinese Sociology] (2004), http://www.sociology.cass .cn/pws/lichunling/grwj_lichunling/t20041222_4091.htm (accessed May 4, 2008).

Li, He. "Middle Class: Friends or Foes to Beijing's New Leadership." *Journal of Chinese Political Science* 8 (2003): 87–100.

Li, Jian, and Xiaohan Niu. "The New Middle Class in Peking: A Case Study." *China Perspectives* 45 (January–February 2003). http://chinaperspectives.revues.org/ document228.html (accessed October 11, 2009).

Li, Jianguo. "Protect the Right to Petition." *Beijing Review,* November 10, 2005.

Li, Lianjiang. "Direct Township Elections." In *Grassroots Political Reform in China,* edited by Elizabeth Perry and Merle Goldman, 97–116. Cambridge, MA: Harvard University Press, 2007.

———. "Political Trust and Petitioning in the Chinese Countryside." *Comparative Politics* 40, no. 2 (January 2008), 209–26.

———. "Political Trust in Rural China." *Modern China* 30, no. 2 (2004): 228–58.

Li, Lianjiang, and Kevin O'Brien. "The Struggle over Village Elections." In *The Paradox of China's Post-Mao Reforms,* edited by Merle Goldman and Roderick Mac-Farquhar, 129–44. Cambridge, MA: Harvard University Press, 1999.

Li, Linda Chelan. "Working for the Peasants? Strategic Interactions and the Unintended Consequences in the Chinese Rural Tax Reform." *China Journal* 57, no. 1 (January 2007): 89–106.

Li Peilin. "Zhongguo jingji shehui fazhan de wenti he qushi" [Issues and Trends in China's Economic and Social Development]. In *2004 nian: Zhongguo shehui xingshi fenxi yu yuce* [2004: Analysis and Forecast on China's Social Development], edited by Ru Xin, Lu Xueyi, and Li Peilin. Beijing: Shehui kexue wenxian chubanshe, 2004.

Li Peilin, Guangjin Chen, and Wei Li. "A Report on the Situation of Social Harmony and Stability of China in 2006," in *2007 CASS Blue Book*. Boston: Brill, 2008.

Li Qiang. "Guanyu siyingjingji de ruogan ziliao" [Some Data on the Private Economy]. *Zhenli de zhuiqiu* [Seeking Truth] 5 (2001): 18–19.

Li Qin. "Dui woguo nongmin fudan zhuangkuang de fenxi" [Analysis of Peasant Burdens]. *Zhongguo nongcun jingji* [Chinese Rural Economy] 8 (1992): 47–51.

Li S. "Shuju xianshi woguo zhongchan jieceng zhan jiuye renkou 11%" [Data Show That the Middle Strata Make Up 11% of the Working Population of Our Country]. *Zhongguo Qingnian Bao* [China Youth], September 2, 2005.

Li, Shi, and Hiroshi Sato, eds. "Introduction." In *Unemployment, Inequality and Poverty in Urban China*, edited by Shi Li and Hiroshi Sato, 1–16. New York: Routledge, 2006.

Li, Yuwen. "Lawyers in China: A 'Flourishing' Profession in a Rapidly Changing Society?" *China Perspectives* 27 (2000): 14–23. http://www.cefc.com.hk/pccpa.php ?aid=1605 (accessed March 29, 2009).

Li Zhidong. "Dangdai daxuesheng zhengzhiguan, daodeguan, jiazhiguan diaocha yanjiu" [Investigation and Study of Contemporary University Students' Political Views, Ethics, and Values]. *Guangxi shifan daxue xuebao, zhexue shehui kexue ban* [Journal of Guangxi Normal University, Philosophy and Social Sciences] 38, no. 3 (2002): 52.

Liang Dong. "Zhongguo dangzheng ganbu ji ganqun guanxi de diaocha fenxi" [Analysis of a Survey on Party and State Cadres and Cadre-mass Relations in China]. In *2004 nian: Zhongguo shehui xingshi fenxi yu yuce* [2004: Analysis and Forecast on China's Social Development], edited by Ru Xin, Lu Xueyi, and Li Peilin. Beijing: Shehui kexue wenxian chubanshe, 2004.

Liddle, R. William. "Indonesia: Suharto's Tightening Grip." *Journal of Democracy* 7 (October 1996): 58–72.

Lipset, Seymour Martin. "Some Social Requisites of Democracy: Economic Development and Political Legitimacy." *American Political Science Review* 53 (March 1959): 69–105.

Liu, Amy Y. C. "Markets, Inequality, and Poverty in Vietnam." *Asian Economic Journal* 15, no. 2 (2001): 217–35.

Liu, Haoting. "Private Firms Propel Innovation." *China Daily*, September 6, 2007.

Liu, Junyan. "Chinese College Students." In *Chinese Youth in Transition*, edited by Jieying Xi, Yunxiao Sun, and Jing Jian Xiao, 145–63. Burlington, VT: Ashgate, 2006.

Liu, Sida, and Terence Halliday. "Dancing Handcuffed in the Minefield: Survival Strategies of Defense Lawyers in China's Criminal Justice System." Paper presented at the Law and Society Association Annual Meeting, Montreal, Canada, May 29–June 1, 2008.

Liu, Ya-ling. "Reform from Below: The Private Economy and Local Politics in the Rural Industrialization of Wenzhou." *China Quarterly* 130 (1992): 293–316.

Lu Xueyi. *Dangdai Zhongguo shehui jieceng yanjiu baogao* [Research Report on Social Strata in Contemporary China]. Beijing: Shehui kexue wenxian chubanshe, 2001.

———. *Dangdai zhongguo shehui ge jieceng fenxi* [An Analysis of Various Strata in Contemporary Chinese Society]. Beijing: Shehui kexue wenxian chubanshe, 2002.

Luo, Gan. "Bolstering the Teaching of the Concept of Socialist Rule by Law: Conscientiously Strengthening the Political Thinking of the Political and Legal Ranks." *Seeking Truth* 433 (June 16, 2006). http://www.qsjournal.com.cn/qs/20060616/GB/qs^433^0^1.htm (accessed October 16, 2006).

———. "The Political and Legal Organs Shoulder an Important Historical Mission and a Political Duty during the Construction of a Harmonious Society." *Seeking Truth* 448 (February 1, 2007). http://www.qsjournal.com.cn/qs/20070201/GB/qs%5E448%5E0%5E1.htm (accessed March 6, 2007).

"Lushimen de hushing: xingshi bianhu nanti duo" [Lawyers' Cry: Many Difficulties in Criminal Defense]. *Fazhi Ribao* [Legal Daily], July 8, 1988.

Ma, Josephine. "Create a Uniform System for Village Polls, Says Jimmy Carter." *South China Morning Post*, September 9, 2003.

———. "'Make Sure Migrant Workers Get Paid.'" *South China Morning Post*, January 8, 2005.

"Manager Killed During Protest Over Steel Plant Privatization." *China Labour Bulletin*, July 26, 2009. http://www.china-labour.org.hk/en/node/100520 (accessed October 10, 2009).

Manion, Melanie. "Democracy, Community, and Trust: The Impact of Elections in Rural China." *Comparative Political Studies* 39, no. 3 (April 2006): 301–24.

Mann, James. *The China Fantasy*. London: Viking, 2007.

Marquand, Robert. "After Dark, Remembering Zhao." *Christian Science Monitor*, January 31, 2005.

———. "Zhao Remembered, But Cautiously." *Christian Science Monitor*, January 31, 2005.

Marx, Karl. *The Communist Manifesto*. Frederic L. Bender, ed. New York: W. W. Norton, 1988.

"Members of Communist Party of China Grow to 70.8 Million." *Xinhua*, June 19, 2006.

Meyer, David. "Protest and Political Opportunities." *Annual Review of Sociology* 30 (2004): 125–45.

Michelson, Ethan. "Climbing the Dispute Pagoda: Grievances and Appeals to the Official Justice System in Rural China." *American Sociological Review* 72 (June 2007): 459–85.

———. "Justice from Above or Below? Popular Strategies for Resolving Grievances in Rural China." *China Quarterly* 193 (2008): 43–64.

———. "Lawyers, Political Embeddedness, and Institutional Continuity in China's Transition from Socialism." *American Journal of Sociology* 113, no. 2 (September 2007): 352–414.

———. "The Practice of Law as an Obstacle to Justice: Chinese Lawyers at Work." *Law and Society Review* 40, no. 1 (March 2006): 1–38.

Miller, Tom. "Hukou Reform: One Step Forward." *China Economic Quarterly* Q3 (2005): 34–37.

Mok, Ka-ho, and Cai He. "Beyond Organized Dependence: A Study of Workers' Actual and Perceived Living Standards in Guangzhou." *Work, Employment, and Society* 13 (March 1999): 67–82.

Moore, Barrington. *The Social Origins of Dictatorship and Democracy*. Boston, MA: Beacon Press, 1966.

Morin, Richard, and Nilanthi Samaranayake. "The Putin Popularity Score." Pew Research Center Publications, December 6, 2006. http://pewresearch.org/pubs/103/the-putin-popularity-score (accessed June 13, 2008).

Murillo, M. Victoria. "From Populism to Neoliberalism: Labor Unions and Market Reforms in Latin America." *World Politics* 52 (January 2000): 135–74.

Murphy, Rachel. "Introduction." In *China Along the Yellow River*, by Jinqing Cao, 1–16. New York: Routledge, 2005.

Nathan, Andrew. "Authoritarian Resilience." *Journal of Democracy* 14, no. 1 (2003): 6–17.

———. *Chinese Democracy*. Berkeley: University of California Press, 1986.

"NBS: China's Rural Population Shrinks to 56% of Total." *Xinhua*, October 22, 2006.

Ngai, Pun. "Becoming Dagongmei (Working Girls): The Politics of Identity and Difference in Reform China." *China Journal* 42 (July 1999): 1–18.

"Non-public Economy Blooming in China." *People's Daily*, July 29, 2004.

North, Douglass, and Barry Weingast. "Constitutions and Commitment: The Evolution of Institutions Governing Public Choice in Seventeenth-Century England." *Journal of Economic History* 49, no. 4 (December 1989): 803–32.

"Number of CPC Members Increases by 6.4 Million over 2002." *China Daily*, October 8, 2007.

O'Brien, Kevin. "Implementing Political Reform in China's Villages." *Australian Journal of Chinese Affairs* 32 (1994): 33–59.

O'Brien, Kevin, and Lianjiang Li. "Accommodating 'Democracy' in a One-party State: Introducing Village Elections in China." *China Quarterly* 162 (June 2000): 465–89.

———. "Campaign Nostalgia in the Chinese Countryside." *Asian Survey* 39, no. 3 (May–June 1999): 375–93.

———. *Rightful Resistance in Rural China.* Cambridge: Cambridge University Press, 2006.

O'Brien, Kevin, and Rongbin Han. "Path to Democracy? Assessing Village Elections in China." *Journal of Contemporary China* 18, no. 60 (June 2009): 359–78.

O'Donnell, Guillermo, and Phillipe Schmitter. *Transitions from Authoritarian Rule: Tentative Conclusions About Uncertain Democracies.* Baltimore, MD: Johns Hopkins Press, 1986.

Oi, Jean C. "Realms of Freedom in Post-Mao China." In *Realms of Freedom in Modern China*, edited by William Kirby, 264–84. Stanford, CA: Stanford University Press, 2004.

———. *Rural China Takes Off: Institutional Foundations of Economic Reform.* Berkeley: University of California Press, 1999.

———. *State and Peasant in Contemporary China: The Political Economy of Village Government.* Berkeley: University of California Press, 1989.

———. "Two Decades of Rural Reform in China." *China Quarterly* 159 (September 1999): 616–28.

Oi, Jean, and Shukai Zhao. "Fiscal Crisis in China's Townships: Causes and Consequences." In *Grassroots Political Reform in China*, edited by Elizabeth Perry and Merle Goldman, 75–96. Cambridge, MA: Harvard University Press, 2007.

Organic Law of the Villagers Committees of the People's Republic of China. http://www.china.org.cn/english/government/20729.htm (accessed May 29, 2008).

Pan Duola. "Ye tan 'ru dang dongji'" [More on 'Motivations for Joining the Party']. *Nanfang Zhoumo* [Southern Weekend], September 27, 1996.

Pan, Philip. "Thousands Mourn Chinese Ex-Leader." *Washington Post*, January 30, 2005.

Parish, William, X. Zhe, and F. Li. "Nonfarm Work and Marketization of the Chinese Countryside." *China Quarterly* 143 (1995): 697–730.

Park, Albert. "Rural-Urban Inequality in China." In *China Urbanizes: Consequences, Strategies and Policies*, edited by Shahid Yusuf and Anthony Saich, 41–63. Washington, DC: World Bank Publications, 2008.

Parris, Kirsten. "Local Initiative and National Reform: The Wenzhou Model of Development." *China Quarterly* 134 (1993): 242–63.

Pearson, Margaret. *China's New Business Elite: The Political Consequences of Economic Reform.* Berkeley: University of California Press, 1997.

Pei, Minxin. *China's Trapped Transition: The Limits of Developmental Autocracy.* Cambridge, MA: Harvard University Press, 2006.

———. "How Will China Democratize?" *Journal of Democracy* 18, no. 3 (2007): 53–57.

Peng Cong and Liu Lantao. "Zhongguo fuhao zai renda" [Wealthy Chinese in the People's Congress]. *Mingxin Caixun,* June 27, 2003.

Perry, Elizabeth. "Casting a Chinese 'Democracy' Movement: The Role of Students, Workers, and Entrepreneurs." In *Popular Protest and Political Culture in China,* 2nd ed., edited by Jeffrey Wasserstrom and Elizabeth Perry, 74–92. Boulder, CO: Westview Press, 1994.

———. "Studying Chinese Politics: Farewell to Revolution?" *China Journal* 57 (January 2007): 1–22.

Pierson, Christopher. *Hard Choices: Social Democracy in the 21st Century.* Cambridge: Cambridge University Press, 2001.

Planning Department of the Ministry of Agriculture. *Nongye jingji ziliao, 1949–83* [Materials on the Agricultural Economy, 1949–83]. Beijing: Ministry of Agriculture, 1984.

Proctor, Kelly, and Tina Qiu. "Lack of Professionals Hampers China." *International Herald Tribune,* August 16, 2006.

Prosterman, Roy, and Brian Schwarzwalder. "From Death to Life: Giving Value to China's Rural Land." *China Economic Quarterly* Q1 (2004): 20.

Przeworski, Adam. "Some Problems in the Study of the Transition to Democracy." In *Transitions from Authoritarian Rule: Comparative Perspectives,* edited by Guillermo O'Donnell, Philippe Schmitter, and Lawrence Whitehead, 47–63. Baltimore, MD: Johns Hopkins Press, 1986.

Przeworski, Adam, and Fernando Limongi. "Modernization: Theory and Facts." *World Politics* 49, no. 2 (1997): 155–83.

Putnam, Robert. *Bowling Alone.* New York: Simon and Schuster, 2000.

Qiao Jian. "2003 nian: Xin yilun jiegou tiaozheng xia de laodong guanxi" [Labor Relations in 2003, Under a New Round of Structural Adjustment]. In *2004 nian: Zhongguo shehui xingshi fenxi yu yuce* [2004: Analysis and Forecast on China's Social Development], edited by Xin Ru, Xueyi Lu, and Peilin Li. Beijing: Shehui kexue wenxian chubanshe, 2004.

Ran, Tao, and Ping Qin. "How Has Rural Tax Reform Affected Farmers and Local Governance in China?" *China and World Economy* 15, no. 3 (2007): 19–32.

"Recognize the Essence of Turmoil and the Necessity of Martial Law." *Renmin Ribao,* June 3, 1989.

Reed, Christopher. Review of *Back-Alley Banking: Private Entrepreneurs in China*, by Kellee S. Tsai. *Enterprise and Society* 4, no. 3 (September 2003): 552.

Rose, Richard, William Mishler, and Neil Munro. *Russia Transformed: Developing Popular Support for a New Regime*. Cambridge: University of Cambridge Press, 2006.

Rosen, Stanley. "China in 1987: The Year of the Thirteenth Party Congress." *Asian Survey* 28, no. 1 (January 1988): 35–51.

———. "The State of Youth/Youth and the State in Early 21st-century China: The Triumph of the Urban Rich?" In *State and Society in 21st Century China*, edited by Peter Gries and Stanley Rosen, 159–79. New York: Routledge, 2004.

———. "The Victory of Materialism: Aspirations to Join China's Urban Moneyed Classes and the Commercialization of Education." *China Journal* 51 (January 2004): 27–51.

Rowen, Henry. "When Will the Chinese People Be Free?" *Journal of Democracy* 18, no. 3 (2007): 38–52.

Rueschemeyer, Dietrich, Evelyne Huber Stephens, and John D. Stephens. *Capitalist Development and Democracy*. Chicago: University of Chicago Press, 1992.

Rui, Xingwen, and Ray Cheung. "State Media Silent as Former Aide to Zhao Ziyang Dies." *South China Morning Post*, June 8, 2005.

Saich, Tony. Review of *Remaking the Chinese Leviathan*, by Dali Yang. *China Information* 19, no. 3 (October 2005): 539.

Sanderson, Henry. "Rights Group: Chinese Lawyers Face Harassment, Restrictions." *Associated Press*, April 29, 2008.

Scipes, Kim. "International Income Inequality: Whither the United States?" *Z-Net*, August 18, 2004. http://www.zmag.org/content/showarticle.cfm?ItemID=6061 (accessed February 2, 2008).

Shi, Jiangtao. "Select Few Flout News Blackout." *South China Morning Post*, November 17, 2005.

Shi, Tianjian. "Cultural Values and Political Trust: A Comparison of the People's Republic of China and Taiwan." *Comparative Politics* 33, no. 4 (July 2001): 401–19.

———. "Village Committee Elections in China: Institutionalist Tactics for Democracy." *World Politics* 51, no. 3 (1999): 385–412.

Shih, Victor. "Factions Matter: Personal Networks and the Distribution of Bank Loans in China." *Journal of Contemporary China* 13, no. 38 (2004): 3–19.

Sil, Rudra, and Cheng Chen. "State Legitimacy and the (In)significance of Democracy in Post-Communist Russia." *Europe-Asia Studies* 56, no. 3 (May 2004): 347–68.

Sisci, Francesco. "Fiscal Democracy: From Taxation to Representation." *China Economic Quarterly* Q3 (2007): 34.

"Siying yiyezhu shi jianshezhe haishi xinxing zichang jieji?" [Are Private Entrepreneurs Builders or New Bourgeoisie?]. *Liaowang xinwen zhoukan* [Outlook Weekly], December 21, 2002.

Skocpol, Theda. *States and Social Revolutions.* Cambridge: Cambridge University Press, 1979.

Social Trends Analysis and Forecasting Topic Group, Chinese Academy of Social Sciences. "Zhongguo jinru quanmian jianshe hexie shehui xin jieduan" (China Enters a New Stage in Building a Harmonious Society). In *2007 nian: Zhongguo shehui xingshi fenxi yu yuce* [2007: Analysis and Forecast on China's Social Development], edited by Xin Tuo, Xieyi Lu, and Peilin Lin. Beijing: Shehui Kexue Wenxian Chubanshe, 2006.

Solinger, Dorothy. "China's Floating Population." In *The Paradox of China's Post-Mao Reforms*, edited by Merle Goldman and Roderick MacFarquhar, 220–40. Cambridge, MA: Harvard University Press, 1999.

———. *Chinese Business Under Socialism: The Politics of Domestic Commerce, 1949–1980.* Berkeley: University of California Press, 1984.

———. "Clashes Between Reform and Opening: Labor Market Formation in Three Cities." In *Remaking the Chinese State: Strategies, Society, and Security*, edited by Bruce Dickson and Chao Chien-min, 103–31. London: Routledge, 2001.

———. *Contesting Citizenship in Urban China: Peasant Migrants, the State, and the Logic of the Market.* Berkeley: University of California Press, 1999.

———. "Labour Market Reform and the Plight of the Laid-off Proletariat." *China Quarterly* 170 (2002): 304–26.

———. "The New Crowd of the Dispossessed." In *State and Society in 21st Century China*, edited by Peter Gries and Stanley Rosen, 50–66. New York: Routledge, 2004.

———. "Path Dependency Reexamined: Chinese Welfare Policy in the Transition to Unemployment." *Comparative Politics* 38, no. 1 (October 2005): 83–101.

———. "Urban Entrepreneurs and the State: The Merger of State and Society." In *State and Society in China: The Consequences of Reform*, edited by Arthur Rosenbaum, 121–41. Boulder, CO: Westview Press, 1992.

———. "Why We Cannot Count the 'Unemployed.'" *China Quarterly* 167 (2001): 671–88.

State Administration for Industry and Commerce Statistical Collection, 2003. Beijing: State Administration for Industry and Commerce, 2004.

St. John, Ronald Bruce. "End of the Beginning: Economic Reform in Cambodia, Laos, and Vietnam." *Contemporary Southeast Asia* 19, no. 2 (September 1997): 172–89.

Tan, Angie Ngoc. "Alternatives to the 'Race to the Bottom' in Vietnam: Minimum Wage Strikes and Their Aftermath." *Labor Studies Journal* 32, no. 4 (2007): 430–51.

Tang, Jie, and Anthony Ward. *The Changing Face of Chinese Management.* New York: Routledge, 2002.

Tang, Wenfang. *Public Opinion and Political Change in China.* Stanford, CA: Stanford University Press, 2005.

Tang, Wenfang, and William Parish. "Chinese Labor Relations in a Changing Work Environment." *Journal of Contemporary China* 5, no. 13 (November 1996): 367–89.

Tanner, Murray Scot. "China Rethinks Unrest." *Washington Quarterly* 27, no. 3 (2004): 137–56.

Tao Mao, et al., eds. *Lushi shiyong daquan* [Applied Encyclopedia for Lawyers]. Hebei: Hebei renmin chubanshe, 1993.

Thireau, Isabelle. "From Equality to Equity." *China Information* 5, no. 4 (1991): 42–57.

Thireau, Isabelle, and Linshan Hua. "The Moral Universe of Aggrieved Chinese Workers." *China Journal* 50 (2003): 83–103.

Thorgersen, Stig. "Through the Sheep's Intestines—Selection and Elitism in Chinese Schools." *Australian Journal of Chinese Affairs* 21 (January 1989): 29–56.

"Three Million Chinese Farmers a Year Expected to Lose Land." *Xinhua,* July 24, 2006.

"Tiananmen—Ten Years On." *China Labour Bulletin* 48 (May–June 1999): 3.

Tomba, Luigi. "Creating an Urban Middle Class: Social Engineering in Beijing." *China Journal* 51 (January 2004): 1–26.

———. "Residential Space and Collective Interest Formation in Beijing's Housing Disputes." *China Quarterly* 184 (December 2005): 934–51.

Trinh, Tamara. "China's Pension System." *Deutsche Bank Research,* February 17, 2006. http://www.dbresearch.com/PROD/DBR_INTERNET_EN-PROD/PROD000000 0000196025.pdf (accessed February 5, 2008).

Tsai, Kellee S. "Adaptive Informal Institutions and Endogenous Institutional Change in China." *World Politics* 59, no. 1 (2006): 116–41.

———. *Back-Alley Banking: Private Entrepreneurs in China.* Ithaca, NY: Cornell University Press, 2002.

———. *Capitalism Without Democracy: The Private Sector in Contemporary China.* Ithaca, NY: Cornell University Press, 2007.

———. "Capitalists Without a Class: Political Diversity Among Private Entrepreneurs in China." *Comparative Political Studies* 38, no. 9 (2005): 1130–58.

Tsai, Lily. "Cadres, Temple and Lineage Associations, and Governance in Rural China." *China Journal* 48 (July 2002): 1–27.

"240 Million Chinese Covered by Social Pension System." *Xinhua,* December 5, 2007.

Unger, Jonathan. "Introduction." In *The Pro-Democracy Protests in China: Reports from the Provinces,* edited by Jonathan Unger. Armonk, NY: M. E. Sharpe, 1991.

Unger, Jonathan, and Anita Chan. "Inheritors of the Boom: Private Enterprise and the Role of Local Government in a Rural South China Township." *China Journal* 42 (July 1999): 45–74.

"Urban, Rural Residents Income Up Over 15% in 2007." *Xinhua*, January 24, 2008.

"Urbanization Is Reducing China's Rural Population." *People's Daily*, February 23, 2006.

"The U.S.–China WTO Accession Deal." *FAS online* (U.S. Department of Agriculture), February 9, 2000. http://www.fas.usda.gov/info/factsheets/China/deal.html (accessed May 25, 2008).

Van Arkadie, Brian, and Raymond Mallon. *Vietnam: A Transition Tiger?* Canberra: Australian National University Press, 2003.

Vermeer, Eduard. "Egalitarianism and the Land Question in China." *China Information* 18 (2004): 107–40.

Walder, Andrew. *Communist Neo-traditionalism: Work and Authority in Chinese Industry.* Berkeley: University of California Press, 1986.

Walder, Andrew, and Xiaoxia Gong. "Workers in the Tiananmen Protests: The Politics of the Beijing Workers' Autonomous Federation." *Australian Journal of Chinese Affairs* 29 (January 1993): 1–29.

Walder, Andrew, and Litao Zhao. *Political Office, Kinship, and Household Wealth in Rural China.* Stanford, CA: Asia-Pacific Research Center, 2002.

Wang, Chunguang. "The Changing Situation of Migrant Labor." *Social Research* 73, no. 1 (Spring 2006): 185–96.

Wang, Feng. "Boundaries of Inequality: Perceptions of Distributive Justice Among Urbanites, Migrants, and Peasants." University of California, Irvine Center for the Study of Democracy Paper 07-09 (2007).

Wang, Irene. "Incidents of Social Unrest Hit 87,000." *South China Morning Post*, January 20, 2006.

———. "Public Praise for an Overdue Celebration." *South China Morning Post*, November 17, 2005.

Wang, Shaoguang, Deborah Davis, and Yanjie Bian. "The Uneven Distribution of Cultural Capital: Book Reading in Urban China." *Modern China* 32 (2006): 315–48.

Wang, Xu. "Mutual Empowerment of State and Peasantry: Grassroots Democracy in Rural China." *World Development* 25, no. 9 (1997): 1431–42.

Wank, David. *Commodifying Communism: Business, Trust and Politics in a Chinese City.* Cambridge: Cambridge University Press, 1999.

———. "Private Business, Bureaucracy, and Political Alliance in a Chinese City." *Australian Journal of Chinese Affairs* 33 (January 1995): 55–71.

Weber, Max. *Sociology of World Religions: Introduction,* 1920. http://www.ne.jp/asahi/moriyuki/abukuma/weber/world/intro/world_intro_frame.html (accessed March 30, 2009).

Wei Jingsheng. "The Fifth Modernization," December 5, 1978. http://www.geocities .com/capitolhill/7288/fifth.htm (accessed January 13, 2008).

Wei, L. "Wider Market Access Opened to Private Business Sector." *China Daily,* August 2, 2004.

Weston, Timothy. "The Iron Man Weeps: Joblessness and Political Legitimacy in the Chinese Rust Belt." In *State and Society in 21st Century China,* edited by Peter Gries and Stanley Rosen, 67–86. New York: Routledge, 2004.

Whyte, Martin King. "The Changing Role of Workers." In *The Paradox of China's Post-Mao Reforms,* edited by Merle Goldman and Roderick MacFarquhar, 173–96. Cambridge, MA: Harvard University Press, 1999.

———. "Chinese Popular Views About Inequality." *Woodrow Wilson Center Asia Program Special Report* 104 (August 2002).

Whyte, Martin King, and William Parish. *Urban Life in Contemporary China.* Chicago: University of Chicago Press, 1984.

"Why the Chinese Income Gap Is Widening." *People's Daily* Online, May 16, 2000. http://english.people.com.cn/english/200005/16/eng20000516_40916.html (accessed May 17, 2008).

Williams, James H. "Fang Lizhi's Expanding Universe." *China Quarterly* 123 (September 1990): 459–84.

"Woguo nongmin gong de shengcun xianzhuan" [How Migrant Workers in Our Nation Subsist]. *Banyue tan* [China Comment], in *Xinhua,* May 18, 2006.

Wong, Christine, ed. *Financing Local Development in the People's Republic of China.* Oxford: Oxford University Press, 1997.

World Public Opinion.org and the Program on International Policy Attitudes, University of Maryland. "World Public Opinion on Governance and Democracy." May 13, 2008. http://www.worldpublicopinion.org/pipa/pdf/may08/WPO_Governance_May08_packet.pdf (accessed June 4, 2008).

World Values Survey. Various years. http://www.worldvaluessurvey.org/ (accessed October 11, 2009).

Wright, Teresa. "The China Democracy Party and the Politics of Protest in the 1980's– 1990's." *China Quarterly* 172 (December 2002): 906–26.

Xiao, Ma. "Private Firms Crucial for Employment." *China Daily,* December 14, 2005.

Xiaoping, Deng. "Speech at the Opening Ceremony of the National Conference on Science." In *Deng Xiaoping wenxuan, di san juan* [Selected Works of Deng Xiaoping, Volume 3]. Beijing: Renmin Chubanshe, 1993.

Yang, Dali. "Economic Transformation and Its Political Discontents in China." *Annual Review of Political Science* 9 (2006): 143–64.

———. *Remaking the Chinese Leviathan.* Stanford, CA: Stanford University Press, 2004.

———. "State Capacity on the Rebound." *Journal of Democracy* 14, no. 1 (2003): 43–50.

Yeh, Andrew. "Rural Policy: New Leaf or Old Hat?" *China Economic Quarterly* Q1 (2004).

Young, Susan. "Policy, Practice, and the Private Sector in China." *Australian Journal of Chinese Affairs* 21 (January 1989): 57–80.

Yu, Jianrong. "Conflict in the Countryside: The Emerging Political Awareness of the Peasants." *Social Research* 73, no. 1 (Spring 2006): 141–58.

Yu Jianrong and Xiao Tangbiao. "Ershinian lai dalu nongcun de zhengzhi wending zhangkuang" [The Stable Conditions of Mainland Peasants During the Last 20 Years]. *Ershiyi Shiji* [The 21st Century] 4 (2003).

Zhang Houyi and Liu Wenpu. *Zhongguo de siying jingji yu siying qiye zhu* [Chinese Private Economy and Private Entrepreneurs]. Beijing: Zhishi Chubanshe, 1995.

Zhang Houyi, Ming Zhili, and Liang Zhuanyun, eds. *Zhongguo siying qiye fazhan baogao* [Blue Book of Private Enterprises], vol. 4 (2002). Beijing: Shehui Kexue Wenxian Chubanshe, 2003.

———. *Zhongguo siying qiye fazhan baogao* [Blue Book of Private Enterprises], vol. 5 (2003). Beijing: Shehui Kexue Wenxian Chubanshe, 2004.

Zhang, Jianjun. *Marketization and Democracy in China*. New York: Routledge, 2008.

———. "Marketization, Class Structure, and Democracy in China: Contrasting Regional Experiences." *Democratization* 14, no. 3 (2007): 425–45.

Zhang, Michael. "The Social Marginalization of Workers in China's State-owned Enterprises." *Social Research* 73, no. 1 (Spring 2006): 159–84.

Zhang Ping. "Zhongguo nongcun jumin quyujian shouru bupingdeng yu feinongjiuye" [Regional Income inequality and Non-agricultural Employment in Rural China]. *Jingji Yanjiu* [Economic Research] 8 (August 1998).

Zhang, Yiguo, and Yuanheng Yang. "The Evaluation of People's Living Level of China." Shandong Province Statistical Bureau of China. http://isi.cbs.nl/iama member/CD2/pdf/542.PDF (accessed May 19, 2008).

Zhao, Ling. "Significant Shift in Focus of Peasants' Rights and Activism (Interview with Jianrong Yu)." China Elections and Governance online, September 16, 2004. http://www.chinaelections.net/PrintNews.asp?NewsID=3123 (accessed May 28, 2008).

Zhao, Renwei. "Increasing Income Inequality and its Causes." In *China's Retreat from Inequality*, edited by Carl Riskin, Renwei Zhao, and Shi Li, 25–43. New York: M. E. Sharpe, 2004.

Zhao, Yaohui. "Foreign Direct Investment and Relative Wages: The Case of China." *China Economic Review* 12 (2001): 40–57.

Zheng Geng et al., eds. *Zhonghua renmin gongheguo lushifa quanshu* [Encyclopedia of the Law of the PRC on Lawyers]. Beijing: Blue Sky Publishing House, 1996.

Zheng, Yongnian. "The Party, Class, and Democracy in China." In *The Chinese Communist Party in Reform*, edited by Kjeld Erik Brodsgaard and Yongnian Zheng, 231–60. New York: Routledge, 2006.

Zhong, Yang. "Democratic Values Among Chinese Peasantry: An Empirical Survey." *China: An International Journal* 3, no. 2 (2005): 189–211.

Zhongguo tongji nianjian [China Statistical Yearbook] (various years). Beijing: Zhongguo tongji chubanshe [China National Bureau of Statistics Press].

Zhongguo xiangzhen qiye nianjian [China Rural Enterprise Yearbook] (various years). Beijing: Zhongguo nongye chubanshe [China Agricultural Bureau Press].

Zhuang, Congsheng. "New Social Strata Has a Vital Role to Play." *China Daily*, October 16, 2007.

INDEX

Accountants, 77, 81–82

Adaptability, Chinese Communist Party (CCP) and, 23, 24–25, 34

Administrative villages, 208n20

Age, 17, 19, 34, 113–114, 176–177

Agriculture, 118, 128, 150, 154. *See also* Farmers

All-China Federation of Trade Unions (ACFTU), 132

Alpermann, Bjorn, 53, 54–55

Arbitration committees (*zhongcai weiyuanhui*), 104, 131, 206n69

Attorneys. *See* Lawyers

"Authoritarian resilience," 25

Bar exams, 78, 80, 195n104

Barro, Robert, 22

Beijing Social and Economic Sciences Research Institute (SERI), 73, 74

Bellin, Eva: capitalism and democracy, 21; private entrepreneurs and, 55; state-led economic development and, 27, 28, 29, 30, 175; state sector workers, 114

Benefits: former state sector workers and, 93, 95, 103–104; for retirees, 95–96; state sector workers and, 87–88, 88–89, 101–102. *See also* Social welfare policies

Bernstein, Thomas, 157

Birth control policies, 140, 142

Blair, Tony, 22

Boix, Carles, 20

Brazil, 30, 55, 175

Buckley, Christopher, 68

Budget transfers, local government and, 151

Bueno de Mesquita, Bruce, 23–24

Burkhart, Ross, 20

Bush, George W., 22

Business associations, government-sponsored, 50–51

Cai, Yongshun, 83, 99

Capitalism and democracy: Chinese experience and, 1, 21–26; economic development and political change, 19–21; pressure for democratization and, 179

Capital mobility, 27, 28

Carlson, Allen, 16

Chen, Jie, 13, 15–16, 176

Chile, 175

China Blue (film), 205n30

China Democracy Party (CDP), 11, 70, 82

Chinese Communist Party (CCP): adaptability and, 23, 24–25, 34; college students and, 70; democratization in China and, 22–23, 26; economic crisis (2008) and, 177; farmers and, 158; former state sector workers and, 109–110; intellectuals and, 75; pensioners and, 112; political status quo and, 1, 10–11; private entrepreneurs and, 6, 37, 41–42, 43, 48–49; private sector workers and, 117, 132; socialist legacies and, 102–103; state dependence and, 162–163; state sector workers and, 91, 107. *See also* Party membership

243